BATTLE ON THE HUDSON

THE DEVILS, THE RANGERS,
AND THE NHL'S GREATEST SERIES EVER

BATTLE ON THE HUDSON

THE DEVILS, THE RANGERS,
AND THE NHL'S GREATEST SERIES EVER

Tim Sullivan

TRIUMPH
BOOKS

Library of Congress Cataloging-in-Publication Data

Sullivan, Tim, 1972-
    Battle on the Hudson : the Devils, the Rangers, and the NHL's greatest series ever / Tim
        Sullivan ; [foreword by] Stephane Matteau.
    p. cm.
    ISBN 978-1-60078-727-0 (hardback)
1. New Jersey Devils (Hockey team) 2. New York Rangers (Hockey team) 3. Sports
rivalries—United States. I. Title.
    GV848.N38S85 2012
    796.962'640974—dc23

                                         2012016993

This book is available in quantity at special discounts for your group or organization. For further information, contact:
    Triumph Books LLC
    814 North Franklin Street
    Chicago, Illinois 60610
    (312) 337-0747
    www.triumphbooks.com

Printed in U.S.A.

ISBN: 978-1-60078-727-0

Design by James Slate

Photos courtesy of AP Images unless otherwise indicated

*In loving memory of Timothy J. Sullivan Jr. and Katherine D. Paullet,
looking down on us, always. Thank you for the inspiration and motivation.*

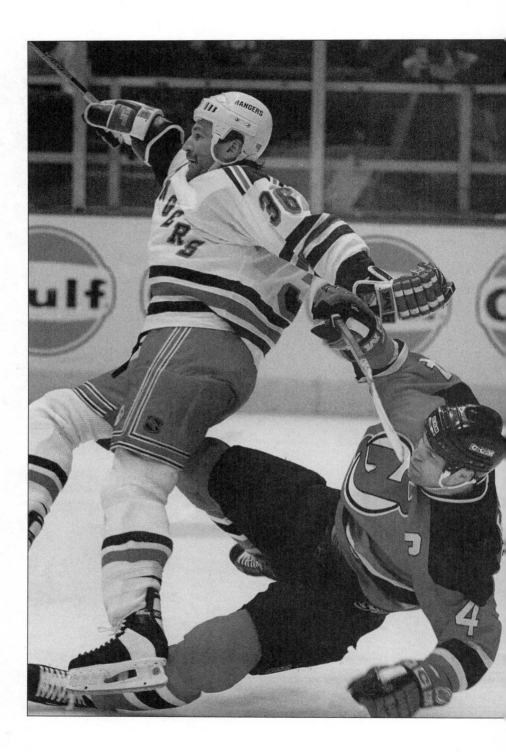

Contents

○ ○ ○ ○

Foreword

○ ○ ○ ○

"All season long, I heard it from Mike Keenan: 'Matteau. Matteau. Matteau.' And that was before that famous radio call about him. He just loved Stephane; he took him everywhere he coached. And I liked him, too. I remembered him from his draft year. But it sunk in for me, for sure. It became increasingly obvious to me that, at some point in the season, I was going to have to trade for Stephane Matteau."
—NEIL SMITH, GENERAL MANAGER, NEW YORK RANGERS (1989–2000)

WHEN I FIRST heard the news that I had been traded from the Chicago Blackhawks to the New York Rangers in 1994, I was a little skeptical. The Rangers were first overall and were really cruising. It seemed like no one could get near them. They had goal scorers, great defensemen, terrific goaltending—they had it all. It was their year. Everyone knew that.

So, when I got traded there, I was like, *Well, they traded for me to be there just in case somebody gets hurt. Great.*

That was the feeling I had on my way to Calgary. We were scheduled to play the Flames on my first night with the team, and I remember being so nervous when I got off the plane to meet my new teammates. But Mike Keenan was there waiting for me, a coach who knew me, and he knew where I might be able to fit in.

We had a quick meeting. I remember he said, "You're going to play with [Steve] Larmer and [Alexei] Kovalev." Which wasn't too bad, right? When I looked up at the bulletin board and saw my name a little bit later, I was like, *This is going to be okay. Let's go to work.* For hockey players, it's a great feeling to look up at the board in the locker room, see your name, and know where you're going to play that night. That's what it's all about.

So, Mike put me on the second line, which I really appreciated, and I never moved from that line the rest of the season.

When we pulled the goalie late in that first game against Calgary, Mike put me out there and I scored a goal. What a feeling to be able to contribute to such a great team right away. The next night, still on the road, we played the Edmonton Oilers and I scored again, and everything settled in. I was fortunate to be around great players, and we all knew what the ultimate goal was.

There were times when things came easy for us in '94, but we knew those times were over when the New Jersey Devils showed up in the Eastern Conference Finals. They were big, strong, physical, tough in their own zone, and had great goaltending. No one in our room—no one—took that team lightly. And right off the bat, Stephane Richer scored for them in double overtime, and we lost Game 1 in Madison Square Garden. We knew right then and there that we'd be in for a long and tough series.

From there, the whole series was a roller-coaster ride. We'd win, they'd win. The momentum swings in that series were unlike anything I had ever seen before. We were very focused against that team, because we knew how good they were. But they were better than us on some nights. There's no doubt about it. The drama was unbelievable.

By the time we made it to Game 6, obviously, things had changed. We knew that if we slipped up just a little bit against those guys, we'd lose the series and be out of the playoffs. On that morning of Game 6, it dawned on me that if we lost, we'd be labeled the biggest chokers of all time, and we'd be gone just like that. All of that work, the trades, the great season, all gone.

I tried not to think about the pressure. I didn't read the papers at all. Being a young player, I had to concentrate on the things I had to do. But that's what made that Rangers team so special—we had an incredible group of older players who had been in all of those situations before, especially the guys from the Edmonton Oilers. And everything was smooth and focused, even during those tough times.

We never panicked. Never.

Things didn't start great for us in Game 6. We were down 2–0 after one period. We had to do something quick, and Mark Messier's line did it for us. He guaranteed the win, and away we went. Messier did it in that one, just like he did throughout the postseason.

Who knew that I'd be the one to do it in the next game? Certainly not me. But to score two double-overtime goals, and three in the series overall, I'd say that was a pretty good stretch for me. I will always feel fortunate for that. It's easily the most dramatic series and stretch of my career. I knew I'd never match that feeling again, and that was okay, because I knew how important what we did was to New York and to the Rangers organization.

In Game 7, when I scored in double overtime to end it, people started calling me "Mr. Overtime." Me? "Mr. Overtime"? Yeah, right. It took me 56 playoff games to score my next playoff goal! Seven years to finally score in the postseason—let me tell you, that's a long time in hockey.

I didn't know [Devils goaltender] Marty [Brodeur] at the time. The Russian players have a bond in this league, and I think the French Canadian players do, too. That was our bond, and it was always professional. Marty was such a good goaltender that I knew he'd bounce back from that. And he did.

As for the goal, yes, you always dream about how you're going to react in that moment. As a kid in the street, you always imagined your celebration, what you were going to do when given the chance. At any level of sports, anyone who wants to succeed thinks he's going to be the one to hit the winning home run in the World Series, or score the game-winning goal in the playoffs. And incredibly, that's what happened for me. The celebration wasn't scripted or planned. All I could think about was that I had a chance now—*we* had a chance now—to play in the Stanley Cup Finals.

When I saw the puck going in the net so very slowly past Marty, I just started going, doing whatever, and was finally mobbed by the team. I will never forget it. To score the winner of such a classic series in Game 7, double overtime…I carry that memory with me every day in my coaching career.

To be an assistant coach now at the junior level is great for me. The Rangers helped me get to this point, but my whole NHL career helped, too. Being on six different NHL teams, I was able to play for a lot of coaches and see a lot of different management styles. I always show respect for the player and tell him where he stands. You cannot be afraid to tell a player, any player, that we need more when the time is right. That's my job.

Sometimes I can be hard on the guys. Respectful, but hard. But the relationship I have with the players as an assistant coach is perfect. I love what I do, and I think the kids respect that. They know I've been there and done that.

I would love to be an assistant coach somewhere in the NHL. Being a head coach is tough. I'm way too nice for that. Right now, I'm enjoying my junior career as an assistant coach. I love it, but if a team comes calling, I'd think very hard about going back to the NHL.

No matter what happens, no matter where I go, I will never forget that '94 team, the bond we had, and the battles we won. The Devils series was such a classic, memorable series for everyone, especially the fans in the area, and I will always be appreciative of the chance I had to have an impact on it.

Looking back, who would have guessed that a French Canadian kid from Rouyn-Noranda would become an unsung hero for the Rangers in such a momentous year?

I'm part of the past now. I'm part of that tremendous series, and I'll never forget that. I'll always be grateful for that. It was great for me and my career. And I cannot thank the Rangers organization, the fans, and the staff enough for giving me that opportunity. It will never be forgotten.

When my son, Stefan, read this foreword and relived some of these memories with me, he was so excited. "I just want to make it to the NHL," he told me. "I can't wait." So, it's amazing that five months after I wrote this—and 18 years since 1994—Stefan was selected in the first round of the 2012 NHL Draft by...the New Jersey Devils. I suppose the Matteaus are destined to be a part of this rivalry forever.

—Stephane Matteau

Introduction

○ ○ ○ ○

"It was hockey at its greatest. It was the most exciting time in my career, and I've been singing in the Garden for 31 years. I will never forget that 1994 series, because it went down to the wire, almost every game! If you were fortunate enough to be in the buildings for those games, you have memories that will last a lifetime. Believe me."
—JOHN AMIRANTE, NEW YORK RANGERS NATIONAL ANTHEM SINGER

IF, AS THE SAGES SAY, "Pain and progress are inseparable," the unforgettable 1994 Eastern Conference Finals offered plenty of both commodities.

Having seen my first hockey game at the old Madison Square Garden on Eighth Avenue between 49th and 50th Streets, I can assure you that I have witnessed many playoff gems. But this 1994 best-of-seven was one for the ages.

Mind you, I did not view it as a dispassionate critic. In those days, Devils games were telecast by SportsChannel, and I was an integral part of the crew covering the series. My role involved the pregame show, in-between-periods interviews, and postgame "sound" from the Devils' dressing room.

I had been involved with the Garden State sextet before Lou Lamoriello took over the managership for the 1987–88 season, and suffered through the club's long and difficult growth period, which culminated in a "miracle" homestretch run. It wasn't until the final night of the season that Jim Schoenfeld's skaters ousted the Rangers from a playoff berth on the strength of a John MacLean overtime goal in Chicago.

Meanwhile, the Rangers—no matter how competent they might have been—still had to cope with the endless "19-40" chants that resounded like the drone of bagpipes. There was only one way that that noise could be stilled...and that required winning the Cup.

Which brings us to the spring of 1994, and the collision of two remarkably competent—yet diverse—hockey clubs.

No matter how you shook it, the Rangers *always* were the patricians among the three metropolitan-area teams—as well they should have been. Although the Blueshirts were not the first National Hockey League team in New York—that distinction belonged to the long-defunct New York Americans—it was the Rangers who popularized hockey in Gotham. Before the Amerks folded in 1942, the Rangers had won three Stanley Cups and were led by one of the game's most distinguished executives, Lester Patrick.

With that head start on the Islanders and Devils, it was no wonder that the Rangers were regarded as *the* team while the others were the Come-latelies.

That said, the Devils, in 1993–94, had become distinguished in their own right. They completed the 84-game schedule with 47 wins, 25 losses, and 12 ties for a club-record total of 106 points. What's more, their coach, Jacques Lemaire, already had taken on the air of genius. All you had to do was ask the players.

"Jacques is the best coach I ever played for," goaltender Chris Terreri said. "He's so good that sometimes it's scary."

Defenseman Scott Stevens seconded the notion.

"I've never been on a team before where, when the coach is talking, everybody looks at him and listens!" he said.

Those words were underlined by results. First, New Jersey beat Buffalo in a heart-throbbing opening round, and followed that with an equally pulsating triumph over the Bruins.

Awaiting the Devils was a mighty Rangers team whose architect was a former Islanders scout, Neil Smith, and a coach, Mike Keenan, who earned the nickname "Iron Mike" for good reason. Keenan was a practitioner of tough love, with the accent on the former over the latter. Insightful and unpredictable, Keenan was a bundle of contradictions, but, above all, he was a winner and respectful of the opposition.

"We have a great deal of respect for the Devils," he said on the eve of the opener, and he didn't mean *maybe*, either.

What I remember most is that the tension enveloping Game 6 was unlike any I had experienced, especially in the hours leading up to the opening faceoff. One incident still stands out in my memory and remains as bizarre in its recollection as it did at the time.

About two hours before the game was to begin, Rangers publicist Barry Watkins approached me and asked if I would take a moment to chat with Keenan. Of course I would, since Mike and I had been good friends and he was especially kind to our family when—during the previous summer—he visited my younger son, Simon, who was suffering from heart failure. The two Mikes—Keenan and his goaltender, Richter—visited the 15-year-old lad at Columbia-Presbyterian Hospital as Simon awaited a heart transplant.

I still can feel Keenan's powerful embrace and the encouragement both brought to Simon, my wife, Shirley, and me. (Simon received his "new" heart a month later, and now lives in Israel, the father of three children. He's still an Islanders fan, a Keenan fan, and a Richter fan.)

After Watkins summoned me, I was hard-pressed to figure out what Keenan wanted, but I entered the empty room next to the studio and sat down. The coach entered, obviously upset about something, but not about me. All of a sudden, Keenan went into a fervent tirade about how the officials have not been kind to the Rangers and this was wrong, and that was wrong. From my side, there was no room for rebuttal. So, I listened, nodded, and listened some more until Mike had gotten all the beefs off his chest. To this day, I'm not sure what he had hoped to obtain from our tête-á-tête but it sure was interesting.

Looking back on it, consider what this series gave birth to: two teams that won the Stanley Cup just more than one year apart, one team completing its long-awaited quest, and the other merely starting it, all within a six-mile radius.

Indeed, they will talk about this one forever.

—Stan Fischler

The Rivalry

○ ○ ○ ○

"Whenever we played the Rangers, you knew it beforehand. Everything was different. Preseason, regular season, playoffs, home, road, it didn't matter. Records? Throw them out. They were New York. We were New Jersey. They were established. We weren't. There was always a feeling that if we're going to do anything in this league, we're going to have to go through them. They were our biggest rival."
—BILL GUERIN, NEW JERSEY DEVILS (1991–98)

Dr. JOHN McMULLEN brought the new kid to school on June 30, 1982. He wasn't all that talented to begin with, he wasn't a hit with the others at recess right off the bat, and he always showed up in a strange red-and-green outfit.

Clearly, the New Jersey Devils arrived with a few strikes against them.

Indeed, it was tough for McMullen's dream on ice to find its way in the New York–New Jersey metropolitan area, much less in the National Hockey League. Formerly the Colorado Rockies, and the Kansas City Scouts before them, this was a vagabond franchise that McMullen purchased, one that had never truly tasted success. And even if it had, no one would have cared.

"We were a mess in the early years," said former Devils defenseman Ken Daneyko, who is now a television analyst for the franchise. "We had a lot of learning to do, a lot of growing. And most people around the National Hockey League thought we'd never reach our potential."

But McMullen, a New Jersey native who gained his fortune in the shipping business, always saw promise in moving the team to East Rutherford, a gritty commuter town of some 8,000 residents in Bergen County, over-looking the skyline of Manhattan. He saw opportunity in the Meadowlands Sports Complex, where the NFL's New York Giants and the NBA's New Jersey Nets had already taken up residence.

It didn't matter to him that the Meadowlands was built on swampland, smack dab in the middle of major highways, a hub for exhaust, waste, and traffic with very little fanfare around it. Let's face it—the place didn't scream out "hockey heaven" to anyone.

It didn't matter to him that the franchise had only produced one playoff season in eight years in Kansas City and Colorado.

And it definitely didn't matter to him that the New York Rangers, an Original Six franchise with as loyal a following as you'll find in the NHL, played just six miles away in the heart of the biggest city in the world.

But it probably should have.

"Say what you will, it was a tough hill to climb," said Gary Thorne, a former television play-by-play man for the Devils. "They were the redheaded stepchildren. No doubt about it. It was going to take a long time for them to gain the respect of the area, and certainly of the Rangers."

Indeed, the Rangers saw the Devils as nothing more than a gnat on their windshield in the 1980s. Wipe 'em off and move on down the New Jersey Turnpike. Heck, before the Devils were even allowed to migrate to New Jersey under McMullen's wing, the Rangers had to grant them permission through the NHL due to the proximity to New York.

They granted it, of course, without hesitation. What did they have to lose, right?

That was an attitude that carried from the locker room to the ice to the stands. While the team that called Madison Square Garden home hardly was a giant success among hockey circles, the Rangers and their fans certainly acted as if they were. You would think that sort of smugness and a cocksure attitude would be supported by layers of championships. But, no. While New York had three Stanley Cup titles to its name, the last one had come in 1940, the same year that Abbott & Costello debuted ... on radio.

But none of that mattered to Rangers fans. They were sure of themselves, year in and year out. In fact, in the early 1980s, the Rangers were a consistent playoff-caliber team, make no mistake. But the New York Islanders, tucked away in Uniondale, New York, were the league standard. The Isles were on their way to four straight Stanley Cup championships, a run unmatched today in any major professional sports league.

The Islanders were the kings of hockey. But not the kings of their own city.

That title belonged to the cult and the culture of the red, white, and blue: the Broadway Blueshirts could walk around town with their heads held high in good times and bad, no matter what. They gathered the headlines and the hugs, and there wasn't a thing anyone could do about it.

"Throughout the years, you had to give the Rangers fans credit," said Mike Francesa, the afternoon talk show host for WFAN-AM 660 in New York. "They suffered through all the years of heartbreak, but kept coming back. They loved that team and loved to tell people about it."

To be sure, in that suddenly crowded schoolyard that was New York–area hockey, the Islanders were the whiz kids, the Devils were the new kids, and the Rangers? Well, they were the cool kids.

"They were an annoyance at first, really. Nothing more," Joe Benigno said of the Devils, echoing the sentiment of legions of Rangers fans at the time. Benigno should know. He cultivated a talk show career at WFAN based on his loud, proud—and often panicked—view of his teams, which includes the Rangers. "All the Devils really provided, at first, was a place to see the Rangers a few more times."

Which was true, of course. Rangers home games were always a tough, pricey ticket—even in the city's lean times—so a few more contests on the other side of the Hudson River allowed Rangers fans the chance to infiltrate someone else's building and watch their pride and joy take the ice. It was truly a bizarre environment to witness, and the phenomenon continues to this day. Whenever the Rangers and Devils meet in New Jersey, there are always a large number of New York fans in the building.

From 1982 through 2007, the Devils called the Meadowlands home. They played in what was originally called the Brendan Byrne Arena, named after the New Jersey governor, which was eventually changed to Continental Airlines Arena.

Whatever the official name was, it was often given a bad name around the league because of its poor ice conditions, lack of atmosphere, and far too many empty seats among its capacity of 19,040.

But it was different when the Rangers came to town. You have to remember that the Rangers, in many ways, were a regional team, and still are. And you have to understand the perspective from which Rangers fans— some of whom may have actually lived in New Jersey—approached this new team, this new era of hockey.

There were some converts, clearly. The Devils' presence, for many New Jersey hockey fans, meant a more affordable, more convenient way of seeing the sport they loved. But for those born and bred into Rangers Nation, those who lived and died with their team, there was no turning back.

"Once they are your team, they are your team," Benigno said. "Doesn't matter the team, doesn't matter the sport. We talk about this all the time. When they are your team, it's for life. I don't know how it can be any other way. For the Rangers, that's a lot of people. Doesn't matter who came into the league after them."

A lot of fans flocked to the Byrne Arena in that first season, if only out of curiosity. And although the Devils, complete with their red-and-green uniforms that often drew comparisons to Christmas trees, defeated the Rangers 3–2 on October 8, 1982, in the first installment of this feud—a surprisingly shining moment for the inaugural club en route to a dismal 17–49–14 season—the New Yorkers were never deterred from coming back.

"It took some getting used to, but they did make us feel at home, yes," former Rangers forward Stephane Matteau said of the New York fans. "As a hockey player, you're raised to be prepared for home games, and then road games. They are different, of course. But when you played there, it was almost as if we were at home. Took some getting used to, but it was fun."

Not for the Devils...most of the time.

"Yeah, it was frustrating," former Devils forward Corey Millen said. "We'd come back from a road trip, and maybe we had won three or four in a row, and we'd be feeling good about ourselves. And then we'd play the Rangers at home, and forget it. We'd look around, and we'd be like, *Are you serious? This is a road game!*"

But such was life for a team that had to start from scratch in a tough environment. In the 1980s, if you were a hockey fan in this market, you either supported the Islanders, who rewarded you with championship after championship, or the Rangers, who were solid most years, played under the bright lights of the big city, and had tradition to fall back on if all else failed.

Who had time for the Devils?

If a lack of respect in their own region wasn't bad enough, the Devils developed an odious reputation that began to filter out across the league.

The team posted the same win total in their second season as it had in its first: 17…to go along with 56 losses and seven ties. It was a dreadful 41-point season. They opened up on October 5, 1983, with a 6–2 loss to the Rangers at the Garden, followed it up two nights later with a 3–1 loss to the same team at the Byrne, and before you knew it, they were 2–20.

Yep. 2–20.

On November 28, two months into the season, they had *four points*.

One of those losses will live in infamy for many reasons. On November 19, 1983, while on a swing through Western Canada, the Devils ran into the fast, furious, high-wire act known as the Edmonton Oilers. Wayne Gretzky and the team that became the standard for success in the 1980s, along with the Islanders, showed no mercy against the road-weary Devils, pummeling them with a video-game-like score of 13–4.

After the game, in his locker room press briefing, Gretzky's hits kept on coming.

"Well, it's time they got their act together, folks," Gretzky said. "They're ruining the whole league. They had better stop running a Mickey Mouse organization and put somebody on ice."

In today's day and age, with social media, blogs, live Internet updates, and 24-hour sports television and radio stations, his comments might have been even more colorful.

As it was, the point was made. Gretzky, who later apologized for his comments, was probably not alone in his thinking. And the Devils, as they tried to gain some momentum on the ice, now had the label of being something of a joke in North American sports.

That image proved to be a tough one to shake.

All this meant more fodder, of course, for Rangers fans. Whether it was at games, in front of the water cooler, on the subway, or in the cafeteria, Rangers fans had another weapon to wield against their New Jersey counterparts. It was debilitating. It was demeaning. It was degrading. It was perfect for Rangers fans.

"There was plenty of that, and in many cases, the Devils were an easy target. But eventually, they found their way," said Chris Russo, a sports talk show host on Sirius-XM Satellite Radio who rose to fame on WFAN in the 1990s partnering with Francesa. "They made the playoffs in 1988, and things started to change. Were they the Rangers at that point? No. And they never will be. But they started a process of gaining respect. And with that, the rivalry with the Rangers gained a little more juice, yes."

Indeed, 1988 was when the rivalry rose to a new level. Cute no more, something to joke about no longer, the feud gained some fire on the regular season's final night. In Chicago, with the anonymous, never-say-die Devils clinging to postseason life and needing a win or else, forward John MacLean beat Blackhawks goaltender Darren Pang in overtime with a shot from the slot to post a 4–3 win not long after the Rangers blanked the Quebec Nordiques 3–0 in New York.

The shutout, though, became null and void at that point, as the Devils clinched the Patrick Division's final playoff berth with the stunner at old Chicago Stadium.

New Jersey played on. New York went home. The tables were turned, and a rivalry was born.

That was April 3, 1988. Easter Sunday. Things haven't been the same since.

"I still say it to this day. I'd like to take some credit for the beginning of the New Jersey Devils franchise and what it is today," said a smiling Pang, who also graduated to a career in broadcasting. "I gave up one of the most famous goals in their history, and that team really started to turn the tide for that organization. You could see it slowly starting to build, and that particular team had a lot of talent."

"But yeah, that one is on me," he added, laughing. "They owe me."

The Devils, under the direction of coach Jim Schoenfeld, would go on to orchestrate a Cinderella-like run that landed them on the brink of the Stanley Cup Finals. They won some fans over, they created a buzz, and in defeating the Islanders and Washington Capitals before finally succumbing to the Boston Bruins in seven games, they established a New Jersey brand, an identity of their own—one that didn't sit well with Rangers fans.

"By that time, we hated them, yes," Benigno said. "Everything about them. Hated 'em."

At the head of the turnaround was general manager Lou Lamoriello, a no-nonsense, all-business executive who had a plan, a mind-set to turn this laughingstock into a playoff staple, one that would be respected and feared at the same time across the league.

Players would wear suits everywhere they went. They would shave every day. They would be professional. They would be proud. They would be passionate at all times.

Or else.

"I always hate to use the word *I*," Lamoriello said. "Around here, it's *We*. And we just felt like a change was needed."

Many in the business thought Lamoriello, who had cut his teeth in sports management building up the athletics program at Providence College, was crazy to think his ways would work in the NHL. But he didn't care.

"Lou was and is his own person," said former Devils forward Jim Dowd, a gritty, hard-nosed center from Brick, New Jersey, who became the first Garden State native to play for the team and truly epitomized Lamoriello Hockey. "He had his ways. And it was his way or you're out.

"It wasn't that hard to get used to; people ask that all the time. It wasn't that hard: it was hockey, and it was hockey his way. You did it, because if you didn't go along with him, you'd be out of work."

McMullen hired Lamoriello in April of 1987 as team president. He then named himself general manager and went to work. A year later, the Devils engineered that miraculous postseason run and stamped themselves as playoff contenders every year going forward.

"Lou held everyone accountable in that organization," former Rangers center Mark Messier said, "and success followed."

They didn't always make the postseason, of course, but the building blocks were in place. They were a tad slow in 1988–89, in fact, failing to make the playoffs with just 66 points. But as Lamoriello continued to install his culture within the organization, the team bounced right back. And as he continued to stockpile players through trades and the draft—and as a testament to just how stable a talent base he had established—the Devils made the playoffs in four straight years after that while employing four different coaches.

Imagine that in today's league.

"He was the perfect man for the job," said Barry Melrose, a former NHL coach and now a television analyst. "That's what they needed. Even in those early years, people around the league knew that Jersey had players—John MacLean, Bruce Driver, that group—but they just needed some stability up top."

They got that…and then some.

"Not just as a player, but as a fan who was aware of what was going on around the league, you began to notice the change in Jersey, sure," former Rangers forward Steve Larmer said. "If you played them at that time, you kind of said to yourself afterward that 'Hey, they have good goaltending, good defense, and they're making it work.' That was their thing. That was what was going to carry them to the next level. And obviously, they did a good job of that for a long time to come."

But all along, the Rangers were still the Rangers. They weren't winning titles yet, but they maintained their superiority complex over the Devils. And after the 1991–92 season, they finally had their chance to exact some revenge for the 1988 Easter Night Massacre.

After the Devils went 38–31–11 for 87 points and the Rangers barreled through the Eastern Conference to finish 50–25–5 with 105 points, the two teams were to meet in the first round of the playoffs for the first time.

It was graduation day for the Hudson River Rivalry.

"In 1992, it was a tough series and a lot of things were happening. There was a lot of emotion out there," Messier said. "Lot of back and forth in the games. In the end, what that means is that both teams were evenly matched and both had the will to win."

But without question, the Rangers were the favorites. Messier led a group that was loaded on offense, finishing the regular season with 321 goals as dreams of erasing the Stanley Cup curse started to gain traction in the Big Apple.

On defense, the top-seeded Rangers were deep and balanced, led by superstar Brian Leetch, who truly began to come into his own. At the time, he was the prototypical, new-era, two-way defenseman. Leetch finished with 22 goals and 102 points. Consider that with regard to today's game: a blueliner with a triple-digit point total.

Along came the Devils, a typical Lamoriello group coached by Tom McVie. They battled their way to 38 wins and 289 goals. Rugged winger Claude Lemieux scored 41 of them, but in the end, it was a mixed bag of players fighting for the same cause. That was Lamoriello Hockey. No one player seemed bigger than the next, and in the net—get this—they used four different goaltenders.

"You can say what you will about Lou, that he was a micromanager, and that he wanted to get his hands on everything," former Devils forward Randy McKay said. "But you can't argue with the success. And that's all that mattered to us. Winning."

Look no further than the net in 1992. Yes, Chris Terreri, Craig Billington, Chad Erickson, and a fresh-faced rookie named Martin Brodeur all saw time between the pipes as the scrap-iron Devils secured a playoff bid and made a date with the flash-and-dash Rangers in Round 1.

Whatever it took.

"We knew we had to play our game, and how not to be intimidated," said Driver, a longtime Devils defenseman who also would see time with the Rangers before his career ended. "They had quite a team, the Rangers, and they had the points and statistics to prove it. Everyone knew that."

With Messier in charge, the Rangers won the Presidents' Trophy for most regular season points with ease. Their total of 105 was seven points better than the rest of the league, and they were 15 wins over the NHL average of 35. Messier, 31, thought of as the missing link to the Rangers' undying quest for a championship, delivered 35 goals and 107 points that season, and combined with Leetch for 209 points.

"When you look back on those teams and that era in Rangers Hockey, it starts with Mark," said Kenny Albert, the Rangers' current radio play-by-play man. "When they brought in Messier in 1991, from that moment on, things changed, obviously."

Messier had already won five Stanley Cup championships with the Oilers by the time he arrived in New York. The last, in 1990, truly cemented his legendary status, as that title was Edmonton's first—and last—without Gretzky.

So, in many ways, Messier was the quintessential New York sports addition: the proven leader and unquestioned star overnighted to the big city with a hefty price tag on his wrist, so that a title-starved franchise, too, could enjoy the many benefits of success. The big-money names before him that landed in the city under similar circumstances were plentiful, with varied results, of course, across many New York sports platforms. Reggie Jackson and Dave Winfield were brought in under the same terms with Major League Baseball's Yankees.

Jackson won. Winfield didn't.

It's just something that New York teams did to satisfy their fans, to fill seats, and to raise banners. And Messier was next in line.

The Rangers had stars, sure. They always did. But now, they had *the* star.

"There was no question about it," Albert said. "And he took on that role well. Things just changed with Mark. And in 1992, with that team, they were well on their way."

Surely, this Messier-made machine wasn't going to slip up against the Devils, right? A tough, balanced team capable of stringing together wins in the regular season, New Jersey wasn't going put up much a fight in the first round against these guys, were they?

"Well, they had a shot. It was the Rangers, and you knew, everyone knew, that anything was possible," Russo said. "When the Devils made the conference finals in 1988, you began to see the franchise take hold in Lamoriello's image, the way Lou wanted to build it. They lost that series to Boston, and I was there in Game 7. Did a show there, will never forget it. You could see it in their faces. They were proud of what they had become, and they didn't want to see it end. It was a tough loss for them, but one that they could build off of. And a few years later, versus the Rangers, they did that."

While New Jersey battled valiantly—and actually led the series at one point 2–1—the Devils eventually succumbed in a rock 'em, sock 'em Game 7 at the Garden that saw the Rangers flex their muscle, once and for all. On May 1, 1992, Messier and forward Adam Graves combined for four goals as the Rangers destroyed the No. 4 seed Devils 8–4. The rivalry's first playoff series ended with an angst-filled Game 7 that featured plenty of offense and far too many odd-man rushes for Lamoriello's liking.

The series also raised the level of animosity between the two teams— there were 156 minutes in penalties in Game 6 alone. It was in this stretch of 13 days that people across both states began to see the feud in a new light. Headlines were made, drama was publicized, and for the first time in a long time, hockey mattered.

When it was over, the ceremonial handshakes were still professional, of course. It is, after all, a hockey tradition. But everyone who walked out of the Garden that night knew that these two teams would look back on that series for a long time.

It was hard not to.

For the Rangers fans, the overriding feeling was one of relief. What mattered to them most, at the time, was that their team was still in the hunt for the Stanley Cup—no matter how tough the test was versus the Devils— and that Messier had delivered, at least for one round. All the moves were paying off and the ship was still pointed in the right direction.

But for Devils fans, there was also a measure of satisfaction. No. 4 seeds in the division—comparable nowadays to No. 8 conference seeds, as the playoff format has since changed—don't often win first-round series, especially against teams with 105 points. (Unless you're talking about the 2011–12 Los Angeles Kings, of course.) But while losing to the Rangers was a tough pill to swallow, the Devils did prove to their region that they were no longer pushovers in this rivalry.

They were gnats no more and, more importantly, they showed that Lamoriello's strategy was working.

"Yeah, we lost that one, and it hurt, no question," Daneyko said. "And that's a tough thing to do when you're in it and you're going through it. When you retire, and you're older, you can look back on it. But when you're in the moment, it's tough to see the big picture, it's tough to believe that the tough times will eventually lead to the good times."

Which is exactly where the Rangers thought they were headed: onto bigger and better things. With the Devils behind them, they needed just 12 more wins for The Curse to be buried forever.

Twelve wins. With that team? With Messier? Not a problem, right? Wrong.

"Yes, it just so happens," Albert said, "that they then ran into one of the best teams of all time in Pittsburgh."

And just like that, doubt, dread, and disbelief had returned to New York.

The Penguins, loaded on offense themselves with future Hall of Fame forwards Mario Lemieux and Jaromir Jagr, plodded their way through the regular season in 1992 to the tune of just 39 wins and 87 points. It wasn't an effort that came to be expected in Pittsburgh, especially after the Penguins won the Stanley Cup for the first time the season before.

The Pens scored 343 goals in the regular season, tops in the league, and simply tried to outscore teams with their skill. But they truly kicked it into gear as a complete unit versus the Rangers. After surviving a seven-game series against the Capitals in the opening round, Lemieux and Co. woke up and upset the Rangers with relative ease.

A 4–2 win at the Garden in Game 1, in which Lemieux had two assists, showed everyone that playtime was over for Pittsburgh. The Penguins eventually scored 24 goals in six games, and buried the Rangers' hopes for good with a 5–1 whitewash in New York on May 13.

The series turned, though, when Graves slashed Lemieux with his stick in Game 2, breaking the Pittsburgh captain's wrist. The Penguins, angered at the loss of their leader, used it as a rallying cry. The Rangers, on the other hand, were deflated to the point of no return when Graves was suspended.

For all intents and purposes, the season ended there in Game 2, as did New York's Stanley Cup dreams. Yes, after just 13 playoff games, the

Garden had gone dark once again, and the quest to kill The Curse would have to wait at least another season.

Meanwhile, Lemieux recovered, finished the postseason with 16 goals and 18 assists, and the Penguins again skated off with the big, silver mug that seemed destined for New York just four weeks before.

How did this all happen?

"I really thought that was the year," Benigno said. "A great regular season, you really start to feel it, and then that terrible series against Pittsburgh. That Rangers team had it all. You really start to wonder at that point, *Is it ever going to happen?* But hey, at least they beat the Devils in that playoff year. That was a series, a great one, that doesn't get a lot of credit."

It's offerings like that, from the die-hard fans, that encapsulate the power of a rivalry. Not unlike the Yankees and Boston Red Sox in baseball, the Green Bay Packers and Chicago Bears in the NFL, or Auburn and Alabama in college football, you know that a rivalry is truly intense when beating the other team in an otherwise unsuccessful year is a quality consolation prize.

Of course, Rangers fans were used to consolation prizes. In fact, they were probably sick of them. Still, at least they didn't have to slog back to work in 1992 and hear it from Devils or Islanders fans. That would have been the ultimate nightmare for them. At least they had one feather in their cap, though it wasn't the one they were looking for.

"To understand the Rangers and their fans and the relationship is truly an unbelievable thing. The Rangers and their fans transcend their sport," said Steve Somers, also of WFAN, who used to work the overnight shift under the moniker "Captain Midnight." It was his airtime, a session which he referred to as "the Schmooz," in which many area hockey fans would come out of their shells and hit the phones. "Hockey fans, and Rangers fans in particular, are limited in number compared to baseball and football, but they could care less. They are as passionate as any out there. They are No. 1 with their hockey team, and as passionate and knowledgeable as any other fan might be. Their voice may be louder than most."

And while Devils fans certainly had something to be proud of in 1992, the fact remained that they hadn't been out of the first round since the magic carpet ride of 1988, and insult was added to injury by losing to a

Rangers team that couldn't even get out of the second round—and out of their own way—two weeks later.

Somers felt that. After all, his show was often a gauge for local hockey interest. The pulse of New York Hockey ran through his overnight shows and often created great radio for those who could stay up late. During that 1992 postseason, with regard to the number of Devils calls, his answer was swift and simple: "Not many."

But that was life as McMullen and Co. came to know it. Though progress was being made under Lamoriello, turning around public opinion is like trying to turn around a battleship. To truly make their mark, the Devils were going to have two do one of two things, or both: defeat the Rangers in a postseason series, and/or win the Stanley Cup.

Through 10 years of existence in the swamps of East Rutherford, they had done neither.

"That's definitely something that was in our minds. We didn't let it affect us, but it was there," former Devils forward Bill Guerin said. "In that area, with the long history that the Rangers have had and the tons of fans, it was certainly understandable. We had to get used to that. But I think we did, and it started at the top. We were thick-skinned, and we just didn't let it bother us. We accepted it for what it was. That doesn't mean we had to like them."

Slowly, as time went on, the rivalry began to gain some notoriety outside of the hockey world, too. Yankees–Red Sox it was not, but there was appeal in the entertainment world, believe it or not. Credit NBC and the team that orchestrated the hit series *Seinfeld* for bringing it to the forefront.

"The Face Painter" was the 109th episode of perhaps the most famous sitcom series of all time. In the 23rd episode of its sixth season, directed by Andy Ackerman and with a teleplay by Larry David, *Seinfeld* featured a crazed Devils fan and New Jersey native who happened to be Elaine Benes' boyfriend. His name was David Puddy, and he loved the Devils so much that he'd often paint his face before attending games.

In the episode, Puddy attended a Devils game with Benes against the Rangers at Madison Square Garden. The show aired on May 11, 1995. Puddy was played by actor Patrick Warburton, who indeed is a native of the Garden State, having been born in Paterson, New Jersey.

"In the realm of half-hour television that I've done across two decades, it is clearly one of the most memorable, most rewarding episodes that I have ever done," Warburton said. "It was just so much fun to be that fan, to be that character, on that show. That was the second episode of *Seinfeld* that I had done, and after it, people recognized me as if I was a regular. The Devils and Rangers have been with me, I suppose, my entire career."

The show ends at another Devils-Rangers game, for which—after Elaine said Puddy couldn't paint his face anymore—he paints his chest instead.

"For the love of the Devils," he said with a laugh. "Looking back on it now, it was just a wonderful experience. The franchise did everything first class, which is not a surprise, and again, to even be mentioned with them, to have a small part of that, is not a bad thing. Especially since I really had nothing to do with anything they've ever done! But I do get requests all the time, from fans all over, especially hockey fans, and fans of the Rangers and Devils. I play along, absolutely. You can tell how much the rivalry means, and it's something they get a kick out of. I've never been one to shy away from that, and I do my character in voice. I have no qualms about that. Just don't expect me to have face paint with me at all times."

Back in the real world, a year before "The Face Painter" aired, a real-life series was about to commence. Some 24 months after the first postseason installment between these two clubs went the distance, the 1994 Eastern Conference Finals were about to try to top that first thriller.

Little did anyone know that the 1992 series, as dramatic, passionate, and intense as it was, would only serve as an opening act for a larger-than-life headliner that would live in hockey history forever.

Building the Rangers

○ ○ ○ ○

"When you look back on things, there are so many ways to describe that particular team. But what sticks out to me was just how deep it was. When you look at some of the players who didn't get to dress almost on a nightly basis, it was amazing. That group was just so incredibly tough and inspiring, and above all else, full of character."
—KEVIN LOWE, NEW YORK RANGERS (1992–96)

STEPHANE MATTEAU AND a quality Chicago Blackhawks team strolled into Madison Square Garden on March 18, 1994, and didn't quite know what to expect. They had heard about this dynamic, dominant, win-it-now-or-else Rangers club that was busy tearing through the rest of the league. And New York entered this particular game off a 4–0 win over the Hartford Whalers, so there was a fresh example on film staring right at Matteau and Co.

But the Hawks were content to reserve judgment for themselves, thank you very much. This, after all, was a deep, skilled team from Chicago that would eventually rack up 87 points and head to the Western Conference playoffs.

They had a lot of pride, too. And like any other NHL team, they didn't want to give the Rangers *too* much respect. These were, after all, still just the Rangers.

But even though Matteau posted three assists and the Blackhawks cruised to a surprising 7–3 victory in front of a disgruntled New York crowd, the rugged forward walked out of the Garden quite impressed. The Rangers had played without captain Mark Messier that night, and goaltender Mike Richter was just a bit off his game.

"But you could just tell," Matteau said. "We caught them on a good night, we were able to beat Richter a few times, but you walked away believing what you had heard. They were good, they had four lines, they had a great building to play in, and you just knew, at full health, that team was going to be tough to beat."

Little did Matteau know that, just three days later, he'd be a member of that team.

Indeed, Rangers general manager Neil Smith and coach Mike Keenan were not pleased with the club throughout the four-game stretch that ended with the Blackhawks game. New York had lost three of those games—allowing 15 goals during that run—and the rival New Jersey Devils, in second place in the Atlantic Division most of the season, were gaining momentum and confidence.

All of a sudden, something wasn't right in the Big Apple, in a season where the Rangers could do no wrong. Smith and Keenan had to turn things around…fast.

"It was said so many times in the regular season, from Mark Messier to Brian Leetch to the media, that it had to be done now. Now or never," said Gary Thorne, who at the time was the national NHL play-by-play man for ESPN. "They had to win the Cup. It was such a big deal for them and New York, and as a result, it became a huge deal to the National Hockey League."

Smith felt the same way, and how could he not? Two years removed from having the best regular season mark of any team in the NHL—only to fall on their faces in the second round versus Pittsburgh—Keenan's Rangers were as talented as ever and were not getting any younger. The Eastern Conference, with upstarts such as New Jersey, Washington, and Boston, not to mention the 1990s staple of command and consistency in Pittsburgh, was not going to be an easy ocean to navigate, one way or the other.

So, with a struggling team and a 54-year Stanley Cup curse enveloping him, Smith—with close guidance from Keenan, of course—burned up the phone lines on March 21, hobnobbed with other general managers, and pulled no punches.

Smith wheeled and dealed in a manner the league wasn't used to. When a team this good has aspirations this high, sure, you make a small tweak here and there as the playoffs near. Maybe acquire a fourth-line center or a penalty-killing defenseman. Maybe add a little depth for the power play.

But Smith, as candid and as open as any executive in the league, took it to a new level. After all, Keenan wouldn't have had it any other way. Smith was the I-just-need-a-few-things guy at the grocery store who grabs a basket on his way through the door, starts shopping, and then realizes the basket just won't do. So, he goes back to the front, scraps the basket, and snares a cart.

And then, he strolled down the aisles and filled it to the top.

Do not discount Keenan's role here. Theirs was not an ordinary coach–general manager relationship. This is how things had to be under Keenan. While Smith purchased the groceries, Keenan picked a lot of them off the shelves.

"Those guys that they acquired, Mike Keenan knew them, and knew he could abuse them," said Bill Clement, at the time the national hockey analyst for ESPN. "Mike whipped everybody. He brought in guys that he knew would respond when he did that. And those were the guys that he wanted."

And so the dominoes began to fall.

Mike Gartner, a high-scoring veteran forward who had 28 goals in 71 games and figured to have a major role in the postseason? Gone. Traded to Toronto for another veteran forward, Glenn Anderson, the rights to Scott Malone, and Toronto's 1994 fourth-round draft choice.

"Keenan hated Gartner," Smith said. "Hated him. And he flat-out told me, 'If you don't trade him, I'm not going to dress him…ever.' And this was Mike fucking Gartner, a proven goal scorer in this league! But Keenan was adamant. And Anderson was having a down year, so I called and asked Toronto, would you give me Anderson for Gartner? Looking back on it, Gartner was still a better player, but Anderson came in and fit in with all of the old [Edmonton] Oilers."

But Smith and Keenan were far from done.

Todd Marchant, a rising center who worked his way through the organizational ranks and figured to give the Rangers some youthful enthusiasm during any potential lengthy series? Gone. Traded to Edmonton for veteran center Craig MacTavish, a faceoff demon who the team hoped would win those crucial draws at crunch time.

"What I wanted to find was good players, in their last years of their contracts, who were playing on bad teams, teams that would want to talk to us. For instance, Craig was becoming an unrestricted [free agent] and Edmonton was awful that year," Smith said. "I had had a bunch of trades in the past with [then–Oilers general manager] Glen [Sather], so there was a rapport there, and a good relationship. And we had talked and talked and talked about Craig, but Glen always put it off. He was like the last-minute Christmas shopper, and then you turn around and you have to get everything on Christmas Eve."

There's that shopping analogy again.

"Anyhow, last minute, we make the deal for Marchant," Smith said. "And Glen calls me back later, and he's pissed. 'You fucked me on the trade! You fucked me! The kid, Marchant, is 5′5″!' I was confused myself, because I thought he was 6′1″! So, I looked it up. And I replied to him, 'What are you talking about? This kid, Marchant, was on the U.S. National team. He's a player!' So, he goes back and looks at the book, and he was thinking about the wrong Marchant! He was looking at his brother, not Todd. 'Oh, okay,' he said. And it turns out Marchant has a great career in Edmonton. Funny how that stuff happens."

And then, finally, the big one.

Tony Amonte, a right wing sniper and career Ranger who had scuffled a bit with this flash-and-dash team, posting just 16 goals and 38 points? Gone. Traded, along with the rights to Matt Oates to Chicago for gritty forwards Brian Noonan and, yep, Stephane Matteau.

"Mike had those guys in Chicago, so he knew them well, and knew what he could get out of them," said Clement. "I don't think Neil did very much, though. Mike demanded that he do it. I don't want to take any credit away from Neil. But Mike Keenan was a pretty demanding coach. 'Give me this guy, give me that guy. Get rid of this guy, get rid of that guy.' Whatever it was, it worked for them. It was another step toward breaking the jinx."

Smith recalls the conversations vividly.

"All season, Mike did not like Amonte. Just didn't like him. And he loved Matteau. Loved him," Smith said. "Anyhow, Steph was in Chicago, and the deadline was close, and they were looking to deal him. Chicago wanted Amonte, and there was just no fucking way I was doing that deal straight up, Stephane for Amonte. No way. I had to get more than Matteau. So, I took Noonan, and that's still a horseshit trade. I mean, we won games, and everything is okay when you win, and they helped us win, but Matteau and Noonan for Amonte? It was a horseshit trade. From a GM standpoint, it was just bad. But it did help us."

Of course, room needed to be made to create space for these players, so Smith and Keenan cut more bait without any hesitation. Veteran forward Phil Bourque, who had no goals in 16 games and was relying more on his background, having won two Stanley Cups with the Penguins, than his actual skating ability? Gone. Traded to Ottawa for future considerations. Seldom-used defenseman Peter Andersson, who was a minus-3 in just eight games and didn't figure into any of Smith's long-term plans? Gone. Traded to Florida for future considerations.

"They definitely made a statement," Clement said. "They had put together a strong team already, and if they didn't think these moves were the right ones, they wouldn't have made them. What they did was pick up players who knew how to win. And when you talk about those Rangers in that season, the more of those, the better."

In the mode the Rangers were in, they felt they needed as many players with Stanley Cup experience as possible. To Smith and Keenan, it wasn't enough that Messier, Adam Graves, Kevin Lowe, pesky forward Esa Tikkanen, and bruising defenseman Jeff Beukeboom came from the flourishing fraternity that was the Edmonton Oilers, a franchise that had won five Stanley Cup titles and played in a town that, to this day, still calls itself the City of Champions.

Those players certainly had been through the wars and were sure to be able to man the postseason fort during the tough times. But hey, this was New York. And enough is never enough.

So, Smith and Keenan welcomed two more Oilers castoffs in MacTavish and Anderson. Though their better days were clearly behind them—Anderson was 33 and MacTavish 35—try to see it from Smith's perspective, especially considering Keenan's nudging.

How could you turn down a guy like Anderson, who was on his way to the Hall of Fame and had two 50-goal seasons on his résumé? And how could you not snag a guy like MacTavish, who was a career plus-34 player and was so much more than the "last player to not wear a helmet on the ice," as he had come to be known?

"Mike and Neil wanted a strong work ethic on the ice. They wanted very competitive players who were strong on the boards," said former Rangers forward Steve Larmer, who had 21 goals and 60 points at age 32 during that season. "He wanted the grind-it-out, blue-collar type players, like Brian Noonan, and Stephane Matteau, and Craig MacTavish, and myself. Mike always seemed to have a few of those guys, so they just figured, let's get some more. We knew his program, on and off the ice, and if you sprinkle enough of us in there, among the stars, it usually finds a way to work out."

Larmer would know. He was traded to the Rangers from Hartford earlier in the season, and was thrilled with his get-out-of-hockey-no-man's-land card.

"Mike didn't like [longtime Rangers defenseman] James Patrick and [forward Darren] Turcotte," Smith said. "And I wanted to get Steve Larmer; he was a fit and he was just what we were looking for. But he was a holdout in Chicago and he was disgruntled. But we knew, with us hiring Mike Keenan after being in Chicago, there might be some tension there. So, we had to get creative. We didn't think Chicago would deal with us, but we knew we wanted him. We knew that much. So, I called [Hartford general manager] Paul Holmgren, and set it up so they'd trade for Larmer, and we'd give them Patrick and Turcotte. It was a good deal. He also wanted me to take [forward Nick] Kypreos. We wanted Larmer enough to make the deal. And it ended up working out. He was a great guy for a team, and that's a deal that gets lost sometimes in all of the deadline deals."

There's a downside to so many transactions, though. There are players who are shown the door, and sometimes, they are lifelong Rangers.

Enter Turcotte.

"It was certainly one of the hardest days in my career when I got that call, because having gone through with the Rangers, I had never been traded before. When you finally get that first call, you lose something," he said. "You're going somewhere, and you don't know much about that place, and it's just a different feeling. But it was just something you have to live with."

But Turcotte didn't leave without a firm sense of what life was like with Keenan. By the time the relationship ended, it was clear that it wasn't going to work. But if nothing else, he had a few stories to take with him to the Whalers.

"Mike did some things that were a little strange," Turcotte said. "Things were good, then we lose to Anaheim for their first road win in franchise history, and the next day, we're out there for practice and there were no pucks on the ice. None. We skated for about 45 minutes straight. Then he proceeded to kick everyone off the ice. When we got back to the room, he was waiting there with our five-game bonus paychecks, and he made everyone come up to him individually, to shake his hand. And that was right after drilling us for about 45 minutes. But that was Mike. And Mike had his ways of motivating. For me, I was just going to work as hard as I could because I wanted to be a Ranger, and you know, when there's a change in coaches, that's something that could happen, so I wanted to do everything I could to stick around. All in all, it was Mike's team, and he was going to go with the guys who he felt could get the job done. And if you look back, the guys like Gilbert and Noonan and Matteau really helped. And I suppose I couldn't prove that to him in two months."

Matteau wasn't so sure, however, that he would be one of "those guys," at least not at first. In fact, it might surprise most Rangers fans to learn that Matteau, who had never won a Stanley Cup and had never been a part of a team with this much potential, was not thrilled to be headed to New York. It was no disrespect to the franchise, by any means. But to know Matteau is to know every hardworking, earn-everything-you-get, never-say-die French Canadian kid who is fortunate enough to get through what they call The League.

In the end, players want to play. But Matteau wasn't so sure where he fit in on this team of stars.

"I knew there was a chance I could be traded, but I had no idea where," he said. "You heard the reports, though, you knew that your name was being mentioned, and that's all part of the game."

On the day of the deal, Matteau took part in a Blackhawks optional practice in Chicago and kept to himself. A few minutes into it, he could hide no longer.

"I saw assistant coach Paul Baxter coming my way, and I knew something had happened," Matteau said. "He comes to me and says, 'Management needs to talk to you upstairs.' I figured I'd play along, you know, try to have some fun with it. I told Paul, 'I'll just see them in the morning.' But I knew I had to go up, and I knew I was on my way out."

All kidding aside, Matteau made it up to the office and was informed of the deal. Indeed, the team he helped to beat just three days before liked what it saw in him and wanted him. It could have been seen as flattering. It could have been seen as an opportunity to win the Stanley Cup. Truth be told, Matteau didn't see it that way at all.

"Disappointed, at first, no question. I was disappointed," he said. "We had just seen this team, we were aware of what they had been doing all year, and really, I just didn't think they needed anything at that point."

Matteau immediately feared the worst, that he'd be relegated to the fourth line or even be made a healthy scratch at times. There he'd be, he figured, in a new situation in a new city—the biggest one in the world, no less—on an outstanding team without much of a role.

But Keenan changed all of that. Quickly.

The coach had a history with Matteau. He knew his strengths, his weaknesses, and how he'd mesh with the Rangers' mission, even before Matteau did. And so Keenan did what good coaches do in the NHL—he showed confidence in the veteran, right off the bat. He made Matteau a key cog in the team's quest from Day One.

Matteau made his debut on March 22 and had a goal, two shots, and was a plus-2 in a 4–4 tie against the Calgary Flames. The new-look Rangers opened up a swing through Western Canada by extracting a point. But more important, Keenan made the new guys feel not so new.

He gave Matteau an opportunity, and Matteau capitalized on it.

"Just goes to show you what kind a person Mike is," said Matteau, who was placed on the second line without hesitation. "Right off the bat, he puts me on a line with Alex Kovalev and Steve Larmer? I mean, just great, great players."

They were great players, and above all else, they were Keenan players. It took a while—there were only 12 regular season games left when the major moves were made—but Keenan finally had a roster that he could call his own, and to no one's surprise, everyone, at least at the time, was buying into the program.

"Mike was his own person, and did things his own way. And he didn't care what people thought about it," Larmer said. "He'd do his thing, and he'd do it without explanation. We knew that going in. We were all after the same thing, so it was never a problem. And it all worked out at the end of the day."

The Rangers went 8–2–2 after the deadline-day trades.

"Even before the trades, you knew this was a team that could go far. And then, of course, they added so much," said Kenny Albert, who grew up a Rangers fan and now lives out his dream calling their games on the radio. "At that point, you had so many players who had already played for Keenan, and that had a lot to do with that. They knew what the coach wanted from them."

The finish put enough distance between the Rangers and the Devils for that all-important No. 1 seed. New York, which swept New Jersey in the regular season, ended up six points better than the Devils.

"We had to respect them and we did respect them, because of the job they had done and because we had such a hard time with them in the regular season," former Devils forward Tom Chorske said. "We were focused on us, no question. But we certainly respected the season they had over there. They had so many great players. Kovalev, Graves, Messier, [Mike] Richter, just a great, great lineup."

And it all comes back to Keenan, perhaps Neil Smith's most important move.

During the 1992–93 season, the Rangers were not the Rangers. Losing has been a large part of this franchise's culture, but that collection of players—especially given they had won the Presidents' Trophy the season before—would not be allowed to use that as a crutch. They were too good for that.

But that season, under coach Roger Neilson, the team wasn't performing. In fact, a 5–2 start was quickly swallowed up by a four-game losing streak in November. There were injuries. Morale was sinking like the team's place in the standings. It felt like there was a dark cloud hovering over the Garden.

Smith sensed it, and took action at the 40-game mark. Neilson, who was overmatched versus Scotty Bowman and the Penguins in the second round of the playoffs the season before as the Rangers bowed out in six games, had clearly not recovered, taking the Rangers to just a 19–17–4 mark with a terrific collection of talent.

Just like that, his run was over.

"To think back to 1992, well, it was not a good situation," Lowe said. "There were fingers being pointed, we were not playing well, and ultimately, we did not make the playoffs. That's a tough thing to deal with in New York."

In came Ron Smith—who turned out to be worse than Neilson. He compiled a 15–22–7 mark, including closing the season with seven consecutive losses as the Garden became nothing more than a fan forum for fretfulness and frustration. The Rangers lost 11 of their last 12 games, and they did so painfully. Along the way, the defeats to some of their rivals only poured salt in the open wounds. In that final stretch, they lost to the Flyers and Capitals twice, as well as the Penguins, Islanders, and Devils.

"To be as good as they were the year before, yes, it was a bad environment for them," said Chris Russo, who at the time co-hosted an afternoon show on the Rangers' then-flagship radio home, WFAN-AM 660. "Nothing went right, and people always went back to the fact that, hey, that's what the Rangers do. But something had to change."

Neil Smith made sure that something did.

"I loved Roger, I really, really did. It was just one of those things that wasn't meant to be. Ron Smith came up from the minors, and he had done a great job in the system, but he couldn't turn around this team," Smith said. "So, I needed to make a change, and when you look at the roster we had, with Mess and Leetch and Richter and Esa, we needed someone who was at their level as the coach. Someone with a coaching résumé that could equal their playing résumés.

"As the 1992–93 season winded down, and we weren't going anywhere, I went to work on it. There were three coaches that were a part of the equation: Al Arbour, who was still working in the Islanders organization; Scotty Bowman, who was still with the Penguins; and Mike. Those, to me, were the real winners that were out there. The top coaches, for sure. I wanted to have it in place, just as the season ended, so instead of everyone talking about what had just happened, we could look ahead. We wanted everyone to forget about the year, and there was no better way to do that than to introduce Mike, and kind of answer one of the big questions before it was even asked. We wanted to build the excitement right away."

As teams around them—including the rival Islanders and Devils—moved on to the Patrick Division playoffs, Smith and Keenan went to work on what would ultimately be one of hockey's great reclamation projects.

Keenan was as stubborn as they came in the NHL, but the record of success was there. Although he had yet to win a Stanley Cup, he did bring the Flyers and Blackhawks to the Finals a total of three times. In fact, his 1991–92 Blackhawks, who had just 87 points and finished in second place in the Norris Division, made it all the way to the Finals on grit and guts before they lost to the Penguins.

So, Smith clearly felt he had his guy.

But where to begin?

Well, the American goaltending duo of John Vanbiesbrouck and Richter made for a cute storyline. From one aging star to another on the rise, the Rangers indeed had the U.S. market on goaltenders seemingly covered. But there aren't many teams that win Cups playing musical chairs between the pipes. And with an expansion draft coming anyway, a decision had to be made.

"That was my call," Neil Smith said. "I figured Mike [Keenan] hadn't been there long at all, and I just felt Mike [Richter] had more potential for growth. John was still a great goalie, but with the expansion draft, you could only protect one goalie. I wanted to trade John before the draft. I felt that could cover us, and he still had some trade potential. So, we talked with Vancouver. They had Kirk McLean and Kay Whitmore, and [general manager] Brian Burke didn't want to lose either one. So, I told him, 'Take Vanbiesbrouck, and Florida will draft him first overall in the expansion, and you won't lose your two goalies.' And if that didn't happen, then we had a deal with Winnipeg already lined up.

"But it happened, and I told Burke that if it played out, give me [veteran defenseman Doug] Lidster. I'll take Lidster. So, he becomes a part of our team, Vanbiesbrouck goes to Florida, and who's on the ice for us in some big spots in '94? Lidster. So, it's amazing how things like that happen. Players can end up being such important figures, and it often happens by serendipity and circumstance."

The 1993–94 team began to truly take shape in the early summer, when Vanbiesbrouck hit the road. He was shipped to the Canucks on June 20, 1993, and five days later, back came Lidster, a smooth-skating quarterback for the power play, equipped with a rifle shot.

"I knew the kind of situation I was getting into," Lidster said. "I give everyone credit there with the Rangers, and this was where Mike was great. He didn't shy away from it. We were going for the Cup, we're going to attack it, and we're going to live by certain rules. It was academic—we had to do what was assigned. I was ready to go."

Vanbiesbrouck, as expected, never played for the Canucks, and became a full-time starter in Florida instead. But what mattered to the Rangers was that it was Richter's ship now, a 26-year-old who was coming off a 13–19–3 season but had as much promise and as much upside as any netminder in the league.

"The funny thing about the Rangers, and that year, was that team was very businesslike. Came to the rink and everyone knew what to do. Mike was a part of that in net, and a big one, obviously," Lidster said. "You had your role. It was up to you to go out and do it."

Smith sat tight with that roster, for the most part, and Keenan took it to training camp. Of course, that was before the true shuffling began.

"I think, when you looked at the Rangers' success in 1991–92, and the pieces they had from that team still, with Mess, Gravey, and Leetch—and we didn't even know about Kovalev and [defenseman Sergei] Zubov and how good they were going to be—we knew we should have been a pretty solid club. And we just weren't in 1992–93," Lowe said. "So, 1993–94 comes, and we needed to make amends. We had talent, we went through a bit of a feeling-out process, and then we made a surge and just never let up. We knew that this was the year, and at that point, it was pretty much up to us where it was going to go."

The Rangers bridged October and November with a 14-game unbeaten streak that included 11 wins and sent an early message to the rest of the league that 1992–93 was a Blueshirt fluke.

Keenan was here, and the Cup would soon follow. At least, that was the plan.

As the team's confidence started to soar, some of the final scores began to resemble those usually found in video games:

- November 24, 1993: 7–1 over the Ottawa Senators. Messier, Lowe, and Larmer with a goal each
- December 26, 1993: 8–3 over the Devils. Sergei Nemchinov with two tallies. Backup goalie Glenn Healy with 23 saves
- January 25, 1994: 8–3 over the San Jose Sharks. Messier and Larmer with two goals apiece

The points kept piling up in the standings, as did the smiles on the bench and in the stands. Keenan and Smith were clearly onto something, and the rest of the league knew it.

"We sure did," said Kelly Hrudey, a CBC analyst and former NHL goalie with the New York Islanders, Los Angeles Kings, and San Jose Sharks. "I remember playing the Rangers that year with the Kings during the regular season in Madison Square Garden."

Hrudey battled a Rangers onslaught on October 24, 1993, in New York. He made 38 saves before finally succumbing to Richter and Co. 3–2.

"We played well. And even then, we were fortunate just to be in the game…and we knew it. And as I looked at what they were doing at the end of the season and into the playoffs, I said to myself, 'Wow, it's not a surprise. It was early when we saw them, and they were already playing so well.' Once they added the other players and continued to build some confidence, I said to myself, 'No one's beating them now. When we look back on it, we're going to be proud that we found a way to play the way we did against them, even if it was the regular season.' They were *that* good."

Strong words from a goalie on a Los Angeles team that also featured Hall of Fame forwards Wayne Gretzky and Jari Kurri, and had made the Stanley Cup Finals just a season before. But Hrudey wasn't alone in his opinion.

"The great thing about that Rangers team was that year, the game really started to slow down," Clement said. "But those Rangers were still playing that freewheeling, up-and-down style. With Mike Keenan behind the bench, and Mark Messier's charisma and presence, well, you had just a little bit of everything with that team."

And never was that more on display in the regular season than against the Devils, a sore spot for New Jersey's faithful. Considering the position the Devils were in, the frustration was clearly understandable. Here was a franchise, some six miles away from the Garden, that was finally set to break the shackles of anonymity, mediocrity, and malaise under their new regime—coach Jacques Lemaire and assistant Larry Robinson. The Devils, with a defensive approach second to none in the NHL, were on their way to their best season in franchise history. They had depth, they had drive, and they had determination. And if it wasn't for the Rangers—of all teams, it had to be them, *over there*—the Devils would have been the best team in the league.

But it was those six regular season meetings between the two teams that showed the Devils how far they still had to go:

October 31, 1993: Rangers 4, Devils 1
November 30, 1993: Rangers 3, Devils 1
December 5, 1993: Rangers 2, Devils 1
December 26, 1993: Rangers 8, Devils 3
February 24, 1994: Rangers 3, Devils 1
April 2, 1994: Rangers 4, Devils 2

Season series? Rangers 6, Devils 0.

"It was pretty simple for me," former Devils defenseman Ken Daneyko said. "I could not stand that team."

He and the Devils weren't the only victims in the Rangers' redemption, though. On the other side of New York, the Islanders had themselves a decent season, but had the unfortunate task of facing the Blueshirts in Round 1 of the playoffs. Things got ugly in a hurry.

"This town loves winners and loves to see teams and players win the big event," said Mike Francesa, who co-hosted New York's top afternoon show at the time with Russo on WFAN. "And, clearly, the Rangers were playing with that in their minds."

Just ask the Islanders, who had 36 wins and 84 points and seemed like a team that could at least keep things close, if for no other reason than the passion inherent in the rivalry.

In classic New York-ese: fugghedaboutit.

The Islanders lost one of the most lopsided series in NHL history in the blink of an eye. Messier had a goal and two assists in Game 1 as the Rangers cruised 6–0 at the Garden, only to repeat with the same exact score in Game 2. By the time the series shifted to Long Island, Richter had made 50 saves, Messier had four points, and the Rangers were up by a combined score of 12–0.

The rout was on.

Shifting to the Nassau Coliseum did not change things for the Islanders, other than finally getting a few pucks past Richter. In the end, though? It was all academic, as the Rangers won Games 3 and 4 by a combined score of 10–3. Graves had two goals in Game 3. Messier had two more in Game 4, and mercifully, the Islanders went home for the summer without a postseason victory on their résumé.

"That first series, we went through pretty easy. We found a way to dominate them," Larmer said in the understatement of the season. "But for some of us, we hadn't been through that process with the Rangers, and I suppose you can kind of slip into a different mind-set, and say, 'Oh, that was nothing, this is going to be easy.' We had to stay sharp."

They did.

The Capitals, with 39 wins and 88 points, were up next in Round 2. They had a little more zip than the Islanders, with former Rangers center Mike Ridley leading the way. He had 26 goals and 70 points in the regular season, and was one of four Capitals to reach 20 tallies on the year, joining Dmitri Khristich, Randy Burridge, and Peter Bondra.

But Washington was among the weaker postseason teams in net, and though the Capitals outlasted a game Penguins team in the first round in six games, the Rangers were clearly a different animal. Washington used four netminders in the regular season—Don Beaupre, Rick Tabaracci, Byron Dafoe, and Olaf Kolzig—with different levels of success, but it didn't matter who they tapped against the Rangers. They didn't have the defense to keep up with them anyway. Beaupre and Tabaracci combined on the losing effort, as the Rangers won in five games and cruised into the Eastern Conference Finals with an 8–1 postseason record.

Perhaps relieving themselves of the pressure of trying to mount back-to-back sweeps, the Rangers dropped Game 4 to the Capitals after taking a 3–0 lead in the series, as Sylvain Cote had three assists in a 4–2 Washington victory.

But that could not erase what the Rangers had already done, punishing the Capitals to a combined score of 14–5 in the first three games. The wealth began to be distributed in Keenan's system in this series, too, as Noonan scored two goals in Game 1, Tikkanen had two points in Game 2, and Leetch had a goal and an assist in Game 3.

"It took me a while to learn the kind of pressure that we had on us to win the Stanley Cup, because when I got there, it was right on the ice, go play," Matteau said. "So, you really didn't have time to worry about that, and even if you did, the leaders on that team wouldn't let you dwell on it too long. And we were playing really well in those two series, so everything was good."

So good that the Rangers were able to rest in between these series. While New York needed only nine games to reach the third round, the Devils, across the river, were chugging through a seven- and a six-game series, respectively, just to reach the league semifinals.

"That was good for us, sure, but we were well conditioned. Mike's teams were always well conditioned," Larmer said. "And we knew, as the rounds moved on and we advanced, that each opponent was going to be tougher than the next. I don't think anyone thought for a second that the conference finals were going to be easy for this team, no matter who we played."

Well, that team, ultimately, was their neighbor from the Garden State. The Devils survived a classic, first-round thriller against Buffalo, and then rallied from an 0–2 hole versus Boston in Round 2, collecting four straight victories and setting up a regional rematch of a first-round beauty some 24 months before.

As the postseason moved along, the New York media began to wrap its long arms around this story. Not to be fooled by the Rangers again, the tabloids waited to see just how legitimate the team was before splashing it all over the pages.

Two easy series victories and a date with the Devils in the third round sealed the deal. Indeed, hockey mattered in New York, unlike it ever had before.

"I don't know that the Devils had a lot to do with that. Some, but not a lot," Russo said. "They were an excellent, excellent team, one on the cusp of a championship. But if it was someone else playing the Rangers—say, the Penguins—I still think there would have been the same juice. The hype, the buzz, was because of the Rangers. This was their year, and they were playing like it. They had a long way to go still, but boy, were they playing well."

Just how Smith and Keenan imagined it the spring before.

Building the Devils

○ ○ ○ ○

*"With Jacques Lemaire and Larry Robinson on the bench, with
their background in Montreal, they just knew we were going to
win. There was never a question about it. With that team, to me,
we had the greatest goalie ever, and the defense was unbelievable.
We knew, as a team, we were going to win every night. Of course,
we didn't every night. But that was the feeling we had."*
—BERNIE NICHOLLS, NEW JERSEY DEVILS (1993–94)

Lou Lamoriello is a man of phrases, sayings, quotes, and comparisons.
He has a few printed and hanging in his office. He uses some when speaking
to the media. He has still more for simple, everyday life. When it comes to
his hockey team, his most important analogy is one of elegance, rhythm,
harmony, and collaboration. And his Devils, more times than not, usually
played along.

"I had a philosophy in college, that the definition of a team for me is
an orchestra. Getting the most talented people to understand their role to
make the music sound good," he said. "If someone doesn't do their job,
they're going to bring down the team. I've always compared a team to the
most sophisticated and the most talented people in the world: the musicians
in the orchestra. They practice harder than any player can practice. And if
they can do it, so can you."

Well, in 1993–94, the Devils played sweet music.

They were dedicated, driven, and dominant. And, sartorially, the league
was still getting used to their new look, too. One season earlier, Lamoriello

scrapped the team's original colors and uniforms. Out went the old Christmas-tree look, the famous—or infamous, your call—red-and-green jerseys, socks, pants, and helmets that often drew laughs in league circles.

The original logo—an *NJ* with horns and a tail surrounded by a circle—stayed, of course. The red stayed, as well. But in 1992–93, the green was replaced with a more serious, more suitable, more marketable black, a uniform that has persevered to this day, while other teams switch every few years.

"My earliest memory is going to see them play the [Minnesota] North Stars one year, and they had those green breezers on," Zach Parise, a first-round draft pick of the Devils in 2003 who eventually became the franchise's captain on October 5, 2011, said of New Jersey's pants at the time. "I remember I liked those uniforms. Those green breezers. Say what you will about them, they were unique. But I'm sure Lou just wanted a change."

If the team's uniforms changed in 1992, its direction did likewise in 1993.

At the helm of this new-look orchestra was a set of conductors, shipped in from Montreal on a whim from Lamoriello, that would change this morose, mediocre franchise forever, and install a culture, a way of life, that was second to none in the National Hockey League.

Jacques Lemaire and Larry Robinson, with an air about them and more Stanley Cup championships on their résumé than one cared to count, made the Devils players at the high-stakes table. And they did so almost instantaneously.

"We felt we had the talent, and what happened in the playoff series of the previous seasons was we got close but we didn't get it done," Lamoriello said. "What was lacking, I felt, was belief. Not belief in each other, but belief that we could win. The mind is a very powerful tool, and I can remember when I sat down with Jacques Lemaire for the first time and we talked about him coming to coach here. I knew what kind of competitor he was, and I knew of his abilities to coach. After that conversation—and I still remember it to this day—I knew he was the man to do it."

Lemaire, a Hall of Fame forward for the Canadiens who was a part of eight Stanley Cup titles in Montreal as a player and two more as an assistant general manager, was hired as coach in 1993 after the Devils bowed out—again—in the first round of the playoffs.

With Herb Brooks—the American icon who led Team USA to the "Miracle on Ice" gold medal in the 1980 Olympics—unable to extract the absolute most out of this New Jersey group, Lamoriello felt the change was needed, though it was a difficult one. Brooks, after all, was a legend. His career was based on turning an overwhelming underdog into an unforgettable champion, leading a scrappy set of American college players in an upset of the USSR en route to the gold in Lake Placid.

But in 1993, after Brooks' Devils lasted just five games against Pittsburgh in the first round of the playoffs, something had to be done. The Penguins were a quality team, of course. There was no great shame in losing to Pittsburgh, the two-time defending Stanley Cup champions at the time. But in that season, after captain Mario Lemieux had battled back from Hodgkin's lymphoma, they were beatable. A round later that proved true, as the New York Islanders orchestrated a seven-game upset and ensured there would be no three-peat in Pittsburgh.

It could have easily been the Devils moving on, though. There was talent up front, with a quality mix of veteran goal scorers and up-and-coming standouts, as well as depth on defense. Remember, those 1992–93 Devils managed 40 wins and 87 points. The pieces were in place. Lamoriello just needed the right person to put together the puzzle.

Lemaire seemed to have the answers. He promised strong, defensive-minded hockey, in which he would maximize the talent of each and every player on the roster. Joining him in the cause was Robinson, a Hall of Fame defenseman who helped the Canadiens to six Cup championships. Robinson came on board as an assistant coach in charge of the back line. His mission was to get a talented, balanced set of defensemen to take another step forward in the Lamoriello process.

"Without a doubt, they came right in and something changed overnight," said Bill Guerin, one of those bright young forwards who had been hand-picked by Lamoriello. A smooth skater with a quality shot and a mean streak to complete the arsenal, Guerin was the fifth overall pick in 1989, and was one of many American sharpshooters who Lamoriello felt could change the culture in New Jersey.

"I don't think there's any doubt. Lou knew American hockey, and it was a thing, at the time, that a lot of other people running teams in the NHL didn't know too much about," former Devils forward Corey Millen, another American, said. "Lou's an American, he had been around USA Hockey, had been around college hockey, and that helped tremendously. We used that to our advantage. It was a Canadian game back then, and a lot of people who were running the league were Canadians. Lou took pride—and still does to this day—in knowing a lot of the American players, about where they grew up, and what kind of skills they had. And we took pride in that. We belonged with the Devils."

Guerin concurred.

"With Jacques and Larry, everyone knew where they fit in," he said. "We were ready for them, right off the bat. We listened, and let's face it, we all wanted the same thing. To win."

The Lemaire era officially began on October 6, 1993, with a textbook, standard-fare 2–1 victory over the Tampa Bay Lightning at the Meadowlands that would ultimately be a microcosm of Devils Hockey:

- A stifling defensive effort that swallowed the Lightning whole, and allowed just 18 shots total
- Constant cycling of the puck that maximized attack time in the Tampa Bay zone, which eventually resulted in 43 shots on net
- A set of two timely goals, one from a forward, Valeri Zelepukin, the other from a defenseman, Ken Daneyko
- Trusted, reliable goaltending in the form of veteran Chris Terreri, who made 17 saves

All in a day's work.

"We knew of [Lemaire's and Robinson's] track records, certainly, and it didn't take long for us to buy in. We started playing their type of hockey right away," said former Devils forward Tom Chorske, another highly skilled American, who, like Lemaire and Robinson, had spent time with the Montreal Canadiens. "We knew immediately that we were in the presence of great hockey minds."

From the outset, it seemed that knowledge was rubbing off. The Devils opened the season with seven consecutive wins, many of which showed the team was more explosive than anyone would have thought. In four of those wins, New Jersey scored six or more goals, and on October 12, they whacked the Winnipeg Jets 7–4.

"It was working so well. We had it going," Guerin said. "And I remember with that start, being at [defenseman and captain] Scott Stevens' house one night. Scott turned to me, and he said, 'It feels like we're never going to lose, doesn't it?' And it truly did. The confidence just kept growing."

The league began to take notice, especially on the defensive end. It did not take long for people to realize the kind of hockey the Devils were playing. In those seven games, the opposition topped 30 shots just twice. In two of the wins, they didn't even get to 20.

What were the Devils doing so differently? How did this change happen so quickly, so efficiently?

"It was a team that played responsibly, is the best way I can put it," said Mike Miller, the Devils' radio play-by-play man at the time. "But, yes, Jacques was always asked about the way they played, and really, it was smart, defensive hockey. I've never been associated with a team that when they had a one-goal lead, it looked like a three-goal lead."

But how? Well, it wasn't long before critics had labeled Lemaire's style the "neutral-zone trap." In this system—one that was not new, just seldom used—four skaters take up residence in the neutral zone, while one drifts into the offensive zone. The object is to clog up the neutral zone, filling lanes so that the opposition either turns the puck over or simply dumps the puck into New Jersey's zone and proceeds to chase it. A turnover in the neutral zone often creates an offensive opportunity for the neutral-zone-trapping team, as that unit already has numbers moving toward the blue line and only has the half the ice, or less, to travel.

Others simply saw it as a 1-2-2 forechecking system, the one Montreal used ages ago with similarly successful results.

Either way, it was viewed as a way a team with less offensive talent could handle opponents with highly skilled forwards. For many of those teams with pure goal scorers, it was a frustrating experience.

"It was terrible hockey," said Howie Rose, the radio voice of the Rangers at the time. "Horrible."

But the Devils didn't care. They were winning. They were scoring goals. And they were getting used to it.

"To me, I take offense to the term *trap*. Larry taught us all how to be better defensemen, and Jacques taught the forwards how to be more sound defensively, to be more responsible, and the chances will come off that," Daneyko said. "The trap was something, to me, created by the media. People wanted to stereotype us. We were winning, and they didn't like it. But when you broke it down, it was consistent defense, scorers who made the most of their opportunities, and great goaltending. It was as simple as that."

Ah, the goaltending. A staple of any championship-contending team at any level. You need depth there. You need skill. And you need consistency.

These Devils had all of that and more.

Terreri was the veteran, a pint-sized, scrappy American who had been through those good-but-not-great years under McVie and Brooks. After a standout career at Providence College, a program that Lamoriello once orchestrated, Terreri found a home in New Jersey and carved out a half-decent career in the NHL. What he lacked in his 5'9" frame, he made up for in athletic skill, skating ability, and an unbelievable degree of flexibility within the crease.

Terreri was a fifth-round pick of New Jersey back in 1983, and he would go on to win 151 games in a career that ended in 2000–01. His best season was in 1990–91, when he went 24–21–7, with an .893 save percentage and a 2.91 goals-against average for the Devils.

But in 1993–94, as the new culture began to take over the organization, Terreri was merely keeping the net warm for a first-round pick out of Montreal who would eventually change the face of goaltending forever. He was a lengthy, rangy, butterfly netminder who slipped through the cracks and past enough NHL general managers that Lamoriello was able to deal down a few spots and select him with the No. 20 choice in 1990.

"In my eyes, Martin Brodeur is the best goaltender to ever play this game," Lamoriello said with ferocity. "And how smart are we? We traded down to get him."

Born and bred to be a goaltender, Brodeur was 6'2", 215 pounds, and grew up in and around the—you guessed it—Montreal Canadiens organization, like so many in Lamoriello's empire had done. Brodeur's father, Denis, was a team photographer for the Canadiens, and so Martin had access to one of the game's most prestigious franchises.

But his talents overrode any special treatment he may have received as a child. After moving around Canada's private schools to get himself into the best possible hockey situation, Brodeur was clearly among the best prospects in the world by the time he became property of the Devils, and a player who represented the new age of his craft.

"I think Marty was already one heck of a goaltender by the time he made it to the league," said former Rangers goaltender Mike Richter, who battled Brodeur countless times in the NHL as well as in international play, including the gold medal game at the 2002 Olympics. "He was young in 1994, but he was so composed. And to play at that level in that organization? What a combination. I have loved watching his career, have always loved his ability, and loved playing against him."

In the 1980s, some NHL goaltenders, though not all, began to experiment with stickhandling a little more. Gone were the days, scouts and coaches thought, of using the stick just to make saves and to leave the puck for on-rushing defensemen. As the league became more offensive-minded, goaltenders were required to be a little more adept at handling the stick. Ron Hextall, who cut his teeth in the NHL with the Flyers, was best known for this, and he became something of an industry standard. But Brodeur would eventually take it to a new level.

In many ways, Brodeur was looked upon by many opponents as a third defenseman on the ice. In 1993–94, after riding the shuttle between New Jersey and its minor league affiliates, he was finally in the Swamp to stay.

On October 8, 1993, in New Jersey's second game of the season, Brodeur stopped 23 of 26 shots as the Devils outlasted the Capitals in Washington 6–3. His season debut wasn't a beauty, but it was a win, and that's all that mattered.

The statistics were insignificant, though. In Lemaire's "everyone matters" system, where all players and coaches were going to be held accountable for the team's fortunes, it spoke volumes that he threw this 21-year-old onto the ice in the season's second game. Brodeur delivered right off the bat.

"We didn't know exactly how much of a role he was going to have. We knew his ability, and we knew where we wanted to go," Lamoriello said. "But it's the old expression, 'the players determine how much they play, and when they play, by what they do.' You can feel that they can do it, but you don't know. You don't know how they'll handle the pressures that go with the roles they've been given."

Brodeur made the most of his opportunity. In fact, when the regular season was said and done, he had the upper hand in the veteran-rookie platoon. He played in 47 games, going 27–11–8 with a .915 save percentage and a 2.40 goals-against average. Was he the clear-cut starter? No, and the early stages of the playoffs would prove that.

But he did enough, easily, to have a say in the postseason. And not long after the playoffs ended, he won the Calder Trophy as the league's Rookie of the Year.

"He was just starting out, but to be able to have those numbers on a team like that as a rookie just shows you where he was headed," said Neil Smith, who had a firm sense of the netminders around the league at the time, having just shopped—and eventually dealt—Vanbiesbrouck. "He had this ability, even then, at going on these spurts, where you just weren't going to get anything by him."

His teammates noticed.

"The amazing thing to me was that nothing fazed him…ever," said former Devils forward Bernie Nicholls, who had 19 goals and 46 points on the 1993–94 team. "Here he was, what, 21 years old? And he'd go out there when called upon, make saves, set us up with breakout passes, and stare down some of the toughest forwards in the game with a smile on his face. Always so relaxed. And he never took anything home with him. To me, he is the greatest goaltender ever."

With that type of tandem in net, the Devils took off like they never had before. A 5–2 win over Ottawa on November 18, 1993, in which Brodeur made 23 saves, gave the Devils a 14–4 record. They never looked back:

- They closed the calendar year and entered the next with four straight victories, part of a 7–2 run
- They had a nine-game unbeaten streak between February and March
- They won 12 games in March, just as the playoff races began to tighten

"Really, a lot of people tried to break down what we were doing, and it was not that hard to figure out," said former Devils center Jim Dowd. Dowd, another American farmhand who was born and raised in New Jersey, became a playoff staple for the Devils in 1993–94 after playing in only 15 regular season games. "The transitioning was simple. Just go play your position. Get the puck and go score. Fundamental hockey that so many other teams weren't doing. Call it the trap, call it what you want. We had the puck all the time. We had talent, and I should know, because I couldn't get in the lineup most nights. But that was never a problem. We were all happy to be there. And when we had a lead on you in the third period, forget it. The game was over."

How good were they? Lamoriello, ever the perfectionist, was so uncharacteristically content with this club that he didn't make any more moves at the trading deadline. And if it hadn't been for the season sweep at the hands of the Rangers, the Devils would have won the Presidents' Trophy and snared the league's No. 1 overall seed.

"It was frustrating that people discounted the Devils as something of a gimmick because they played the trap, when Montreal won Cups playing it," said Don LaGreca, a journalist who is now torn between the rivalry. He is a Devils fan through and through, but he's also Kenny Albert's backup as the radio voice of the Rangers. "I just think it was misunderstood, because people labeled the trap as something that was boring. I never found the Devils boring. They just played it well. Maybe that's just the fan in me. But I think they got a bad rap. I still have people come to me and say, 'I don't follow hockey anymore, because the Devils ruined it for me, because they're boring.' And it became a self-fulfilling prophecy. They got pigeonholed into this stereotype as this bore. People looked at them as if everything that was wrong with the game was their fault."

Parise, a young pup with his eyes on the NHL at the time, concurred.

"They definitely did not have a great reputation throughout the hockey world, just because of how defensive-oriented they were," he said. "And I think once you get here, and you understand the reasons behind everything, you realize that it's just smart hockey, and eventually everyone played that way. No matter what people think, trust me, there isn't one team in the league that doesn't use some form of the trap in the neutral zone. Everyone does it. It just was a case that we got the reputation for it."

Reputations didn't matter to the 1993–94 Devils. Wins were wins, and New Jersey finished with 106 points—six fewer than the Rangers—and took the No. 3 seed in the Eastern Conference with a record of 47–25–12. (Pittsburgh claimed the No. 2 seed as winner of its division.)

"But we were well aware of them, and while we had things to worry about on our own end," former Rangers defenseman Brian Leetch said, "we knew they weren't going to go away. That 1-2-2 they were using was tough. Real tough."

Still, the Devils didn't exactly march into the postseason. The regular season was easily the best in the franchise's history. The finish, though, was just so-so—New Jersey went 2–4–1 down the stretch, including an uncharacteristic three-game losing streak.

The finale on April 14, 1994, however, was a back-to-business, everything-is-okay 4–1 victory over the Senators in which Chorske had two goals and Brodeur made 18 saves. It appeared like onward and upward into new territory for this burgeoning bunch.

"When you reflect on it, that team was something else," said Millen, an often forgotten cog to the 1993–94 Devils, who had 20 goals and 50 points in 78 regular season games before sitting most of the postseason. "It was one of the best defensive corps in the league. And then you had Brodeur and Terreri, which was such a solid tandem in net, and a pretty good group of forwards. Clearly, there was an unspoken confidence about this team. We weren't the kind of guys to go out and show off and strut our stuff. But there was that silent confidence, where everyone knew—if you played your role that night—you were going to win more than you lose."

That carried over to the early rounds of the playoffs. But it was hardly easy.

"When you're talking playoffs, things certainly have to fall into place and every player has to have a pretty good year," said former Devils defenseman Bruce Driver, a veteran mainstay who had 32 points in 66 games in 1993–94. "If one player doesn't have a very good year, it usually doesn't end up working out for that team in the end. For us, to an extent, it went well."

And differently, for sure.

After years of packing up, kissing their wives and children good-bye, and heading out to start the playoffs on the road, the Devils finally had home-ice advantage, at least for one round. Unfortunately for them, with Pittsburgh snagging the second seed, the Devils could conceivably open up Round 2 away from home.

But that was miles away for a franchise that had only made the second round once before in its history. For the time being, all that mattered was that a tough-minded Buffalo Sabres team—one that could play a little defense, too—was on its way to East Rutherford as the Devils prepared to host just their second Game 1 in franchise history on April 17, 1994.

"The thing about this team is that when something went wrong, we learned from it," Nicholls said. "We learned how to take what we needed out of bad beats."

That was a good thing. Because three hours after all the pomp and circumstance that went with a playoff opener, the Devils were in a hole.

Final score: Sabres 2, Devils 0.

Home-ice advantage? Gone. Momentum? Gone. The bustling buzz at the Byrne Arena? Gone.

While the Rangers were busy punishing the Islanders and announcing to the rest of the league that they had arrived once and for all, across the river, the Devils looked as if they were ready to check out.

"Well, if you're going to go anywhere in sports, you're going to have to face adversity," Guerin said. "For us, that started right off the bat."

Take a closer look at the box score, though, and there were signs that New Jersey could bounce back. Certainly, it wouldn't be easy against the Sabres' superb, unorthodox goaltender, Dominik Hasek. But the Devils did, after all, fire 30 shots on net.

"Everyone needs to experience losing first, before winning," Nicholls said. "And we used that as a lesson."

It showed. The Devils regrouped and responded with two New Jersey-esque performances, taking a 2–1 series lead into Game 4 on April 23. Forward Stephane Richer had two goals and Nicholls had two assists as the Devils won Games 2 and 3 by identical 2–1 scores. Brodeur notched both victories.

For a series that featured a No. 6 seed and a No. 3—and the former was clearly better than the seeding indicated—this suddenly was a series that was probably closer than the Devils had hoped. Keep in mind, the combined score through nine periods was just 4–4. Sure, Buffalo had a great goaltender. But through three games, the Sabres had only scored three goals that mattered—the fourth was an empty-netter—and their offensive liabilities were showing.

Perhaps, the whispers said, the pressure was getting to the Devils.

"Nobody cared about what the press said. Nobody cared about what people believed," Lamoriello said. "All we cared about was what we had to do. Eventually, everyone would get into it."

But not before Buffalo tied the series at 2–2 with a thorough 5–3 win at the Memorial Auditorium that saw Brodeur make just 25 saves on 30 attempts.

What transpired over the next six days was something to savor, a time that fans could look back on, no matter where this club eventually landed, and say a corner had been turned.

Forward Claude Lemieux scored twice in Game 5 and Stevens had three assists as the Devils repaid Buffalo with a 5–3 victory of their own. It was, again, a response on home ice befit of a team with championship aspirations.

And even though the Devils failed to close Buffalo out in Game 6— losing 1–0 in a marathon overtime game that pushed the favorites to the brink of elimination and spanned seven periods and 125:43 of game time— New Jersey fired 70 shots on net and controlled long pockets of play during the six-hour classic.

"We learned from it, no question," Daneyko said. "Hasek was playing well, and for a lot of us, this was our first real taste of adversity and negativity. But we knew we played hard, and we knew, going back home, a similar effort would probably get us a win."

Daneyko's assessment was on the money.

In a microcosm of a series the Devils dictated in every aspect but the scoreboard, New Jersey indeed made the most of home ice in Game 7, outshot Buffalo 46–18, and shook off the heartbreaker from 48 hours previous. In the end, a 2–1 victory that was not as close as the score indicated sealed the Sabres' fate and secured a spot in the round of eight for the Devils, a position they had not held since 1988, after they outlasted the Islanders in six games.

Easy? Absolutely not. But satisfying?

"Yes," Daneyko said. "Buffalo provided test after test, and we moved on. Who knew how much that experience would pay off in the long run? But to go through all of that, the overtime loss, falling behind in Game 1, those were all things we could bottle up and use later."

But it didn't take long after reaching Round 2 to realize that nothing was going to come easy for this team. Home ice notwithstanding, these Devils seemed content to make things difficult for themselves and their fans.

Wasn't that supposed to be the Rangers' way of doing things?

Thanks to Washington's upset of Pittsburgh, the Devils became the highest seed remaining behind the Rangers, and so New Jersey would host the second round against the Boston Bruins. With 42 wins and 97 points, the Bruins stood to be a stiffer test than Buffalo, but not a team that should have its way with the Devils.

So much for that.

In the blink of an eye, Boston took the upper hand, winning two games at the Meadowlands in a span of three days, 2–1 and 6–5, respectively. Brodeur took both losses and caused many to wonder if he had finally hit the rookie wall.

Suddenly, the Devils and their breakout season of power, promise, and potential, were on life support. Again.

Sensing a change was needed, Lemaire elected to tap the shoulder of Terreri for Game 3, and possibly beyond, at Boston Garden. Maybe it was a stop-the-bleeding move, or maybe it was permanent. Either way, something needed to be done.

"The playoffs can be a long road and a lot of things happen," Driver said. "But then, something just clicked."

Terreri took the net in Boston, the skaters in front of him responded, and despite being on the road in a hockey-mad town, the Devils woke up and began to play like, well, the Devils.

"In many ways, we always considered ourselves a road team," Driver said. "We liked getting away, bonding together, and silencing crowds a little bit."

Mission accomplished.

Across a run of seven days that will live in Devils history, New Jersey responded with 16 goals in a four-game span, all victories, as this inconsistent, hard-to-figure collection secured a spot in the Eastern Conference Finals for just the second time in franchise history. Three of the series wins were on the road. Three of them were notched by Terreri. One of them came in overtime.

"You know what, I was just happy when they told me to go out and play," Brodeur said. "I knew I'd be ready, but they took me out against Boston, and with good reason. I lost the first two games, and then Chris came in, won us two games, and really turned us around. He was on, I was off, it was a day-by-day operation. And it was fine."

In New Jersey, fans always had the sense that the players meant what they said. The only thing that the Devils cared about was moving on to the next round, no matter who was in net.

Believe it or not.

"What does it take to win? Well, it takes a team full of people that do not want to let anyone down. It takes a team that is not based on individual things," Lamoriello said. "This was a team. It was not about the name on the back, it was about the logo."

And that logo was headed to the third round, one way or the other, where the rolling Rangers were eagerly waiting. While the Devils played the first two series like they were stuck in metropolitan-area gridlock—stop and start, bump and grind, hurry up and wait—the Rangers flew through the first two rounds via the express lane.

New York played nine games. New Jersey played 13.

"I don't think either team really worried about how much hockey they had played, but I suppose it could have been a factor," Richter said. "Different things happen in different series, we all know that. The important thing for both franchises is that they had moved on."

The Devils certainly concurred.

"Absolutely. We went into the playoffs knowing full well that we had two known commodities in net," Guerin said. "And we felt pretty good about either one of them taking the ice in a big game. They both played well, and they both won games for us. We were unfazed through most of it, and not much bothered us."

Would that ring true as a battle of wills, separated by six miles of terrain and the Hudson River, gained in strength? Would that hold water as the pressure of playing the mighty Rangers in what might seem like as many as seven road games mounted?

Only time would tell. For the time being, at least the Devils had given themselves a chance.

"And it was a good one, sure," said Barry Melrose, a former NHL coach with Los Angeles and Tampa Bay, and now an analyst for ESPN. "How could you not have a chance with Marty Brodeur in net, Scotty Stevens and Scotty Niedermayer on defense, Jacques Lemaire on the bench, and that system in place? Sure, they were going up against a lot in the Rangers that year, and the Rangers had a lot going for them. But one thing you always knew about those Devils was, don't ever think they weren't capable of something just because they weren't always pretty."

So, Lamoriello and Lemaire made reservations for the short trip to Manhattan. Less than a year after the two first got together and began to talk about the long-term vision for the franchise, they found themselves in the Eastern Conference Finals against their biggest rival.

"The change of culture was definitive and quick. Was it always a walk in the park? No," Miller said. "But Lou was happy with the group, and Jacques was, too. And before you know it, they were four wins away from the Stanley Cup Finals."

And for the New Jersey Devils, that was rarified ice.

Game 1

○ ○ ○ ○

"The Rangers fans—when I first started at WFAN—taught me
about loyalty to a team. Madison Square Garden was always filled
at 18,200 in the stands, in good times and bad. Every night—old
Garden, new Garden, you name it—the Rangers fans filled it up.
They would often become cynical, like a parent would with a
child. They may have felt at times they needed to ground them.
The parent may have to reprimand them. But they never kicked
them out of their heart. The same goes for Rangers fans with
their team. And 1994 just felt like it was going to be their year."
—STEVE SOMERS, HOST, WFAN-AM 660

I T'S TOUGH TO FAZE John Amirante.

By the time the 1994 NHL postseason rolled around, the longtime New
York singer famous for his rendition of the national anthem had already
seen quite a bit in his day. When you grab the microphone and sing in front
of charged-up crowds at many of the city's sports venues for all kinds of
events, it's often difficult to separate one night from the other.

But not in 1994. Not in the Eastern Conference Finals. And especially
not when the Rangers were set to host the rival Devils in Game 1 on May
15, 1994.

"Electric."

That was the short-and-sweet description of an energized Garden
crowd from a man who uses words for a living. Amirante is a man who uses

good inflection, great tone, and has an even greater vocabulary loaded with descriptives.

Yet, this time, he only needed one.

"Yes. Electric," he said with a smile on his face and a tear welling in his eye, all while shaking his head in amazement. "I cannot tell you how loud that crowd was. They were ready. They could feel it. This was the year. Had to be."

Or else.

As they took the ice versus their rivals from New Jersey in a playoff series for the second time in three years, the racin' Rangers were out of excuses to lean on. The Curse of 1940 needed to end, and it needed to end now.

In two cruise-control postseason rounds, playing just one game over the minimum versus the Capitals and Islanders, the Blueshirts became a victim of their own success. They had made so many headlines that anything less than a Stanley Cup would have likely brought about wholesale changes, top to bottom, and further dragged the franchise's name through the mud.

"The setup was so incredible," Bill Clement said, "because of the rivalry. You knew what Devils-Rangers meant. The hatred that was under all of it. And you had the complete contrast in styles. The Devils, although some people didn't know what it was all about at the time, were 'trapping,' and the Rangers still played the freewheeling, up-and-down style. You had Mark Messier's charisma and presence, and you had the Devils who were, I would call them faceless, but typical of the organization. They were the socialists of the NHL."

It was now or never for the Rangers. Surely the Devils, a ragtag bunch of upstarts aimed at slowing down the game and revolutionizing the NHL with their own tactics, weren't going to stand in the way, right?

"Wrong. And it didn't take very long did it? Here we are, in Game 1, and you're already like 'Oh, shit.'"

Those were the words of Neil Smith, New York's tell-it-like-it-is general manager at the time who, along with Mike Keenan, had sculpted his team at a microwave-like pace.

But the Devils had other ideas, and let them be known as soon as the first puck dropped in Manhattan. In fact, New Jersey dictated the play early on, as veteran center Bobby Carpenter won the opening faceoff from Messier, allowing the Devils to set up their strategy.

"He has taught this team positional hockey," ESPN analyst Brian Engblom said on the broadcast regarding Jacques Lemaire, as New Jersey unleashed their defensive system, intent on draining the life out of that "electric" crowd.

While it worked in the early going, it didn't stop the Rangers from garnering a few chances. New York shook off some rust and got to work three minutes in. The Rangers went on the offensive, made the absolute most of their opportunities, and skated as if they didn't care what scheme the Devils were going to play.

One of the key weapons in the Rangers' arsenal, especially against the tactically sound Devils, was their breakout speed. They would need every ounce of it to burst through New Jersey's system. And that speed, especially on defense, is what helped the Rangers draw first blood.

Carpenter, as Devils centers did in their system, dumped the puck into the Rangers' zone and chased it. Sergei Zubov, a rising Rangers star defenseman from Russia who was fleet of foot and possessed a rifle shot, was able to turn it around and get up the ice quicker than the Devils could set up.

Zubov carried across center ice and passed to Messier, who took it into the Devils' zone. In a quick little exchange that displayed New York's puck skills, Messier left a neat little backhander for Zubov in a give-and-go, and Zubov made the most of his open attack-zone room. He fired a wrist shot that surprised Devils rookie goaltender Martin Brodeur—who returned to the net despite sitting out the finale against Boston—through his gaping five-hole at 3:39 of the first.

Rangers 1, Devils 0.

Cue the crowd.

"The Devils will need to do a better job of getting back against the speed and skill of the Rangers," Engblom said, "or it's going to be a long night."

Brian Leetch kept the pressure up with a slap shot from the point that went wide, but the blast confused Brodeur enough that the rookie actually looked behind him for the puck. A minute later, Kovalev snuck in behind the Devils' dominant defensive pair of Scott Stevens and Ken Daneyko, and let a slap shot fly off a partial breakaway that hit the right post.

New Jersey was scrambling, and Brodeur, who had just turned 22, was feeling some butterflies. The Garden crowd, as only it could, sensed his hesitation. Even though he'd only been around a little more than a year and had never beaten the Rangers during the regular season, the fans started to get on the Montreal native.

"Mar-ty," they yelled in their typical, derisive, sing-song chant that is now famous and is still used today. "Mar-ty."

Not long after Kovalev's near-miss, Brian Noonan and Sergei Nemchinov, a pair of veteran forwards, bolted in on Brodeur, but a wrist shot again sailed wide. Seven minutes in, the Devils' early wave of emotion had long since been erased, and the play was all New York's.

"This is going to build against the Devils," Engblom said, "if they don't get one soon."

The pace was frenetic, frantic, and frenzied, and while that favored the Rangers and the crowd, it wasn't going to last forever. The Devils were too good to let that happen. Nine minutes in, fans finally started to see the team that amassed 106 points in the regular season.

Bernie Nicholls and Bill Guerin, two of the more offensively skilled Devils, created a little room for themselves and picked up the pace. At his own blue line, Nicholls found a streaking Guerin racing past the Rangers defense, and hit him in stride. Guerin got himself alone in on Richter, but his backhander was swallowed up by the sprawling Rangers netminder, which brought a roar from the crowd and an ensuing "Let's Go Ran-gers" chant.

"Ricky was on his game," Guerin said. "He was playing great. But that was okay. We knew if we kept up that pace, and didn't get ourselves down, we could score some goals."

Suddenly, the flow had evened out. Lemaire threw out his fourth line—a rowdy bunch with a scoring touch that featured Bobby Holik, Mike Peluso, and Randy McKay—and they dictated play in the Rangers' zone. Holik had a slap shot blocked, but the mission was accomplished.

New Jersey was back in this thing.

"This," ESPN's play-by-play man Sean McDonough said with 7:35 left in the first, "has become the Devils' pace."

It probably wasn't as slow as New Jersey wanted. With such a pregame emphasis on the chess match between Lemaire and Keenan—and on who would make the most of the game stoppages—there weren't many of them. In fact, 13:30 into the first, there had only been six whistles. But the Devils journeyed onward and slowly worked on the crowd.

With less than two minutes to go in the first, their persistence paid off.

After a soft dump-in from the Rangers for a line change, the Devils gained center ice with some steam. Defenseman Tommy Albelin weaved around the opposition and stopped short at the right point, where he fired a slap shot that Richter stopped. The rebound kicked out to the right faceoff circle, where MacLean gathered and carried behind the net before sneaking a wraparound past Richter with 1:44 left.

It was fitting that in the Devils' biggest series in franchise history, MacLean, a veteran of so many tough times who would later become the all-time leading scorer and the coach of the organization who drafted him in the 1983 first round, scored their first goal. The kid from Oshawa, Ontario, who broke in with the Devils at age 19, and who finished a memorable career with 413 goals and 842 points, tied the score at 1–1 with assists from Albelin and Driver at 18:16.

"Boy," Engblom said with a rise in his voice, "did they need this goal."

The crowd, on the other hand, did not. As the final seconds of the stanza ticked off, and Lemieux let off a slap shot that Richter stopped, the Garden fell silent. The Rangers had thrown everything they could at the Devils, but 20 minutes into the series, the score was tied (1–1), the shots were tied (8–8), and the road team was feeling pretty darn good.

"But that was the key with that team. We had an exceptional group of older players with their leadership," Rangers winger Steve Larmer said. "They were just never going to let us let our guard down."

Larmer's theory rang true in the second period, as Messier won the opening draw from Carpenter and set the stage for a settled-down frame for the home team.

Zubov, who led the Rangers with 89 points in the regular season and became the first defenseman to pull off that feat for a team that finished first overall, showed his gracefulness at center ice as he maneuvered his way through the Devils and left a nice drop pass for Esa Tikkanen, who let a slap shot fly that landed wide of Brodeur. Then, Adam Graves had a nice little tip off a Noonan shot, though both were stopped.

The Rangers were coming, and the Devils knew it. Nicholls hooked Kovalev for a New York power play, and while New Jersey killed it off, the team was scrambling at this point. What's more, veteran defenseman Slava Fetisov was forced to hold Kovalev at the 5:08 mark, creating another Rangers power play. Again, the Devils killed it off, but in terms of pace and dictation of play, this was again the Rangers' game.

"Home ice meant a lot to us," Richter said. "We worked hard for it, and we wanted to protect it."

At 17:50 of the second, they took a big step toward that goal.

Nemchinov, along with three other Rangers and two Devils, was trying to become a member of the first Russian class to get their names on the Stanley Cup. And he helped his own cause as the Rangers' grinding line of their own—Noonan, Nemchinov, and Greg Gilbert—produced.

Noonan gathered a puck in the Devils' zone and pushed it back to Gilbert behind the net. Nemchinov swooped in, took it from Gilbert, and skated in front of Brodeur on his right side. His shot floated wide, but Noonan was in position to gather at the right circle and hit Nemchinov in front for a one-timer that beat Brodeur on the glove side, just under the crossbar.

It was a workmanlike, blue-collar, grind-it-out goal that was more suited for the Devils than the Rangers. But not many in the Garden seemed to mind.

As the Rangers took a 2–1 lead on Nemchinov's first playoff tally after 22 goals in the regular season, a pattern was developing; a book was being formed on Brodeur. Both Rangers goals came from the top of the faceoff circle.

The crowd was jumping at this point, and as the final minute hit, Graves just missed an insurance goal as his wrist shot from the right boards was stopped.

"Those late goals at the end of the period," Leetch said. "They can change things so dramatically."

Considering the fact that the Rangers were 48–0–4 when leading after the second period that year, well, the Devils had quite a hill to climb. But as fans quickly learned, it was wise to expect the unexpected in this series. It was New Jersey that came out as the aggressor in the third period. Here were the Rangers, skilled, swift, and superb at protecting leads, and the Devils took it to them on Garden ice with less than 20 minutes remaining in regulation.

The balanced, diverse line of Stephane Richer, Valeri Zelepukin, and Jim Dowd had some success six minutes in, as Dowd, quickly becoming one of New Jersey's best faceoff options, won a draw and got it to Zelepukin, who carried it into the right side. Zelepukin had more space than he should have in a one-goal game and decided to take an uncontested slap shot that Richter stopped calmly. A quality chance was thwarted, but the heat was on.

Nicholls, a former Rangers forward who was predictably taking heat from the Garden crowd, was also building up some momentum. He was among New Jersey's best backcheckers on this night, he was winning his fair share of faceoffs, and in true "neutral-zone trap" fashion, he swiped the puck from Kovalev and Matteau at center on the same shift, the latter of which paid off.

After turning over Matteau, Nicholls gained the zone and some room, and fed Guerin with a perfect one-timer pass that Guerin deposited past Richter on the stick side to tie the game at 2–2. Guerin's first of the playoffs from Nicholls at 5:50 had again sucked the life out of the crowd, and the Rangers, as they had been all period, were seemingly looking at themselves.

The only difference was that now their lead was gone.

"The neutral-zone trap was clearly evident, and the Devils were good at it," Gary Thorne said. "It was a way for the teams to balance things out. Maybe it was a little boring, but it gave you a chance to win. And from Lou's perspective, that was all that mattered: winning. If you had to play in the neutral zone for 60 minutes a game to win a game? Well, that's what you were going to do. That was Lou's way."

Lou's way was working, as the third-period clock ticked away in a knotted game.

At 12:51, the Devils kept on coming. Scott Niedermayer, like Zubov a swift-skating, smooth-stickhandling defenseman, was often given the green light to leave his post if a scoring chance opened up. It wasn't Lemaire's preference all the time, of course, but on certain occasions, Niedermayer, the third-overall pick in 1991 and a 20-year-old speed demon who had 10 goals and 46 points in the regular season, could go for it.

Sensing a lane he could expose with a burst of speed, Niedermayer fluidly transported from the neutral zone to the attack zone and discovered a streaking MacLean at his side. He fed MacLean with a pretty 2-on-1 pass, but MacLean's potential game-winner sailed wide of Richter. The play was pure precision until the finish, but the intentions were clear. New Jersey was playing to win, and with 12:21 left in the final period, the Devils were outshooting the Rangers 6–0.

But a lack of discipline and uncontrolled emotions cost Dowd and the Devils not long after. In a scene that would be repeated throughout the series, Dowd fell hook, line, and sinker for the antagonistic attitude of the pesky Tikkanen, drawing a 2:00 minor for interference in front of Brodeur that ignited the crowd and gave New York's top-rated power play a chance to snare the lead.

And that's exactly what the Rangers did.

Messier beat Carpenter in the faceoff circle, and a clinic in maintaining the attack zone on a critical power play commenced. Messier to Leetch. Leetch to Larmer. Larmer to Messier. It was efficiency personified. Messier created some space at the faceoff dot and lasered a wrist shot that was kicked out by Brodeur calmly, but the puck landed right on Larmer's stick. With Brodeur slightly out of position, Larmer buried a backhander into a yawning net on the man advantage to again swipe the momentum, the lead, and some confidence.

Rangers 3, Devils 2.

"It quickly turned into a series that was going to have that kind of an edge," Dowd said. "You have to learn from those."

But New Jersey would not panic. That was not Lemaire's way. He had a system, and he stuck to it. At the 5:00 mark, trailing by a goal and needing some offensive skill on the ice, he defiantly sent out the fourth line—a unit that would later be tabbed "The Crash Line"—and Holik, Peluso, and McKay went to work.

"Holik-Peluso-McKay, that line right there tells you it all. That was probably our most important line," Lamoriello said. "They were considered the fourth line, but what they brought was so valuable."

With three minutes left, Lemieux won a faceoff from Messier, and the puck landed with Niedermayer at the point. Surprisingly, Niedermayer had the time to set up his slap shot, yet it floated wide of Richter with 2:38 left.

At this point, "Let's Go Ran-gers" bellowed through the aisles, and the crowd could sense that Win No. 9 was near. Seven more and the Stanley Cup would be theirs. Easily the Rangers' most difficult game in the entire postseason, save for one loss versus Washington, looked as if it would have a positive outcome for the home team.

A frantic Devils team did not lose composure, however, foreshadowing how well played this series was going to be over the long haul. Still the dominant team throughout the period, the Devils gained some speed on a rush after Albelin raced back to break up a 2-on-1 with MacTavish and Noonan.

Albelin's efforts led to a fresh Niedermayer blasting through the neutral zone, as Lemaire pulled Brodeur from his net for the 6-on-5 man advantage. Niedermayer hit center ice with 1:00 left, gained the zone, and dumped in the puck, where MacLean could gather.

"Composure was so big with the Devils," Thorne said. "They never lost it."

MacLean took possession in the right corner and centered a pass to Lemieux in front of Richter, but the puck stayed in the crease as a mad scramble ensued. The fans were all standing at this point as the Devils, with the extra attacker, feverishly whacked at the loose puck. Eventually, Lemieux gained an inch of ice and lifted the puck past Richter's shoulder with just 43 seconds left. The scrappy, veteran New Jersey pest, who always seemed to be in the right place at the right time, had tied the game at 3–3 with his sixth goal of the postseason.

Suddenly, the crowd went numb. Despite likely getting what they deserved for letting New Jersey dictate play in the final period—not to mention letting the Devils outshoot them 13–8—the Rangers and their fans could hardly believe their fate.

"We played them enough times to know they were more than a worthy opponent. There was nothing that was going to sneak up on us with the Devils," Kevin Lowe said. "We knew how good they were, how deep, and how incredibly sound they were defensively. And they showed that right away."

A Game 1 victory had been just 43 ticks away, but the Rangers couldn't close.

The overtime session began as one might expect: the Devils played cautiously, and the Rangers—not wanting to lose home ice—played along. There were quick shifts. There were a lot of long, easily stoppable shots on net.

"It's surprising how quiet this crowd has been, just thinking back to the previous series versus Washington," Engblom said. "It's no comparison, and it's a credit to the Devils controlling the tempo and keeping the crowd out of it."

The best chance for either side came with 8:20 left, after Bobby Carpenter lost his stick. That allowed Gilbert some breathing room to fire a point-blank shot that Brodeur calmly stopped on the blocker side. Thirty seconds later, Brodeur dropped to stop a Messier wrister in his classic butterfly style, one that would soon become the league trend.

Zelepukin gained a little momentum for the Devils a bit later, only to be thwarted by Richter. With 6:46 left, the Russian split a tired Rangers defense and let off a wrist shot that was stopped by Richter, though he could not control the carom. Zelepukin then carried the puck behind the net and fed Richer in front, who was also stopped. This time Richter held on for a faceoff, as the crowd began to chant "Rich-ter! Rich-ter!"

As the players' legs grew heavy and the chances became less frequent, a second overtime was forced. New Jersey outshot New York 11–9 in the first overtime.

"At this point, you're just going," Leetch said. "These were both well-conditioned teams, and you don't have time to worry about how long you've been playing."

Leetch had played 40 minutes by the time the second overtime began, and Scott Stevens had played 30.

But the intermission seemed to breathe a little life into the road team. You can tell a lot by a player's mannerisms and expressions, especially as he begins his fifth period of the night, and the Devils players had shown positive signs. Before the drop of the puck, in fact, MacLean skated over to Brodeur, gingerly punched him in the chest, stared right into the mask of the rookie, and calmly said, "Let's go."

And so they did.

"I wouldn't expect the strategy to change much at all here in the second overtime," McDonough said.

Brodeur was ready, either way. A slap shot from MacTavish two minutes in? Stopped. An opportunity for Graves 30 seconds later? Stopped. A 3-on-2 that ended in a Gilbert wrist shot? Stopped.

While Brodeur was gaining in momentum, the Devils went on the attack. But they, too, were misfiring. Richer missed an open net three minutes in, and then Zelepukin failed to score on a breakaway in which he tried the standard backhand-forehand motion. Zelepukin was fed on the break by Richer.

"I remember No. 44 well," Smith said, referring to Richer. "A goal scorer who was playing smart."

Eventually, the efforts were rewarded. As the game hit the 5:00 mark, and with Leetch working on his 47th minute of game action, the Rangers' defensive leader was surrounded by a swarm of Devils. Rather than take them on, he sent the puck down the boards. With Leetch still a bit out of position, Carpenter turned hard toward the Rangers' zone and quickly shuffled a pass to Richer up the boards.

At that point, the Rangers were caught with Graves, very much an offensive forward, as the emergency defenseman. Richer used him as a screen, blew right by him, and floated in off the right circle. This time, Richer made the most of his chance, lifting a wrist shot over Richter's shoulder as Richter pushed his stick forward to try to deflect the shot.

Richter missed. Richer didn't.

Devils win 4–3.

Devils lead 1–0.

"But give credit to Richer," Smith said. "He knew Graves was there. He knew Graves wasn't a defenseman, and he used that to his advantage."

It was indeed a rewarding night for Richer, who had seven shots on goal. Although they were proud to say their team was one without stars, Richer was as close as one got in New Jersey, and he would always have the expectations on his shoulders that come along with being the principal piece of a major trade.

"This game was not a surprise. We knew they'd come out hard and ready to go, and it just showed us how evenly matched the series was going to be," Matteau said. "Ah, Richer, yes. Double overtime. He was a good goal scorer, and he made the most of it."

He made Lamoriello look awfully smart in the process. In 1991, Richer and Tom Chorske were traded to New Jersey from—where else?—Montreal for former Devils captain Kirk Muller. Forever a fan of the Canadiens' system, Lamoriello pegged Richer, a former two-time 50-goal scorer, as a solid New Jersey fit. He played well enough in the regular season, posting 29, 38, and 36 goals, respectively, in his first three seasons with the Devils. But his playoff total, prior to 1993–94, left something to be desired, as he had just three goals. Meanwhile, Muller helped lead the Canadiens to the Stanley Cup in 1992–93.

But with each new game in this postseason seemingly more critical than the last, a case could be made that Richer had just scored the biggest goal in Devils history.

"The numbers would come and go. One night, it'd be your turn. The next night, it'd be someone else. That's how it was in Jersey, and you learned to accept it," McKay said. "But once in you're in Jersey mode, so to speak, everything changes. You realize you're on a better team, you realize you're on a team that is committed to winning and is successful, and more times than not, those players come around to feeling that. Stephane was certainly one of those."

So, in a game that began on a Sunday but ended on a Monday at 12:03 AM, the Devils took an early series lead, handed the Rangers their first home postseason loss, and sent a long-winded, almost-five-periods-of-play message to the rest of the league and the metropolitan area: if the Rangers were going to win the conference and have a shot to break The Curse in the Stanley Cup Finals, they were going to have to earn it.

"And we knew that," Matteau said. "We had the best team in the NHL, and Mike's way with us was to just go out and play, and use your emotion to get us where we needed to go. It was up to us."

New York's first step in reclaiming the momentum would be reestablishing that Garden buzz, the electricity that had flowed from center ice to the blue seats just five hours earlier. Suddenly, that was gone.

"We go out and lose Game 1, and like I said, it's 'Oh, shit,'" Smith said. "We just lost home ice, and we're going to hear it all over again. 'There go the Rangers...again.'"

Game 2

○ ○ ○ ○

"For the marriage of a coach with huge expectations to a team that had huge expectations, it really was a fit with Mike Keenan and the Rangers. It wasn't good enough to be close, for him or us, and we felt we had the horses to be the best team in the league. And now, we had someone who could help us get there. We had to respond."

—MIKE RICHTER, NEW YORK RANGERS (1989–2003)

JIM DOWD RECALLS the moment as if it was yesterday. It was so out of character for Jacques Lemaire, how could he forget it?

After the Devils rallied from an 0–2 deficit in the second round to set up this dream date with the rival Rangers in the Eastern Conference Finals, Lemaire had himself a moment with his team, a moment that would truly show how much winning this series would mean to the New Jersey organization. Normally reserved and subdued, yet quick to offer up an all-in-good-fun comment from time to time, playtime was clearly over for Lemaire.

The Rangers, after all, will do that to you.

"Getting off the plane from Boston, we had just won it in six games, and we were in the conference finals, and it was just a great feeling," Dowd said. "It was right then and there, I'll never forget it. It was just Jacques and the players as we were about to walk out. He turns to us, and says: 'We're going to beat those fucking guys.' And we just looked at each other, and we knew. It was right then and there that we knew we could beat them, and we knew that we weren't going to let them walk over us. Didn't matter what was in the cards for them. We knew we had what it took to beat them."

And in Game 1, they played like it.

But two days later, it was the Rangers' turn, right? This high-priced, highfalutin collection of skill, speed, and experience simply had to respond to their leader, right? Surely Mike Keenan wasn't going to let this club fall down 0–2 on home ice to a team that clearly felt it had to overcome an inferiority complex, was he?

Fittingly, his captain answered that question for him just a few minutes into Game 2.

Mark Messier, who had two assists but wasn't a huge factor in the opener, stemmed the tide as the Rangers' faithful quickly showed—as they had for 54 years—it can forgive and forget and move on to the next game. Messier won the opening faceoff, and in the first minute, he delivered a one-arm shiver that knocked the normally impenetrable Scott Stevens to the ice behind Martin Brodeur.

In one of the better shifts you're going to see in any series, Messier then checked Ken Daneyko and Bill Guerin in succession as his game-opening hitting spree continued. He kept the puck in the zone, then passed it to the point for Kevin Lowe, who immediately gave it back to Messier. A centering pass for Esa Tikkanen was clean, but the winger fanned on it, perhaps demonstrating to Messier that if you want something done right, you have to do it yourself.

So, that's exactly what he did.

Claude Lemieux gathered the loose puck at the right circle, reversed direction, and tried to clear the zone via the boards behind Brodeur, but he was intercepted by—you guessed it—Messier. The captain carried it in front of the net and tucked a backhand beauty through the goaltender's five-hole, ending a shift for the ages.

The crowd erupted. The Rangers took a 1–0 lead. The Captain delivered, just 1:13 into Game 2.

"When I look back, I can say I learned more about myself, about the game, about what it really takes to win, that year than any other," said Doug Lidster, a 33-year-old reserve defenseman at the time who sneaked his way into this series in Game 6 and never came out of the Rangers lineup again. "And in particular that came from Messier, who just had his way of seizing the moment."

With more than 58 minutes of regulation time to play, it already seemed like the game was over. Messier's 94th career playoff goal was his first of the series, and to no one's surprise, it was unassisted.

"That shift just showed you," Bill Clement said on the ESPN telecast, "that the Rangers are revved to the max."

Keenan recognized it. The man who showed little emotion and little body language behind the bench acknowledged the job well done. When Messier finally came to the bench and sat down, Keenan politely scooted over to him and tapped him on the shoulder.

The "Let's Go Ran-gers" chants were loud and proud, as Messier kept his playoff scoring streak intact at 11 games. His teammates, meanwhile, fed off the emotion. On the next shift, Stephane Matteau and Steve Larmer started taking the body on Bobby Holik and Randy McKay of the Devils. New Jersey's grinding line, a unit often tabbed by Lemaire after an opponent's goal to get physical and shift momentum, was getting beat at its own game by the Rangers' version. Truly, a different team had taken the ice in the home white uniforms.

"Look at the hits levied by the Rangers here," Gary Thorne said on the ESPN broadcast. "And they're doing it against New Jersey's big line!"

The Devils were in a bind. The line changes weren't as crisp, the passes not as accurate. In fact, they didn't have a true scoring opportunity until five minutes in. Stephane Richer created some room for himself and attempted a wraparound wrist shot, but got no air under it. The puck stayed along the ice, and Richter stopped it cleanly and calmly kicked it to the right corner.

It was a sign of things to come for Richter. After facing 48 shots in Game 1, he was going to have much less work in Game 2, as his teammates controlled the play 180 feet from his crease. Even when the Devils reversed the flow, they were firing blanks. Six minutes in, the Holik-Peluso-McKay unit broke in on a 3-on-2, but Peluso missed the net on his shot by about 10 feet. Still, that line deserved credit in the first period—it was clearly New Jersey's best unit in a frame that was not going well.

"We didn't get down on ourselves. No matter the situation, we kept working," McKay said. "For a fourth line, we still played quite a bit. Jacques liked the combination, it seemed to work in a few different situations, and it was one of those things that just stuck."

As disappointing as it may have been for the Devils, it was not a surprise to Daneyko, who grew up in Edmonton and was a longtime friend of Messier. They acted differently on the ice, certainly, but maintained a strong relationship off it. Daneyko was well aware of Messier's big-game, big-performance mind-set, though the latter hardly flaunted it.

"That was not his game, not his style," Daneyko said. "He would just go out there, do what he needed to do, do what his team needed him to do, and he'd move on to the next shift."

Daneyko, though clearly a different type of player playing a different position, always took notes when in Messier's presence. In fact, early in his career Daneyko trained with Messier, Lowe, and some of the other Oilers back in Edmonton. Many of those off-seasons followed unsuccessful Devils campaigns, so it wasn't always easy to show up and be in the presence of greatness.

"But I liked and knew Mark and Kevin so well. And they were instrumental in my development," Daneyko said. "For me, I was very fortunate to have their tutelage, and to learn everything I could from those guys in the summer. They took me under their wing, and that's something they didn't have to do."

Daneyko, a first-round pick of New Jersey in 1982 who played his entire career with the Devils, was one of the more emotional players in the NHL. He was unafraid to fight and scrap, and never worried about his statistics—a good thing for a player who finished with just 178 career points. He battled alcohol problems, but Lou Lamoriello and the organization stuck with him throughout, perhaps basing their faith on the work ethic he had displayed for some 20 years.

"Even back in Edmonton, and I mean during the season, I had followed the Devils quite a bit because of Kenny," Lowe said. "He is such a great friend of ours, and you knew, once they turned it all around there, Kenny was going to be a part of it. He worked hard in the summer and truly wanted it."

Those who know Daneyko, either personally or from watching him on television, know his lighter side as well. And in those summers, in a relaxed atmosphere in Edmonton, he'd let it show. Keep in mind, this was the 1980s, when the Oilers were in the middle of a five-year run that resulted in four Stanley Cup championships. Edmonton had more greats than any opponent would care to admit: Wayne Gretzky. Messier. Jari Kurri. Lowe. Glenn Anderson. Paul Coffey. Grant Fuhr. The list goes on. With all due respect, you can understand how Daneyko, and what would eventually be his career total of 36 goals, might not fit in.

"We had fun with it, always," Lowe said with a laugh. "He never lost his sense of humor, and he was there to work. I remember Kenny always saying during those summers that 'the Devils were going to be the next Oilers. Look out, we're coming.' And it was funny at the time, the way he delivered it, but we knew that it was going to come around at some point. Once Lou took over, and they drafted well, and started to build a foundation, it was just a matter of time."

Daneyko never wavered in his confidence, even among those greats.

"I did, I always told them that. 'The Devils were going to be the next Oilers,'" he said, laughing. "And they always got a chuckle out of that, but I truly believed that. You had to. You had to have faith and trust in what Lou was building, and know that, in the end, the hard work would pay off."

It just didn't seem likely in Game 2 at the Garden.

Despite the fact that the first period ended with the Rangers still up by only a goal, there was never a true feeling that New Jersey was in it. New York outshot the Devils 11–5 in the stanza, and it didn't seem that close. The final few minutes belonged solely to the Rangers as the crowd continued to buzz. Brian Leetch hit a streaking Tikkanen, fresh off a line change, and he broke in on Brodeur and let off a point-blank wrist shot that was stopped.

Larmer kept it in the zone and fired a shot that was also snared. Anderson kept the pressure on and fired a shot from the point with 1:00 left that Brodeur stopped. The surge was on again, as New York posted the final six shots of the period. Brodeur was sharp—and had to be—or the score would have been 4–0 heading into the locker room.

"The Garden stands," Clement said, "as we've completed one."

"But the Rangers played outstanding hockey, and it's only 1–0," Thorne said. "The Devils can be proud of that."

Thorne and Clement, who would become the staple for ESPN's hockey coverage, always had that give and take, that smooth, subtle way of balancing each other out. Clement, a former center for the Flyers, Capitals, and Flames who rose to fame as a member of Philadelphia's Broad Street Bullies teams, was never afraid to call as it he saw it, and was able to draw from years of experience on the ice.

His style always blended well with Thorne, who got his start in the NHL as the Devils' play-by-play voice from 1987 to 1993. So, not only was this series near and dear to Thorne, it also played to his strength.

"A series like that, with the talent out there, and what was at stake, it became a very important series for the growth of the sport and of the league. There was such a tremendous amount of excitement involved," Thorne said. "For us, it was a matter of living up to that standard. Can [the Rangers]do it? Can they get the Cup? Can they break the hex? Or will this upstart team from across the river stop it all? It was truly great drama, and that made it easy for us, really."

From 1992 to 2004, the duo called just about every integral series for ESPN together, but it's hard to find one that had more of, well, everything than this one between New York and New Jersey.

"It was just so easy to rally around," Clement said. "It was so incredibly colorful."

And it Game 2, it was all red, white, and blue.

The second period began the same way the first ended—with the Devils on their heels. In fact, New Jersey's shotless drought reached 12 minutes, bridging the intermission break, before Stevens finally launched a slap shot from center ice that Richter paddled with ease.

While the Rangers weren't exactly keeping the pressure on at all times, the Devils were icing the puck too much and scrambling for their positioning in the neutral zone. It seemed like a matter of time before the home team struck again. With 15:00 left, the shots still favored New York 13–6. Lemaire, searching for answers, kept turning to the fourth line to make the Rangers work a little harder, if nothing else. Later in the period, things got worse for the Devils as Valeri Zelepukin left with an undisclosed injury.

All the while, Keenan stuck to his regular rotation, giving his combinations the opportunity to increase their lead. At the same time, Richter looked sharp and was well rested.

"As we continued to improve as a team, he did too," Richter said of Keenan. "His practices were very, very hard. And so we were in better shape than anyone we played, so in that type of game, we had no problems. We could play a lot of ways—we could go up and down, or we could play a tight, grinding style with the number of tools we had."

Game 2 displayed a little bit of both. There were times when the Rangers would mount one of their patented flurries; there were also times when they would sit back, let the play come to them, and allow Richter the opportunity to make a play. Either way, as the crowd settled down in the second period, the Rangers were in a groove that they had no intentions of breaking out of. New York even calmly thwarted a 75-second, 5-on-3 man advantage for the Devils.

"We still had a lot of confidence in ourselves after Game 1, and to be honest, had we won Game 1, things might have been different," Leetch said. "If we won the opener, we might have continued to roll like we had against the Islanders and Capitals. So, Game 1, I think, went a long way toward that series being what it became. It would have put more doubts in the Devils' heads, too, after we beat them six times in the regular season. But that all ended with Game 1, and we needed to refocus, get back out there, and get a win."

After outshooting the Devils 25–11 in the first two frames, New York all but iced it in the opening minute of the third, going up 2–0 as Sergei Nemchinov buried a rebound into an open net while Brodeur was being hassled by Tikkanen. Daneyko was in position and actually blocked a Leetch shot from the point, but it caromed right to Nemchinov for his second goal of the series. Tikkanen, who was dumped by Danekyo on his way to the net, allowed his momentum to carry himself into Brodeur, allowing for the open net. Under today's video review rules, it was a goal that might have been disallowed. But in 1994, it stood...much to the dismay of Brodeur.

The Devils' rookie was often a picture of poise between the pipes. Not easily rattled and always quick to flash a smile through the thin bars on his facemask, Brodeur never seemed fazed by the Garden chants. After Game 1, he seemed to see the attention as a compliment.

"I have to stop and look around every now and again," he said at the time. "And what a thrill to look up and see the signs, and they're saying it to me. It's great."

But in Game 2, after Goal No. 2, he was not happy, and rightfully so. He slammed his water bottle in frustration on the top of the net, feeling very strongly that Tikkanen should have drawn an interference call. It was the first sign of any angst from Brodeur, who at that point had already stopped 25 shots.

The non-call did not inspire the Devils much, though, and the beat went on for the Rangers. They were the agitators on this night, and New Jersey fell for it: Brian Noonan knocked down Stevens at one point, and the latter countered with a 2:00 roughing penalty. The Devils killed it off, but the result seemed inevitable.

At 6:11 of the third, Anderson, whom Keenan clearly wanted to see more out of, got on the scoring sheet with a little help from Daneyko. Trying to feed a break—and perhaps taking more risks than normal because of the two-goal deficit—Daneyko tried a breakout pass, cross ice, from his own blue line instead of firing it up the boards. A quick-turning Anderson read the pass, picked it clean, and beat Brodeur unassisted.

Rangers 3, Devils 0.

The Garden Party was on. Order had been restored.

The goal was a long time coming for Anderson, and it probably seemed like old times. It may have been his 89th career postseason tally, but it was his first in 1994. Remember, the Rangers gave up Mike Gartner, eventually a Hall of Fame forward who finished his career with 708 goals, for Anderson, a mainstay on the Oilers' title teams and a player who blended in well with Messier, Lowe, Tikkanen, and Co.

As Neil Smith admitted, it wasn't exactly a great trade for the Rangers. Gartner would go on to score six goals in 10 games for Toronto that season, and played four more years in the NHL—crossing the 30-goal plateau in two of them—before his retirement. In 1995–96 with Toronto and 1996–97 with Phoenix, Gartner actually played full 82-game seasons, scoring 35 and 32 goals, respectively. Anderson, meanwhile, never played more than 36 games in any one NHL season to follow, and would only score 18 more goals overall before walking away from the game.

But Keenan likes what he likes, of course, and doesn't what he doesn't. And he didn't like Gartner.

"I really don't think the deadline deals were as strategic as some people make them out to be," Smith said. "In many instances, we just needed *different* players."

That was true, of course. Anderson had won more in his career than Gartner, and that experience helped in the dressing room. He had four goals in 12 regular season games with the Rangers after the trade, and squeezed out three goals and six points in the postseason. Decent numbers, yes, but hardly a fair return on Gartner.

Wins are wins, though, and the Rangers were well on their way to their first of the conference finals.

"If you want to know the definition of a team, it's on the Rangers bench right now," ESPN rinkside analyst Al Morganti said on the broadcast. "As soon as that [Anderson] goal was scored, Messier and Keenan hugged each other. It shows what the players think of the coach."

With their team comfortably in front, the crowd took a turn for the ugly in the third. As New York crowds are wont to do, the fans aimed their fire at the opponent, not their team. Chants of "De-vils suck! De-vils suck! De-vils suck!" reverberated throughout the Garden. New Jersey played along as frustration started to seep out of their red-and-black jerseys. Even the fourth line, the Devils' most efficient of the game by a wide margin, lost its composure as Mike Peluso cross-checked Adam Graves, netting a 2:00 minor and a 10:00 misconduct with 12:42 left.

The Rangers' power play went to work, again putting on a show. Messier held at the point, allowing Leetch to pinch in. The defenseman, showing his gracefulness, skated around Lemieux as Messier hit him in stride. Leetch then cut in between Bernie Nicholls and Lemieux, just as Stevens finally caught up to him. But Leetch, in turn, dropped a beautiful touch pass to

Graves, who one-timed it past Brodeur through the five-hole for a 4–0 lead. Targeting Brodeur's five-hole was becoming a trend—or a problem, depending on which team you were rooting for.

"Is there anything that he does not do?" Thorne said of Leetch on the game call. "He has never played better hockey than in these playoffs."

"I don't care who you have on defense," Clement said. "You just cannot defend plays like this."

It was Graves' eighth of the postseason, which tied a Rangers playoff record. With more than half the period left, chants of "Mar-ty, Mar-ty" had returned as the Garden faithful prepared to celebrate. A few minutes later, Tikkanen fired a slap shot in from center ice so the Rangers could make a line change. As Brodeur stopped the easy, 90-foot play-in, the crowd gave him a full-throated Bronx cheer.

"I wondered if the Rangers could play a whole game the way they have played," Thorne said. "And they have."

Meanwhile, Zelepukin did not return, and before the end of the period, Lemaire pulled Brodeur and let Chris Terreri finish the game. This, of course, would allow an interesting storyline to surface before Game 3 back in New Jersey. Terreri had played in the previous series against Boston, and the two goalies had platooned during the regular season as the Devils set a franchise record for points. Would Lemaire start Terreri after allowing the veteran to get his legs underneath him in the waning moments of Game 2? Or was he just giving Brodeur a breather on a night when there was plenty of blame to go around? It was not as if Brodeur played poorly. He did make 36 saves, and the Devils were assured of going home for Game 3 with a 1–1 split at the Garden. There were certainly worse situations to be in.

The timing was interesting and typical Lemaire. Why would he wait until 4–0 in the third period to make the change, when the game had already been decided? Lemaire, as was often the case throughout the series, gave very little in the way of information and forced the media to speculate.

"I'm going to take it game by game," he said.

Terreri, meanwhile, didn't have much chance to shake off any rust, as he made just one save in the final period. The Rangers called off the dogs, concluded the frame with a 16–5 shots advantage, secured their first victory of the series, and made travel arrangements for their visit to the Swamp.

Final score: Rangers 4, Devils 0.

"By this point, we knew it was going to be a wild series," Larmer said. "And that was something new to us, given the way we were playing going into it."

Larmer and the rest of his teammates knew that no matter what style or complexion the following games took on, the Rangers were secure in net. In one of the more subdued shutouts you'll ever see in the postseason, Richter quietly posted 16 saves en route to the win. It was Richter's sixth career playoff shutout.

"I think that was one thing that got lost in that game," Kenny Albert said. "Richter was a big part of it."

"He was always there," Leetch said.

"You don't win championships without great goaltending. You need to make the right save at the right time. Mike Richter was such a tremendous athlete at the time, and one of the best from a flexibility standpoint, and just a great competitor," said Tom Chorske, one of the Devils' top penalty killers who was a minus-2 in Game 2. "He could win games by himself at times. Now, he didn't have to with that talented of a team all that often. But he was really good on that night."

So, the momentum—fleeting though it may have been—shifted to New York as the series itself shifted to New Jersey. The Rangers had made it a five-game series, and eagerly jumped on their bus knowing full well that they'd have plenty of support waiting for them in East Rutherford among the expected crowd of 19,040.

That said, it was going to take more than a 4–0 win at home against a team Rangers fans did not respect to convince New York that something special was in store.

"Listen, it would have been a disaster if they were to lose that series," Joe Benigno said. "With all those chips on the table? And the fact that they didn't even make the playoffs before it? They had to get it done. So, there was such a long way to go. I felt they were the better team, and they should win this series. But I can't tell you I had any confidence whatsoever."

The team did, though. With so much experience in the locker room, being down a game that early in the series—in any series, really—wasn't the hindrance that it could have been for a younger team.

"There are so many things that happen over the course of a playoff run, but I can tell you that team never lost its confidence," Lidster said. "Never did. That was a point of emphasis and a point of strength, and we built off it. You always knew what to do. There was no question. You had your role. There were a lot of times in the year where we won games without dictating the play, and you'd just get used to it. We could play so many different ways, and win so many different ways, we never really spent too much time breaking things down."

Across the river, it was likely a different story. After losing their sixth game of the postseason, and with the series headed toward a pivotal game on home ice, the focus was now on Lemaire to right the ship, be it with Brodeur or Terreri.

"We had the right mix of players for the system to work, and we never panicked," Chorske said. "We had young, hungry players, and we had veterans who weren't necessarily old, but knew they needed to do whatever was needed to win now. And everybody bought in. We always felt that there was an instant chemistry there."

In Game 3 in East Rutherford, in front of primarily their home fans, that needed to come to the surface.

Quickly.

Game 3

○ ○ ○ ○

"At this point, there was more to it. Two games in, and there's more media, more fans, and the whole metropolitan area was watching us now. So, everyone was involved, and we knew we were going to have to go through them. We had battled hard already, and it was only 1–1. So, it was talked about. We knew going [to New Jersey] was not going to be easy. We knew what we were up against."
—BRIAN LEETCH, NEW YORK RANGERS (1988–2004)

Hugh Randall McKay is not unlike many other rough-and-tumble Canadian players who made their way to hockey's highest level. Born and raised on the game in Montreal but not blessed with the greatest skill in the world, the 6'2", 210-pound forward earned every cent he made in the NHL on grit, determination, desire, and drive.

In short, he was the prototypical Devil.

McKay, a sixth-round draft choice of the Detroit Red Wings in 1985, was always incredibly honest with his teammates, his coaches, the fans, and even the media. It's a trait so often found in hockey players, one that often makes hockey journalists a spoiled lot relative to their brethren covering other professional sports.

You didn't have to read between the lines with McKay, so there is likely no better person than he to help describe what it was like when the Rangers crossed the Hudson River to play the Devils in East Rutherford.

"You play your whole life, and for the most part, when you're at home, you're at home, and you enjoy all that goes with it," McKay said. "With the

Rangers in our building, it was different. Simple as that. There was such a strong presence there for the road team. We always felt like the underdogs, no question, the second-class citizens. It was always in our heads when we played them. That's why each game against them was so big. Preseason, regular season, playoffs, it didn't matter. The Rangers were always the top gun in town."

Well, the top gun came to the Swamp on May 19, 1994, with its eyes on its target. The Rangers prided themselves on bouncing back from rare losses, and this series was no different. Drop Game 1 and home-ice advantage? No problem. Go out, dominate Game 2 at home, and then get ready to do it all over again. That was the Rangers' mind-set when they traveled through the Lincoln Tunnel and made the six-mile trek to the Meadowlands. This was still very much their series, they thought, despite the fact that it was tied 1–1. And with a split crowd of 19,040 watching their every move, they had every intention of taking a 2–1 series lead and improving their overall playoff mark to 10–2.

"We felt good," Rangers forward Stephane Matteau said. "We had played well in Game 2 on both sides of the ice, and there was a confidence there, for sure."

But the Devils did not lack confidence, either, regardless of how much Rangers blue was going to be in the stands. A 4–0 whitewash, it seemed, was not going to derail a train that began rolling in September.

"That's what confidence does to you, and we certainly felt that way under Jacques [Lemaire]," said Scott Stevens, a Hall of Famer who played for three teams across 22 star-studded seasons. "I've said it before, and will always say it. He was the best coach I ever had, and there was just a sense of confidence, of calm, that he made us all feel."

Game 3 at the Meadowlands, with jerseys of both teams scattered throughout the arena, was a spectacle. How much did this game mean to Devils fans? Consider a middle-aged man, sitting in Section 128, wearing a Ken Daneyko jersey over his suit. He looked like he'd come directly fresh from the office, and he probably had to go back there the next day. But that didn't stop him from having "1940" shaved into the sides of his head.

"It was definitely something that was new to me," said Steve Larmer, who hadn't landed with the Rangers until November 2, 1993. "We'd walk into buildings against the Islanders or the Devils that year, the rivals, and some people would be chanting for us, and others would be chanting '19-40! 19-40!' The first few times I experienced that, I didn't know what was going on."

But he and his teammates were steady and sure on this night, at least at the outset. It was the home team that was scrambling around as the Rangers dominated play, attempting to set a tone. Two minutes in, with his defense confused, Martin Brodeur had to make a series of saves on Sergei Nemchinov and Sergei Zubov. But the Rangers kept coming, as Mike Keenan quickly rolled lines, kept everyone fresh, and tried to sustain the pressure.

"He has to believe in his best player. Even though they don't get the last line change [as the road team], he has to think that Mark Messier, his captain, can handle any one checking line that the Devils throw out there," Bill Clement said on the ESPN telecast. "I don't think Mike Keenan does anything different because he's on the road."

As if to prove Clement's point, Keenan gave Messier three shifts in the first four minutes of the game. The captain's fourth shift resulted in a goal.

Off a faceoff win, Messier blew into the zone on the right side, parallel to the Devils bench. He swiftly fed Adam Graves with a cross-ice saucer pass, and Graves' slap shot from 15 feet beat Brodeur over the shoulder, igniting the Rangers fans and immediately putting the Devils in a hole. Graves' second of the series and ninth of the playoffs, from Messier and Jeff Beukeboom at 2:43, gave New York a 1–0 lead, and gave Graves a new Rangers franchise record for postseason goals in a single year.

"It was typical of the New York Rangers," Clement said. "On the board early, again."

He was right. Through 12 playoff games, the Rangers had scored nine goals in the first 5:00 of first periods. The bad news for the Devils? The Rangers were 7–2 in the postseason when scoring first.

"But for us, it was always about how we responded," Jim Dowd said. "Bad things are going to happen in hockey games, in hockey series. They always do. What we took pride in was responding."

New York kept coming in waves, as the "Let's Go Ran-gers" chants gained in volume. It was New Jersey's worst nightmare come to life: all the Devils wanted to do was drain the road team and its fans over the course of three hours, and in less than three minutes of game action, they had only achieved the opposite. It was a repeat, or a continuation, of Game 2, as the Devils found themselves chasing. Dowd's shot from the right point 4:40 into the period was the home team's first.

But the Devils stemmed the tide on the next shift, and it started with McKay. After a faceoff, McKay managed to keep the puck in the corner to Mike Richter's right, and sent it to Viacheslav Fetisov at the point. A veteran, lock-down backliner (who would later be the general manager for his native country's Olympic hockey team, and also serve as the Minister of Sport in Russia) was everything but a goal scorer. In nine NHL seasons with New Jersey and Detroit, he never had more than eight tallies in a single season.

But funny things happen in the playoffs, and Fetisov fired a slap shot from the point that whizzed by Mike Peluso's stick, caromed over to Rangers center Craig MacTavish's skate, and then past a sprawling Richter.

The Crash Line had paid off. The goal was announced as Peluso's, as the puck appeared to graze his stick before reaching MacTavish. But it would later be changed to Fetisov's at 5:48 of the first.

"What a line," Stevens said. "What we were able to get out of Randy, Mike, and Bobby speaks for itself. Not many teams could get that kind of production out of a fourth line, if you want to even call it a fourth line."

The Rangers did not waver, though. They stayed aggressive. They continued to flow in layers. And then, they started to hit.

Less than a minute after the tying goal, Beukeboom caught Bobby Carpenter in the thigh. It was Beukeboom's shoulder to Carpenter's lower waist, and the latter's leg flailed in the air before he spun around and fell to the ice in the neutral zone. Carpenter was eventually helped off the ice by two trainers and into locker room. It was labeled a right leg injury, and suddenly, there was more concern for the home team as Lemaire was forced to scramble his lines.

Carpenter was a loss, for certain. A poster boy for American hockey in the afterlife of the 1980 "Miracle on Ice" in Lake Placid, Carpenter, a smooth skater with a left-handed shot and a terrific knack for winning faceoffs, was a first-round draft choice of the Washington Capitals in 1981. His arrival was so highly publicized that he landed on the cover of *Sports Illustrated*. Deemed the "Can't-Miss Kid" in the February 23, 1981, issue, Carpenter, a native of Beverly, Massachusetts, never truly lived up to the hype. In 1984–85, he scored his career high—53 goals—but in an 18-year career, he made the All-Star Game just once. But after being tossed around the league as a journeyman—making stops with Los Angeles, Boston, Washington again, and even the Rangers—Carpenter found a home in New Jersey.

His acquisition was typical Lou Lamoriello. Give him your tired, your poor, your huddled skaters yearning to breathe free, and he'd turn them into determined Devils, ready to contribute to the cause. Like so many other moves, it worked. Signed as a free agent on September 30, 1993, Carpenter was just another convert who bought into the Lamoriello-Lemaire philosophy. He was a defensive forward who knew his role, who could still win faceoffs, and who could kill penalties with the best of them. In his first season, he played 76 games and had 10 goals, 33 points, and was a plus-7. It was not pretty, fancy, or special. But for the Devils? It was perfection.

"Carp could do some special things," Tom Chorske said. "He took pride in faceoffs, and to get out there and kill penalties at a high level in a series like that took a little extra."

The Rangers knew that, so Keenan's crew stayed aggressive against this shorthanded bunch. The shots came early and often. The play stayed in Brodeur's neighborhood far too much for Lemaire's liking. Indeed, the home team was not itself.

"The Rangers are dictating the play, taking the body, and holding the zone," Gary Thorne said on the broadcast. "Right now, it's Brodeur against the world."

But the Devils began to fight back, and in doing so, a major storyline in the series would develop. With the play in the Devils' zone and the home team in desperation mode, New Jersey had clearly become frustrated. The Devils thrived on keeping the puck out of their half of the ice and controlling the neutral zone. They couldn't do that here, and in turn, things got chippy. Claude Lemieux was snagged at 14:42 for a cross-check, but it was the cross-check that *wasn't* called that would gain notoriety for ages.

With Alexei Kovalev in possession and off to the right of Brodeur's crease, forward Bernie Nicholls took the liberty of pushing him off to the side of the cage. Bruce Driver was behind Nicholls at the time, and had the veteran defenseman been in Nicholls' spot in front of Brodeur, things may have turned out differently. But Nicholls wasn't done yet. He smothered a sprawling Kovalev, who fell to a knee as the puck raced around the boards and out toward the point. As Kovalev gathered himself, Nicholls took a breath, turned his stick horizontally, and cross-checked Kovalev under the helmet and at his neck. The Russian fell backward, landed on his back, and clutched his throat.

No call.

"Emotions were running high in that series," said Nicholls, a career goal scorer who had some grit and toughness, but was never viewed as a dirty player in his 18-year career. "I cross-checked him. I did. But I didn't hurt him."

Suddenly, there was a major edge to the series.

"Nicholls' shot on Kovalev," Thorne said, "I guarantee you will be in the league office soon for a review."

The Rangers journeyed on, seemingly fueled by the non-call. With 3:19 left in the first period, New York held a 14–4 advantage in shots, but with Brodeur as the backstop, the Devils survived. The final seconds of the first period ticked away, the horn went off, and the fans of both teams were pleased—the visitors happy with the pace of the game, the hosts glad there was a break ahead. Carpenter was nowhere to be seen, Bill Guerin was nursing a bad shoulder, Nicholls had dodged a bullet, and the Devils, who had scored on an inadvertent, highly fortunate deflection off a skate, were lucky to be tied at the first intermission.

"No question, the Devils are more banged up than the Rangers are at this point," Clement said. "They are playing hurt."

That would be a secondary theme of the second period, as Carpenter returned but clearly wasn't himself. But players play hurt in the playoffs, and while Guerin and Carpenter were hardly 100 percent, they allowed Lemaire to go back to his normal set of lines in a tie game. Carpenter, in fact, took the opening faceoff as New Jersey began the 10th period of hockey in this series having never led at any point in any game.

But as the puck dropped, the talk in the press box, in the runways, and throughout the arena was Nicholls' hit. And so began the politicking of one Mike Keenan. The Rangers' enigmatic bench general officially inserted himself into this classic tale in between periods of Game 3. Keenan left his team during the intermission and waltzed over to the doorway of the officials' room to complain. He spent nearly the entire break in front of that room, and was heard saying, "We're going to send the tape to the league!"

He clearly wasn't going to get the call back, but Keenan was thinking about the rest of the series, not the rest of this game. This was about working the officials over, making sure they remembered who was doing it, and hoping that the tide turned toward New York's side before it was said and done.

"Both of these coaches have used the press to their advantage, to talk about officiating, after they've lost a game," Thorne said. "So, they're still at it."

But the game had to go on, and regardless of what Keenan said or did, the Devils showed a spark early in the second. Dowd hit the post on Richter's glove side that brought the fans to the edge of their seats. A shift later, Nicholls' slap shot from the left point almost sneaked through, and Richer's rebound tip-in try was also stopped. Richter came up big, but the Devils were finally starting to impose their will. Sensing the mood of the game, knowing what was on the line, and not wanting to let the game escalate out of control, the officials clamped down on both sides, and it stopped that Devils' flurry quickly.

Guerin was sent to the box on a cross-check of Kevin Lowe, and the Rangers pounced.

When New York's power play was clicking, it had a lot to do with Brian Leetch. The quarterback of Keenan's No. 1 man-advantage unit, Leetch was more than just a steadying force on the backline with a rocket shot. He possessed an innate ability to sense holes in a penalty-kill diagram. He knew when to stay at home, fire a shot, look for a pass, or pinch in and take a chance.

Leetch took a chance on this power play, and found himself down low after leaving the puck up top for Graves. Graves' shot was stopped, but Leetch gathered the rebound. With an effortless precision that would help define his career, he lasered a cross-crease pass right by Brodeur's eyes and onto the waiting stick of Larmer. A veteran who would end his career with nine seasons of 30 or more goals, Larmer left no doubts, burying it past Brodeur and igniting the Rangers' portion of the crowd. His 50th career playoff goal in an underrated career that spanned 15 seasons and included 1,012 points was one of his easiest, and gave the visitors a 2–1 lead.

"Leetchy could do some tremendous things with the puck, no question," Larmer said. "So skilled, so smart, and such a leader. We had a lot of them on that team. But Brian was definitely one of them."

The Rangers' momentum began to snowball. Lemaire sent out the Crash Line after Larmer's goal, but to no avail. Messier broke through, got himself in position, and fired a point-blank shot that Brodeur stopped to keep his team within a goal 12:00 into the period. Six minutes later, Messier was back at it. He carried behind the net and offered up a classic Messier backhand pass to a streaking Leetch. Again, Brodeur thwarted the Rangers' attempt.

The Devils were alive…barely. With 6:00 left in the period, the shots were 29–12 in favor of the Rangers, and if it weren't for a rookie netminder too young to know any better, New York would have been on cruise control.

"It was times like that where he always had fun out there," Scott Niedermayer said of Brodeur. "Big series, big moment of the game, and the thing with him is that he has so much fun doing it. Always."

Daneyko concurred.

"You could always see that smile peek through that facemask," he said. "Always smiling."

Leave it to Messier to sense the youngster's calm and confidence. After one whistle right smack dab in the middle of this run, Messier playfully whacked Brodeur in the pants on the way around him. It was nice gamesmanship, but also a pat on the back, so to speak, from one legend to a rookie about a job well done.

What Brodeur really needed, though, was for *his* team to do something in support of him, rather than the other team's captain. And finally, his teammates responded.

"When you make those types of runs, you need special players, and special performances by players," Brodeur said. "During that year, we almost always found a way to get one of those, and it was usually from someone different every night."

One of the things that made New Jersey so strong on defense was that one through six, the blueliners were adept at holding pucks in. Super-skilled scorers they were not, but they could hold the zone with the best of them.

With five minutes left, Bruce Driver corralled a pass on the right point from Richer and, as he'd done a thousand times before in that building, held and controlled the puck, then let loose a cannon shot toward Richter. The Rangers netminder stopped it, but he couldn't diffuse the rebound as it sailed 10 feet in front of him toward Valeri Zelepukin. The Russian quickly gathered the puck and lifted a wrist shot past Richter as the goalie fell backward. With Richter rolling to get up off his back, the Devils' portion of the crowd erupted, and—somehow, some way—the home team had forged a 2–2 tie in a game it had no business being in.

Despite being outshot 31–13, Zelepukin's goal from Richer and Driver at 15:50 knotted this classic up. Suddenly, the Rangers were headed into the locker room having thrown their best hockey at the Devils, and all they had to show for it was a tie.

Sensing his team's precarious situation, Keenan went for the kill in the third period. He used his top three lines almost exclusively and tried to control play with New York's skill players, rather than keep everyone fresh by rolling all four lines.

His counterpart on the New Jersey bench did not follow suit. Lemaire wasn't about to let his fourth line sit out when it had already been one of his most productive units of the game and series. So, the Devils stayed the course and didn't worry about matching lines.

"That's what we could do with [the fourth] line," Lamoriello said. "We didn't have to worry about shortening our bench. They were *that* good."

Whether it was a byproduct of the strategies or not, the game took a turn for the sluggish, as neither team wanted to make a mistake with the puck. As each shift became more conservative than the last, physicality came to the forefront. At 11:08 of the third, Carpenter and his gimpy leg got mixed up with Beukeboom, and each drew 2:00 roughing penalties. Perhaps, with one bum wheel already, it wasn't the smartest move for the Can't-Miss Kid, but his aggressiveness and guts would go a long way toward showing his teammates, and his opponents, that he meant business.

The rough stuff continued, as neither team stockpiled quality scoring chances, and it continued to come from unlikely sources. As the midway point of the period neared, a well-rested MacTavish ran right into Brodeur, most likely on purpose. The Rangers wanted to make sure the rookie knew they weren't going away anytime soon.

Niedermayer, as any good defenseman would do, responded by going right after MacTavish. It didn't stop the veteran forward from going back after Brodeur, and as the helmetless wonder skated through the Devils' crease, he took a swipe at Brodeur's back, drawing an interference call.

"The Rangers series was tough, there were a lot of things going on," Niedermayer said. "But it's in series like that where we really learned how to come together as a team."

As a team, the Devils would milk the clock in the third, and the Rangers hardly stopped them. In fact, during a stretch of 11:40 in what would be a scoreless period, New York was held to one shot. Keenan's three-line approach, perhaps, wasn't working.

"The pace of this game, the energy level is so high," Clement said. "These Rangers, at least some of them, are wearing down."

The good news for New York was that after Richer was stopped by Richter with a sprawling glove save 15:00 into the frame, the veteran Rangers had an intermission to recharge, reset, and resume their push as the two teams headed to another overtime.

Well, perhaps *push* is the wrong word. Neither team truly mounted one in the extra period. In fact, the biggest storyline out of those 20 do-or-die minutes was Nemchinov, a faceoff demon who quickly dispelled the myth that Russians weren't among the game's toughest players. Early in the period, Nemchinov was hit in the head with a puck, immediately drawing blood from his right eye. In today's game, he may have been rushed off to the locker room, never to return. But Nemchinov wasn't about to leave this game, this series. Not a chance. He didn't even leave his shift.

"It's all about sacrifice at that time of the year," Leetch said. "We had some incredible players do some incredible things."

Indeed, Nemchinov stayed out there, even after a whistle. At the stoppage, he simply went over to bench, wiped his bloody eye off with a towel, and returned for the faceoff. As he was skating away, someone from the bench asked him to return. Nemchinov simply turned around, looked Keenan in the eye, and offered an English response that was easy to decipher despite his Russian tone: "I'm good."

It was efforts like his that gave the Rangers a 48–30 faceoff lead with 12:00 left. Yet the Devils continued to battle, despite being outshot 47–26 after 77 minutes of game time. Niedermayer had an open lane for a slap shot midway through, but it was deflected into the crowd. Richter had been ready for it, in any case; he was incredibly relaxed for an overtime game, just as Brodeur was on the other side.

After the Niedermayer deflection, Beukeboom went over to Richter just to check on him, and Richter simply nodded. Through the small cage on his Statue of Liberty mask, he winked with his left eye.

A few minutes later, the horn sounded, and the series' second double-overtime game had been reached.

"This one was a tough game," Matteau said. "There was a lot of dirty play. A lot of hate had started between the two teams. The Devils had their chances. We had our chances. And then there were times where no one had their chances. But in that locker room before the second overtime, Mess just told us to stay focused and go out and play like we had all year."

They did exactly that.

Trying to overcome a 1–7 playoff overtime run that spanned years of mediocre hockey in New York, the Rangers were a determined bunch in the second overtime. New Jersey's best chance came after Lemieux fed Tommy Albelin on a 2-on-1 break, but that was stopped by Richter's leg pad. New York took over, and within minutes, control of the series was in its grasp.

"I'll probably sound like a stupid kid," Matteau said, "but I just had a feeling I was going to score."

After Lowe wrestled the puck away from Chorske at the Devils' blue line, he left it for Glenn Anderson to carry into the offensive zone from the left point. With Matteau on his left side just two feet away from him, Anderson pulled up, wrapped the puck around the net behind Brodeur, and the Rangers went to work.

Fresh off the bench—and showing no ill effects from the Nicholls' cross-check that by then seemed like three days ago—Kovalev stopped the puck and centered it for Matteau, as the Devils scrambled for position. The pass was too sharp, and it bounced off Matteau's skate and off to the circle. But a pinching Leetch—remember, he always knew when to pinch—kept the puck in, and flipped it toward Brodeur with a wrist shot. Brodeur stopped that easily, but couldn't digest the rebound, and possession continued for New York.

The entire building was on edge now; this was one of those classic flurries in which the defensive team just can't get in the right lanes. Despite having their two best defenders—Stevens and Niedermayer—on the ice, the Devils were on their heels, and it seemed like only a matter of time before the Rangers punched one home.

Eventually, the puck passed behind Brodeur. Kovalev fetched it and sent it to Matteau. Matteau then left it for Anderson before breaking to the front of the net as if he was a wide receiver and Anderson was a quarterback on a "go-deep-and-look-back" play.

With Kovalev and Matteau now parked in front of the net, Anderson streaked to the left and slid a centering pass in front of Brodeur to Kovalev. A neat little push by Kovalev was stopped by Brodeur, but again, the difference between winning and losing is often about who controls the rebounds. A prone Brodeur couldn't freeze the puck, and as it caromed amid a scrum from one skate to another stick back to someone else's skate, it eventually landed on Matteau's blade.

"It's hard to describe, because it sounds so simple," Matteau said. "Put your stick down on the ice and good things will happen."

Indeed, Matteau's stick was on the ice, and a quick backhander beat Brodeur for the game-winner. An elated Matteau did two plyometric jumps on skates with his stick up high before eventually getting swarmed by his teammates. Up and down once, up and down twice, landing awkwardly each time, but maintaining his balance as his team caught up to him at the left faceoff dot. A deadline acquisition, Matteau paid off large, and the shift that just wouldn't end for the Devils defense finally did.

Rangers 3, Devils 2.

"In the blink of an eye," Clement said, "Matteau scores the goal of his life."

And so began the Legend of Matteau.

The winner came at 6:13 of the second overtime, from Kovalev and Anderson, and on the Rangers' 50th shot of the night. As the crowd filtered out, the "Let's Go Ran-gers" chants rang triumphant throughout the Swamp.

Brodeur, sprawled out and dejected in a scene we'd see again, looked up to the sky for an answer that wasn't going to come on this night. His teammates immediately trudged off to their locker room, as Lamoriello sat stoically in the press box. Just to his right was the in-house video feed on a 13-inch television. And as he stared straight toward the ice from that lower-level press box known around media circles as having the best view in the league, a shot of a smiling Keenan, ear to ear, stared right back at Lou from the television.

Meanwhile, the Rangers continued to tap Matteau on the helmet in a group hug that looked like it might never unravel. Finally, an exhausted Matteau headed toward the exit bent over from fatigue, with his stick on his thighs and a smile as wide as the Lincoln Tunnel. When he finally stepped off the ice and got his bearings about him, he looked straight ahead into the locker room and just let it all out: "Woooooooooooooooooo!"

Little did he know, this was only the beginning.

As the security guard opened the gate for the dejected Devils, the guard tapped Stevens, the captain, on the shoulder. Despite the disappointing circumstances and the fresh wound the team had just suffered, the guard offered only words of encouragement.

"It's far from over, boys," he told them. "Don't worry."

That guard knew what he was talking about.

Game 4

○ ○ ○ ○

"You have to hand it to Mike Keenan. He's good. I'm sitting in the lounge after the game, and I'm watching the postgame on the TV. All I hear is Mike complaining and demanding a suspension, and it's just going on and on. He's really into it. And I remember saying, 'Who is he talking about?' Sure enough, it was me! And sure enough, I get suspended for it. He definitely influenced that. I don't think that happens in today's game."
—BERNIE NICHOLLS, NEW JERSEY DEVILS (1993–94)

RANGERS COACH MIKE KEENAN had made his displeasure clear during Game 3. As he ranted and raved at the officials between the first and second periods, his message was unmistakable: win or lose, he was going to push to get Bernie Nicholls suspended for his cross-check on Alexei Kovalev. If he created a media circus in the process, so be it. The only thing that mattered, in the end, was the result.

The Rangers made it a production, of course, as Keenan continued his message in the postgame press conference following the euphoric 3–2 double-overtime victory in East Rutherford. The tabloids ran with the story, the talk shows opened up their phone lines, and the Rangers sent a tape to the league for review.

"It was incidents like that, that made for great radio in New York," Chris Russo said. "It was a great time for hockey fans, and let's face it: controversy goes a long way toward making great series. We had that in this series. There was a lot going on there."

Had this happened in a different series, in a different media market, perhaps the outcome would have been different. But with the buzz surrounding this series at an all-time high, in the world's largest media market, Keenan succeeded with his quest. The message was out to the masses, and the league had the evidence.

"Things are going to happen quick," said NHL vice president in charge of discipline Brian Burke.

And boy, did he mean it.

After further review, the NHL concurred with Keenan. Even though no penalty was called, Nicholls, one of the Devils' most consistent offensive players, was to be suspended immediately for Game 4 at home, with New Jersey trailing the series 2–1 and facing its biggest game of the season.

"In that series—in any series, really—you have to go through that kind of adversity," Ken Daneyko said. "The decision was the decision, and you take responsibility for the tough times, learn from it, and know what you need to do the next time out."

Jacques Lemaire wasn't going to let that message slip by his troops. Nicholls—who scored 70 goals in 1988–89 with Los Angeles, made three All-Star teams, and finished his 18-year career with 1,209 points—would be missed. But it was not the Devils' way to make excuses or neglect to have someone ready to fill another teammate's skates.

Enter Corey Millen, an American sparkplug of a forward, all 5′7″ and 170 pounds of him, who could come in, win faceoffs, agitate the opponent, and create some offense from time to time.

Keep in mind, this was one of the deeper teams in the NHL, so Lemaire didn't need to call on a minor league farmhand. Millen, a former Ranger, had scored 20 goals in 78 regular season games for the Devils, marking the third time he reached 20 tallies in an eight-year career. Not bad for a reserve. "Everyone had a role, and everyone knew what to do when your name was called," Lou Lamoriello said. "It didn't matter if you were Scott Stevens or Corey Millen. You were always ready to go."

Millen certainly welcomed the opportunity to show the organization he still belonged. Despite his statistics, Millen didn't have one of his more enjoyable seasons under Lemaire, and it just goes to show you that even when a franchise enjoys a breakthrough season, there are always pitfalls and personality clashes to manage. Millen, a proud, passionate, and experienced player, wanted to play, of course, and felt he could contribute to such a good team. But in the end, he was only in the lineup for seven postseason games.

"I tried my best to just go about my business. Everyone's job with the Devils is to take ownership in what they had to do, so I did that," Millen said. "I had my moments of frustration, certainly. Jacques had his ways and knew what he wanted to see, and if you didn't do it, you wouldn't be used. I had to get used to that, and cater my game around that."

But for a player who was drafted in the third round back in 1982, represented his country in the Olympics twice, and scored 119 goals in a star-studded career at the University of Minnesota—one of the nation's top hockey schools—sitting in the press box watching games in a suit and tie was an adjustment.

"It was probably the most frustrating time of my career," he said. "For me, I never knew from day to day if I'd be in the lineup. Every day in practice, I was on the line with three other guys: Bernie Nicholls, Claude Lemieux, Stephane Richer, and me. And I knew those guys were going to play, so I had to get used to the fact that I wasn't going to be out there. Jacques had me on edge all the time, and I wasn't the only one. It was tough to get into any groove. In the end, as far as the regular season, I was in the lineup most of the time, but out of it just enough to wonder why. But the team was so successful, and he did a great job of managing all the parts. You could not argue with the success."

But none of that mattered on May 21, 1994. He *was* in the lineup on that day, and it was up to him to make the most of it. And oh by the way, he just happened to be walking into an epic series against his team's biggest rival, one that had just taken a 2–1 lead.

"No question, it was a serious time," Millen said. "Every game with the Rangers was serious. But with that kind of talent out there on both sides, this was a new level. And having played for the Rangers, I spent enough time there to know what they were all about and know what they were up against here. When you play there, you certainly get a feel for the fans, and their desire and their love and their hunger to win. You knew, once they got Mark [Messier], it was a whole new ballgame, and they finally had the pieces in place to deliver what the fans wanted. So, it was pretty clear that most people thought this was their year. And it was up to us to stop that."

That wasn't going to be easy, with or without Nicholls. After all, the Rangers were brimming with confidence and knew that they'd have plenty of support in the stands again in Game 4. "It was just a very professional group, with some great characters, but they all seemed to bring a sense of calm to every situation," Mike Richter said. "And we also had the ability to withstand the inevitable—injuries, losses, tough bounces, you name it. We were always prepared."

In a series so even across the board, it was hardly a surprise that the Devils were the aggressor in Game 4, given the fact that they were dominated the game before. With the crowd at another fever pitch, Bobby Carpenter edged Messier on the opening faceoff, and the home team went to work. Stevens and Lemieux let off successive slap shots in the first three minutes that Richter stopped, but the pressure was on.

"I think the Rangers are just being a little sloppy at this point. It's not that the Devils are doing anything fancy, but they are coming," Bill Clement said on the telecast. "I think it's realistic to say that this is the New Jersey Devils' season if they do not win this."

They played like it.

Tom Chorske, one of the Devils' best skaters who had the explosion to take over a game if given the room, was all over the ice in the first period. On one shift, he laid out Jeff Beukeboom, sending an early message, then broke into the Rangers' zone and drew a hooking penalty on Brian Leetch, of all people, at 10:01. It was a foreshadowing of things to come for the Rangers defenseman.

Sixteen seconds later, the Devils had their first lead of the series. Lemaire sent Jim Dowd out for the power-play faceoff, and though he lost it, Bruce Driver—as was his specialty—kept it at the point. He passed the puck to John MacLean, who backhanded it along the boards back to Dowd. Stephane Richer, who was developing a nice bond with Dowd though they rarely played together in the regular season, sensed his center's wont, and broke to the net. He received a neat touch pass from Dowd, and with a little room, Richer went five-hole on Richter for his second goal of the series and seventh of the playoffs.

Richer's 46th career playoff tally finally gave the Devils something to work with: a lead, albeit small, which would allow Lemaire to truly clamp down in the neutral zone.

"The Devils' transition game," Gary Thorne said on the broadcast, "is maybe the best that we've seen in this series."

Indeed, New Jersey—with the Crash Line taking a regular turn, including the shift right after Richer's goal—was able to dictate play. Keenan, hoping for a spark, juggled his lines, and with 6:00 left, he even sent out one of the team's many enforcers, forward Joey Kocur, along with Stephane Matteau and Adam Graves.

It wouldn't be long before the game turned chippy, and with 4:38 remaining in the first, the series' first true fight—a rarity in postseason play—took place between two bruisers at center ice: Beukeboom and Mike Peluso. Peluso, who led the league with 408 penalty minutes in 1991–92 while with the Blackhawks, shed his equipment and tagged Beukeboom with a right to the side of the head that knocked him down. Peluso landed on top of him, the officials stepped in, and they both shuttled off to the locker room with 5:00 penalties.

Valeri Zelepukin continued the physical play 16:00 in as he floored Steve Larmer, who had his head down on the far boards from Richter. It was uncharacteristic of Zelepukin, but only further illustrated the Devils' cause on the night. Larmer shook it off, took a pass at center, and carried into the Devils' zone only to be hooked by Zelepukin, who could have easily drawn a penalty for it. No call, and it was a biggie. Stevens corralled the loose puck, turned, and fed a streaking Bill Guerin on the quick transition at center. Guerin broke in the zone with steam in between Sergei Zubov and Kevin Lowe, who could not catch up. Guerin faked forehand, getting Richter to commit, and then went backhand top shelf over the American's glove hand for as pretty a Devils' goal as one will ever see.

"I think there's different ways to win, and you have to learn how to play to your strengths. You also have to play with the hand that you're dealt. That's where our strength lied, back then on defense, and that's the way we had to play," Scott Niedermayer said. "But we had goal scorers, and there's not just one way to win in this league. If you have talent in one area, you have to take advantage of it in this league. And that's certainly what we did back then."

Guerin, who finished with 13 20-goal seasons in an 18-year career, was one of those snipers who often sacrificed a chance or two to play within the Lemaire system. But when he sensed his opportunity, he had the wheels and the skill set to make the most of it. Though he scored in the opener as well, he is more remembered for a shot that Richter stopped in that Game 1. So, you can understand his excitement.

"It was good to get that one," Guerin said.

Stoned at Madison Square Garden by Richter in Game 1, Guerin made good on his chance in Game 4. The two Americans would later be teammates, friends, and key cogs in Team USA's stunning 1996 World Cup of Hockey championship victory against Canada. But on this night in New Jersey, Guerin stood tall with his second goal of the playoffs, at 16:54, as Richter lay prone on the ice, staring at the rafters.

"Something I learned pretty early on with the Devils: put it behind you and move on," Guerin said of Richter's famous Game 1 save. "I ended up having a good series. I got one back on Ricky there in Game 4."

Guerin raced over to the bench and hugged Lemieux as if a huge weight had been lifted off his shoulders. But it was the activity on the Rangers' bench that was more interesting. As the Devils fans celebrated what seemed like a monstrous 2–0 lead, backup goaltender Glenn Healy began to stretch, and suddenly, a change in goal was in store.

"This is Mike Keenan telling his players, you're not getting it done," Thorne said. "It's a message."

But how serious a message was it? There was only 3:06 left in the first period, so Keenan may have just been playing mind games. Get Richter a little rest headed into the break, get him refocused, and get back at it after the intermission.

"I did think I was going back in," Richter said. "I honestly did. And I probably should have known better."

In fact, Healy and Richter shared a moment at the blue line where each gave the other a vote of confidence, and the latter simply went to the bench and joined his teammates.

"Keenan had a way of sending a message. There are many reasons why you pull a goalie, and he used just about every one of them at some point," Richter said. "But I'd rather be with someone who cared as much as he did. It could be tough at times. In the end, you knew what your job was, and if he didn't feel you were doing it, he'd make a change."

So, in a game the Devils were dominating—with 3:00 left in the first, they held a 10–3 shots advantage—Healy made just his second appearance of the playoffs. And he was able to survive the period, stopping the only shot he faced.

But would he return after the break? Only Keenan knew.

"[Keenan] was not going to just sit there," Richter said, "and let the ship sink."

Well, Keenan thought it'd be better to stick with Healy, surprisingly enough. But Richter wouldn't be the only superstar on the shelf in this game.

"He might have done some strange things," Richter said, "but it was all for the betterment of the team."

Perhaps. But it was hard to fathom why star Brian Leetch would find himself on the bench during the crucial moments of the second period, with the Rangers in an all-out push to stay in the game.

"There always seemed to be something hovering," Leetch said. "It was a dark time, and Mike didn't make it any easier on me, talking about injuries, and suspensions, and sitting myself. There was a lot of stuff going on."

Wasn't that the way of life with the Rangers? As unique as Keenan was, with his mind games and the politics and the strange decisions, it was hard for many to digest the fact that Leetch was being benched in a game of this magnitude. Then again, the suspension demand worked, the Healy decision was working, and at 8:47 of the second period, with a jumbled power play, the Rangers, minus Leetch, even knifed the Devils' lead in half.

Esa Tikkanen, a defensive forward with a scoring touch, manned the point instead of Leetch as the Rangers held the zone off the faceoff. Zubov fed Larmer at the faceoff dot, and Larmer, in turn, shifted it to Messier behind the net. Matteau, who had been the Rangers' best forward for the last three periods going back to Game 3, was in front of Martin Brodeur with his stick down—"Always have my stick down," Matteau said—and Messier saucered a flat centering pass to him. Matteau calmly pushed it past Brodeur with a one-timer through the five-hole as Tommy Albelin fell to the ice.

It was the perfect storm for the Rangers. Had Albelin kept his balance, he would have been able to erase Matteau. Instead, he fell, and Matteau delivered. Again.

"I felt great after Game 3," Matteau said. "I felt that getting that goal was a lot of pressure off my shoulders, and I was able to just go out and play. I parked myself in front of the net and outmuscled Albelin, and was able to get another one."

Matteau's post-goal celebration was a little more subdued than in Game 3, but he was excited nonetheless. He was greeted by a smiling Messier, who picked up an assist, along with Larmer.

"The door," Thorne said, "just crept open."

And the Rangers, as good teams do, built off the momentum change. Sergei Nemchinov fired three shots on net in the next shift, as the Crash Line found itself scrambling for a change. Brodeur stood tall this time, but the Rangers were coming in waves.

On the other end, Healy was playing well in his unexpected appearance. Prone and with his waffle out in the air, he stopped Lemieux point blank on a power-play rebound chance en route to a scoreless period for New Jersey. Any surprise at Healy's performance was no sign of disrespect, of course; Healy played 15 seasons in the NHL and had a career 3.37 goals-against average. But he never had more than the 25 wins he posted in 1988–89 with Los Angeles, and had never come close to winning the Stanley Cup.

As the Rangers continued to push, Leetch eventually made his way back on the ice, though he uncharacteristically drifted into the Devils' zone offside with 4:15 left. "When you look back, we all remember the series vividly for so many reasons," Larmer said. "How can you not? I mean, Brian Leetch was benched!"

"If the rivalry is not established as one that is a terrific rivalry," Clement said in the second period, "then this series will take care of the rest."

As the final seconds of the frame ticked off, the Rangers were clearly back on their game, albeit with different faces in different places. They held a 12–8 advantage in shots in the period, and though they were trailing in the game and had lost the first fight of the series, and despite the soap opera that was building on the bench, they were down by just one goal.

The Devils, meanwhile, had no time for the theater that was being orchestrated by the visitors. They were, after all, in the midst of their best all-around effort of the series, though the Rangers had managed to stem the tide.

"It clearly was one of the most solid games the Devils had played," said Mike Miller, who began his career as New Jersey's play-by-play man on October 6, 1993, and at one time called 1,741 consecutive games. "The way they looked that night—holy smokes—you knew this was a team to be reckoned with."

New Jersey—on home ice, with the Lemaire lockdown system in place—probably felt confident about holding a one-goal lead for 20 minutes and evening the series, especially considering the alternative. As good as the Devils were—complete, skilled, and defensively sound— nobody was going to give them a chance against the Rangers if they had to limp back through the tunnel down 3–1.

"Responsible, defensive hockey, at all times, in all games," Miller said. "There's not much more you can say about it. People didn't like it, at all. But say what you will. That was Devils Hockey. And on most nights, there wasn't much the other team could do about it. This—Game 4—was one of those nights."

While the other New York stars failed to shine, Messier had already put in another solid effort as he took the opening faceoff against Carpenter to start the third. Through two periods, he had won 17 of 20 faceoffs, recorded his sixth point of the series, and showed his typical grit, cross-checking Millen from behind in a play that eluded the officials' whistles.

"The game, overall, was kind of a blur for me," said Millen, with disappointment in his voice even some two decades later. "I twisted my ankle when Mess cross-checked me. It was twisted pretty badly. I tried to play through it, but the coaches could sense it. I wasn't myself. My season ended for me right there."

Like most who ever played for Lemaire, Millen remains complimentary to this day of the Hall of Fame coach. But as he coaches junior hockey now in Alaska, Millen cannot help but stop sometimes to wonder if things could've turned out differently.

"I'd be lying if I didn't say this: Jacques made his mark on me. He was one of the first coaches that made me really be a thinker out there," Millen said. "Before him, I just wanted to drop the puck, get after it, and go. That was the type of player I was. But he was one of the smartest coaches I've ever seen, he taught the game so well, and that has certainly had an impact on me the rest of my life. And I don't think I'm alone with that thinking. Do I wish things worked out better in that season? No question. But we were team players on the Devils; we knew what we were after. And to see the team succeed, well, that was Devils Hockey."

Banged and bruised in the third period of Game 4, New Jersey indeed played Devils Hockey. Chorske, a penalty-killing specialist who was playing his best game, hit a streaking Lemieux for a shorthanded breakaway early in the third. But he pumped a shot right into Healy's glove. It was a critical save at a critical juncture. Healy, well into the game now, was keeping his team in the game. At 11:19, he was back at it again. The Crash Line had returned to its normal tricks, and Bobby Holik fed Randy McKay in front for a wrist shot. Again, stopped by Healy.

But the Rangers were not building off these saves. In fact, Lowe was snagged for his third minor penalty of the game at 9:29, as he held Richer. The Devils didn't threaten on the man advantage, but at this point, they didn't care to. They just wanted to burn two minutes and further frustrate the Rangers.

Enter MacLean, who added a little levity to a tense situation. During the power play after Lowe's call, Beukeboom and MacLean tangled behind Healy, fell down together, and Beukeboom lost his helmet. He responded by shoving MacLean into the back of the net. When MacLean picked himself up and got his bearings about him, he found the loose helmet and tried to throw it into the stands. It was a short toss, or the boards were too tall; either way, the helmet stayed in play.

The Devils finally got to Healy with 6:00 left, and put the game away, once and for all. Dowd dumped in behind Healy, where the goaltender stopped the progression and left it for defenseman Alexander Karpovtsev. Unfortunately for Healy, Karpovtsev didn't see it, and Healy was slow to get back to the net. Zelepukin, who had played with an edge all night, swooped in and scooped the puck up, shoveling a neat wraparound backhand to the left side of the net while Healy was still behind it. It was a simple miscommunication between a backup goaltender and a third-line defenseman who hadn't played together much in the postseason. And it was probably one the Rangers could live with, considering how well Healy played in spot duty. Either way, though, the Devils cashed in at 13:18.

New Jersey 3, New York 1.

Zelepukin, who showed his teammates on this night that he could intimidate the opponent with the best of them, couldn't help but laugh when he arrived at the bench. It was his fourth goal of the postseason, and sent many of the Rangers faithful unhappily headed for the exits.

The Rangers weren't themselves after the goal. Lowe, a calm, steadying force on the backline, even dumped Lemieux, but did not get a penalty. Had he, it would have been his fourth of the game.

"By then, yes, the series was really shaping up," Lowe said. "It was definitely ratcheted up another notch. You could sense that right away."

The home fans, meanwhile, were finally able to sense a comfortable win. With 4:00 left, there was a consistent, if not loud, chant of "19-40," as the Devils readied themselves to improve to 5–4 on home ice in the postseason. After two double-overtime games that sandwiched a 4–0 shutout in Game 2, the Devils were able to take a breath, post a 3–1 victory, even the series at 2–2, and leave the ice feeling good about themselves and their place in the series.

Healy was not pulled in the final minute for the extra attacker, as Albelin calmly shoved the puck down the ice with 10 seconds left to end it. Brodeur, as would be his customary move during his career, took a victory swig off his water bottle and waited for his team to come and celebrate.

In a series already stuffed with momentum swings, Game 4 was the Devils' turn at the plate. Brodeur was sharp, the defense matched him, and by the time Game 5 rolled around, Nicholls would be back in uniform to help the offense.

"I couldn't wait," Nicholls said. "Playing in New York, and knowing the rivalry, I think we had already proved we weren't going to be intimidated there. And we were a better team on the road anyway. Everybody understood that in our room. It became something we fed off. There was nothing better than winning on the road."

On the other end were the Rangers, stone-faced, gathering around Healy, knowing that there were a lot of questions to answer before the Game 5 puck dropped back at Madison Square Garden.

"There was so much going on with the team at the time," Mike Francesa said. "It was classic New York. There was turmoil with the coach and some of the players. It all played a part."

The series, though, was still very much New York's to lose. All the Devils did, after all, was win a game they *had* to win. But keep in mind, these were the Rangers, and with a long history of disappointments weighing on their shoulders, fans weren't sure which team was going show up two days later.

"Most people realized that the Rangers had to do it that year. The Devils were going to have their chances, but with the Rangers, in that year, they had home ice, they had the Presidents' Trophy, a ton of offense, and a great defense," Russo said. "Drama and all, that team was primed to win a Cup. It was now or never. Nobody wanted to hear any excuses."

"Anyone who grew up around the Rangers and with the Rangers as I did, you never felt that anything was going to be easy in the playoffs," said Howie Rose, the Rangers' radio voice at the time. "So, knowing the Devils, and knowing the system that they played, which would be a pretty good counter to what the Rangers' strengths were, I certainly expected a good series. I certainly never anticipated what it would do to people's intestines and nervous systems and probably take 10 years off people's lives. I'm not so sure I didn't sacrifice a few myself."

Maybe it was fitting that the series was headed back to New York tied 2–2.

After all, this enigmatic, theatrical Rangers ensemble seemed best fit for Broadway.

Game 5

○ ○ ○ ○

"My second year with the Devils, I was trying to start fresh. I was. For me, going to the rink every day, practicing with the guys, playing, that was an escape for me. Gradually, it got better with time for me and my family. As the year progressed, I started to move on ever so slowly. But it was tough. It was a struggle at times. It's something that was always there."
—BERNIE NICHOLLS, NEW JERSEY DEVILS (1993–94)

JACK NICHOLLS WAS BORN in Edmonton, Alberta, on November 25, 1992. The third child of Bernie and Heather Nicholls, Jack was premature, arrived by way of Cesarean section, and changed the family's outlook on life immediately. Jack, who weighed just three and a half pounds at birth, had Down's syndrome, a condition that is created by the existence of an extra chromosome and affects about 2 percent of the world's population.

But the profession of hockey can be a difficult one at times, cruel even, as competition and business can often get in the way of real life during what is a marathon of a regular season.

Such was life for Bernie, a marketable, super-skilled superstar forward, who was playing for the Oilers at the time. And just as a strong dose of life and reality hit, along came the rebuilding New Jersey Devils some two months later, and they needed Bernie's scoring touch and flair for the dramatic. The Devils acquired Nicholls, who had eight goals and 40 points in 46 games for Edmonton that season, on January 13, 1993, for forwards Zdeno Ciger and Kevin Todd.

As if moving to a new state wasn't disruptive enough, the trade meant Nicholls had to switch conferences, move to a new country across a couple of time zones, and adapt to new team that was some 2,500 miles away from his previous one.

Jack was nearly two months old when Bernie boarded a plane for Newark, New Jersey, to join his new team. And as difficult as it was going to be, the Nicholls family was just going to have to make it work somehow.

Without much reason to stay in Western Canada, Heather, Jack, and his twin siblings, Flynn and McKenna, did not remain in Edmonton. They returned to Heather's parents' home outside Los Angeles, where Bernie had started his NHL career with the Kings in 1981. But a little more than a week after becoming a Devil, Bernie received more bad news. On January 21, after a practice with his new teammates, Bernie discovered that Jack had developed meningitis, a bacterial infection of the membranes that surround the brain and spinal cord. Meningitis infections—even if treated in some cases—can often quickly result in death or brain damage, especially in children.

"The Devils were just great about the whole situation. I will never forget that," Nicholls said. "They put me on a plane and told me to go take care of my family. That was all Lou [Lamoriello]. I will never forget that."

Nicholls returned home, spoke with the doctors who were treating Jack, and spent some time with his family. When things appeared to have calmed down a bit, Nicholls traveled back to New Jersey. Not long after, he had to return to California.

"To have to go back and forth like that, the Devils could have acted differently, but they didn't. It was all class from them," Nicholls said. "They never held it against me, and Lou covered the flights and everything. I couldn't have been more appreciative."

Eventually, Nicholls settled in with the Devils and coach Herb Brooks, a committed family man himself. With his loved ones across country and in a dire situation, it was admittedly tough for Nicholls to focus on hockey. Being on a new team with new aspirations in a new conference helped.

"Herbie was amazing. He had big plans, and wanted me there, but knew what was most important," Nicholls said. "They wanted me to be with my family. They did everything they could for us."

Back and forth, Nicholls would go. New Jersey. California. New Jersey. California. Surely, the miles weren't a good thing for his 31-year-old body, but he still managed to play 23 games that season in a Devils uniform. He finished with five goals and 20 points in New Jersey and was a plus-3.

"Family is a very important thing to the Devils," Lamoriello said. "We are all family."

The Devils, back in the old playoff format where the seedings went Nos. 1–4 in each division rather than 1–8 in the conference, finished as a No. 4 seed that year, and lost to the Pittsburgh Penguins in five games in Round 1. Outclassed by a Pittsburgh team that was the two-time defending Stanley Cup champion, it was hardly a banner New Jersey postseason run. Nicholls had no points in the five games, and finished as a minus-5.

That summer, Brooks was relieved of his duties, Jacques Lemaire and Larry Robinson came in, the Devils changed their philosophy, and the transformation officially began. Still with an unstable situation at home, Nicholls was expected to be a big part of that culture change. Lamoriello and Lemaire needed him. The Devils needed him.

And he needed them.

"I can't say it enough. Lou was just amazing," Nicholls said. "He treated me like I was his son."

On November 21, 1993, the Nicholls family lost Jack on an early Saturday morning in Long Beach, California. Bernie, again with the Devils' permission, left the team two days beforehand. The long road had ended just four days before Jack was to have his first birthday.

"To think back on it now, it is difficult. But when he died, I had reached a point where I knew that I could move on from there. I knew that everyone would want me to continue on," Nicholls said. "The first year with the Devils, absolutely, it was a huge struggle. But the second year, I knew it would eventually get better."

It did, in so many ways. As the wins began to pile up and the expectations began to rise in New Jersey, playing hockey was fun again for Nicholls. He was inspired. He was motivated. And with a new perspective on life, he cherished every moment he had out there. As his world continued to change, his teammates, many of whom were starting families of their own, truly bonded with him.

Nicholls was not your typical Devil when he arrived in New Jersey. He had played, after all, with the Kings, the Rangers, and the Oilers, much flashier teams that allowed their players a few more liberties. For example, Lamoriello required Devils players to wear suits and ties. That was new terrain for Nicholls, and one day, he simply forgot.

"I fined him," Lamoriello said with a laugh. "It was procedure. It was what we did. But it was funny, too, because you knew Bernie wasn't trying to go against the team. He just wasn't used to it! He paid it and we moved on. We had a laugh over it. There were never any problems."

The same can be said of his performance on the ice. It would have been easy for a career goal scorer to shake his head at the Devils' defensive ways. But that never happened with Nicholls.

"When you think of Bernie Nicholls, you think of a guy who is scoring a lot of goals, a lot of fanfare, the whole nine yards, and even Bernie bought into what we were doing," Bruce Driver said. "When I think of Bernie Nicholls playing for the Devils, I think of goals and the offense, but he'd get in there and block shots all the time. It was unbelievable. And he was great on the penalty kill, too. Bernie was tremendous at sacrificing his body, and I never knew that after all those years of playing against him. He was a penalty-killing, shot-blocking machine!

"It was all those little things that players were doing, and it really added up. As we were going through the playoffs, it really didn't matter who we were playing. We had total confidence in our ability. Bernie was a huge part of that."

Traveling back and forth across the country to be with his family, Nicholls only played in 61 regular season games that season, but his totals were solid. On a team that finished second overall in offense and battled the Rangers all season long for the No. 1 postseason seed, Nicholls had 19 goals, 46 points, and was an impressive plus-24.

"I think Jacques was misunderstood at times," Nicholls said. "On defense, yes, he was strict. He would never let our defense pinch. He was real strict about that. But for offense, he was awesome. As a center, the first out was me, and he allowed us to be creative. In the offensive zone, in the attack, it was great. Were the reins on the defense? Sure. And it worked, and they never got caught, and they were the reason we were winning so easily. But the thing to remember was Jacques was skilled offensively as a player himself. I think he was amazing. He allowed us to do so much offensively. It was so much fun."

Which is exactly what Nicholls needed.

After a poor decision to cross-check Alexei Kovalev in Game 3 of the Eastern Conference Finals, and then after sitting out the Devils' impressive 3–1 win in Game 4 while on suspension, Nicholls was back and ready to go in Game 5. Back at Madison Square Garden, with a chance to put the win-it-now-or-else Rangers on the brink of elimination, Nicholls and the Devils were primed for production as the puck dropped on May 23, 1994.

Nicholls' return to the lineup was just one of many storylines as play began in the first period. Mark Messier and Brian Leetch, who Mike Keenan claimed were mysteriously injured after Game 4, started this tilt at home, causing many to wonder if they were even injured at all. With Keenan's history of mind games, who knew what to believe? Craig MacTavish, another one of the "injured" Rangers, was also out there, so perhaps it was all one, big Keenan smoke screen. Either way, Leetch's playing time was something to monitor on this night, when the Rangers desperately needed to avoid falling into a 2–3 hole.

Suspension or not, the Rangers still weren't happy with Nicholls' antics, and it did not take them long to make that known. Three minutes in, the Rangers played the intimidator card, as Esa Tikkanen sprayed Martin Brodeur with some ice while the goaltender held on for a whistle. In the same sequence, Adam Graves elbowed Nicholls, much to the delight of the Garden crowd.

But the home-team satisfaction would not last long. And you wouldn't believe who delivered the first dose of bad news.

After Tommy Albelin slashed MacTavish at 5:05, the Rangers built some momentum on the power play, but it was short-lived. On the penalty kill, Scott Stevens stood up Messier at the blue line, almost leaving his skates to do it, which would have been another minor. Instead, it was a no-call, and the short-handed Devils went to work. Brodeur's clearing attempt—remember, though still a rookie, he was easily one of the best goaltenders in the league handling the puck—efficiently hit the glass, avoided the reach of Leetch, and sailed out of the zone. Perfect positioning. From there, the Devils' transition game—so strong in Game 4—resurfaced.

A charging Claude Lemieux blew right past Leetch. He took the puck, streaked through the neutral zone, and raced in on a 2-on-1 with Nicholls. Lemieux avoided Sergei Zubov and unleashed one of his patented 20-foot slap shots from the right point, which Mike Richter kicked out. Maybe it was fate, maybe it was destiny, maybe it was just the Devils' precise positional play. Whatever it was, Richter's rebound landed right on the stick of Nicholls, who buried it into the open net as Richter scrambled to get back.

Nicholls' first of the series, and third of the postseason, came on a penalty kill at 6:49 and silenced the crowd. It was the Devils' first shorthanded tally of the playoffs, and with an assist, Brodeur registered his first-ever postseason point.

The Rangers did not respond well to the goal. After a Game 4 in which Keenan deemed the team's effort "unacceptable," it appeared as if nothing had changed, with the exception of Leetch's playing time. The defenseman was taking a regular turn in Game 5, after compiling just 13:04 of time on the ice in Game 4.

New York created some chances as the first-period clock ticked down, but Brodeur was sharp throughout. With 5:06 left, he had stopped all 10 Rangers shots. By the end of the period, the total was at 13, New York was searching for answers, and there was an uneasy feeling throughout the Garden, a feeling that the faithful had felt before—oh, once or twice—in the previous 54 years.

"Being a Rangers fan, I'm always pessimistic," Joe Benigno said. "And I definitely felt that way with Game 5. The Devils were so good at that point, and Brodeur was starting to show you just who he was. Didn't look good."

And it took a turn for the ugly in the second.

In light of Nicholls' suspension, there was talk of retribution, of revenge, of getting one back for the home team during the walkup to the game. Well, the Rangers did not stop with Graves' dump of Nicholls in the first. In the second, it was Jeff Beukeboom's turn. And he decided to target someone else. Stephane Richer broke in off the left wing, and his wrist shot was stopped by Richter. As he turned toward the right boards, Beukeboom rubbed him out and left him flat on the ice, face down.

The crowd loved the hit, but it was clear Richer was hurting. The New Jersey trainers rushed out, as Richer was down for four minutes. While Nicholls complained to the officials, Richer finally got to his feet, a bit woozy still, and was helped off the ice with a clear bruise under his left eye.

"That one could have been costly," Devils radio voice Mike Miller said. "Stephane Richer, the guy may be one of the most talented players I ever saw. He may have never lived up to his potential, but this guy was a force, and he was having a great series."

In a tit-for-tat series that was shaping up to be a great one for the future of the league, it seemed like this hit might draw the same kind of suspension that Nicholls' did, though that still had to be determined. In the interim, like the Nicholls play, there was no penalty called.

Play carried on without Richer, and as the focus moved away from how much playing time the Rangers' stars were getting—Leetch played nine shifts in the first period for a total of 7:34, and Messier also had nine for 6:35—the crowd seemed more interested in booing anyone who was on the ice in red, white, and blue, rather than worrying about *who* was actually on the ice.

"We were what you'd call a road team," Driver said. "That's the way we played. We were never going to be a flashy team. We were just going to go out and do what was needed to give us the best possible chance to win."

Mission accomplished. In fact, as Ken Daneyko and Viacheslav Fetisov touched up on respective icing calls at 12:58 and 12:28 respectively, the boos had never been louder in Manhattan.

"After Game 4, it all took a turn," Leetch said. "That was one of their best games, and they were carrying it over at the Garden. I remember just thinking, *We're really in for something now*. And the doubts started to creep into our heads a little bit."

Play then took a turn for the sluggish on some poor ice on this warm day, with temperatures in the 70s in New York. That was a traditional stumbling block throughout the NHL at this time of year, as the weather warmed in many of the league's postseason cities. This year was no different. Plus, the NBA's Knicks, who were orchestrating their own run for the ages, defeated the Chicago Bulls 87–77 in Game 7 of the Eastern Conference Semifinals the night before at the Garden. That didn't help the condition of the ice.

In the end, the period amounted to a penalty fest.

"Lot of whistles," Stephane Matteau said. "Lot of calls, lot of back and forth in that one."

Esa Tikkanen, high sticking.

Bill Guerin, slashing.

Bill Guerin, elbowing.

The beat went on, and so did the boos, as the Rangers did little with their power-play opportunities. As the period ended, and as the Devils' lead seemed bigger than one goal, the crowd became restless. The fans received little consolation from the "Let's Go Rangers" signs that they were given upon entry.

Meanwhile, no one was going to mistake Richer for Willis Reed—who led the Knicks to an NBA title in 1970 despite an injured thigh muscle— but the Devils' sharpshooting forward did waltz through the Garden tunnel at the end of the second intermission and returned to action. Richer, like Reed, wasn't quite 100 percent. But he was back, which meant Lemaire could steady his lines and fully utilize the trap. Plus, Richer felt comfortable in New York. Remember, he scored the winner in Game 1 in the second overtime, and even though he missed the majority of the second period in Game 5, he still began the third period as New Jersey's leading shooter, with three on net.

"Getting the matchups right and the lines straight, that was so important to Jacques," Guerin said. "And who better to listen to than him with all of his Stanley Cups? We bought into all of that, and were ready for anything. We just wanted to walk out of there with a win."

With a steady flow of line changes and fresh troops abound, the Devils took another step toward that early in the third, thanks to the Crash Line. Bobby Holik won a draw, shoved it toward the net, and Alexander Karpovtsev—the young Russian, all of 24 years old, whose miscommunication with Healy led to a goal in Game 4—goofed again, and the Devils pounced. Karpovtsev fired it past his own goaltender and along the line, instead of whacking it around the boards. Mike Peluso, positioned correctly, pushed it with his stick, as well as Richter's glove, past the line.

It was an ugly goal that Richter probably never should have had to suffer. But Peluso notched it at 2:36, unassisted, and the Crash Line had delivered a 2–0 lead that truly allowed New Jersey to clamp down.

"The Devils had several ways to beat you, and they were doing that," Richter said. "So, we needed to keep improving with each shift, and be ready for anything."

If they were ready on this night, they didn't show it. In fact, Brian Noonan later roughed Scott Niedermayer, snared a 2:00 minor, and the Devils' power play took the ice looking for a 3–0 lead.

They found it.

Down two goals with time ticking away, the Rangers, shorthanded or not, were going to have to take some chances. Kevin Lowe moved in to forge a 3-on-2, but got caught as the play turned around, and the Devils went on the attack. An aggressive John MacLean was able to streak past the benches as Nicholls caught up to create a 2-on-1 against Zubov.

A younger player might have panicked and decided to shoot or pass too early, giddy over his good fortune on the road. But MacLean had been through the battles with the Devils all too many times. In fact, at 29 years old and with nine years of experience in the organization, you can make the case that this series meant more to him than anyone. Perhaps for those reasons, MacLean's patience and perseverance paid off. He cruised to the right faceoff dot and waited for Zubov to lean his way. When the defenseman did, MacLean hit a turning Nicholls at the crease, who had his stick down and in position for a tip that eluded Richter's left, sprawling skate. Nicholls lifted the puck into the net, then lifted his stick to the sky as he skated backward around the boards, waiting for his teammates to join him.

Nicholls, who quite possibly had experienced more than any one hockey player in the last two years, gave his Devils a 3–0 lead, with an assist from MacLean at 10:37. It was Nicholls' second of the game, and fourth of the playoffs. To be sure, folks, Bernie was back.

"Leave it to Johnny MacLean," Nicholls said, quick to deflect any of the credit. "What a pass. What a great feeling."

The boos, at this point, gave way to silence, as the fans could not believe what was occurring in front of them. Sure, there were some Devils supporters out there, but not enough to break what seemed like a painful hush, 54 years in the making. As the teams strolled to center ice for the faceoff, many of those fans discarded those free signs, and headed for the exits. Indeed, in *the* year that The Curse was supposed to die, the Rangers were about to be on the brink of elimination, courtesy of their formerly harmless neighbors from the Garden State.

The Devils were not about to take their foot off the gas, however, and soon would add insult to injury. Bobby Carpenter and Tom Chorske, New Jersey's penalty-killing duo, teamed up on a tally at even strength for the Devils' third goal of the period. Out of a lazy scrum at center ice, as the Rangers were merely going through the motions, Carpenter broke in on a 2-on-1 with Chorske. Carpenter simply stopped at the circle and drew in Beukeboom, who laid out to stop the rush. But Carpenter stayed patient, and waited for Chorske to set up. With more time than he needed, Chorske stopped at the dot, took the pass, and lined up his shot. The slap shot from 25 feet out beat Richter on his glove side, top shelf, in a play that seemed out of a video game.

Just like that, with six minutes still to play, it was 4–0 New Jersey, and the Garden had turned into a ghost town.

"We really developed a lot of chemistry," Chorske said of his partnership with his fellow American forward. "We sat with each other on bus rides, plane rides, on the bench, you name it. And that's so important on penalty killing, to know each other, to know where each other will be on the ice. I was still learning the role, but to get that kind of ice time on a team like that was great, and to know you're contributing to the success, and to be counted on and trusted, was amazing. I think everyone realized what we did for the team, and that's what it's all about in pro sports: to gain the respect of your teammates and coaches."

With the way the bench exploded after that goal, you could tell that all of the Devils had that respect for both of those Killer C's.

Meanwhile, the clock couldn't turn fast enough for the home team, a group that no longer had time for the soap opera that had been building over the past week. Forget playing time, and injuries, and working the officials over, and sending messages. The Rangers needed two wins in the next two games, or the dream would be dead.

In the first 15 minutes of the third, it appeared as if the Rangers didn't even believe in themselves anymore. In that span, they totaled all of two shots as Brodeur continued to build confidence and moved closer toward taking that victorious swig off the water bottle that sat behind him.

New York did avoid complete embarrassment, though. Tikkanen let one fly in frustration from the Stanley Cup logo in the neutral zone, five feet away from the blue line, and it sneaked by Brodeur and through his legs, stunningly. It was a five-hole trickler that many of the paying customers did not see, and the shutout was erased. Tikkanen from Zubov, with 3:27 to go, concluded the scoring at 4–1, as the focus turned to Game 6 at the Meadowlands.

When the "last minute to play in the third period" announcement went off, the Garden crowd let out a Bronx cheer as it had done so many times during the Rangers' lean years. It was a stunning reminder of just how fast a team can fall, and how fast a fan base can forget that a series is never over until it's over.

It didn't look good, of course. But remember what the Meadowlands security guard said to Stevens just two games ago: "It's far from over." And until one team registered four wins in this unreal series, that phrase worked both ways.

"To have that happen in Game 5, at Madison Square Garden, it was really hard to take," Matteau said with disappointment in his voice. "Guys were bummed. I'm not going to lie to you."

But there were hints of optimism as the series shifted back to East Rutherford. There were things to hang their hat on, albeit small, if the Rangers so elected to:

- The Rangers had only lost three in a row twice during the regular season

- The Rangers still had only lost four postseason games total across three series
- The Rangers, if you combined the regular season with this series, were still 8–3 against the Devils

While all of those factors could help motivate the Rangers, it was hard to think the Devils wouldn't be prepared for anything, knowing they had two chances to win one game to get to the Stanley Cup Finals for the first time.

"It's hard to say, because you know it's such a cliché, but we really thought about things as one game as a time. We didn't look very far down the road," Randy McKay said. "The next game was the new game to worry about, and there really wasn't any time to look at the future and the past. Lou and Jacques would not stand for that."

As the final seconds ticked away, MacLean threw a shot in from center ice, which was stopped by Richter, and finally, it was over. It was so silent— and empty—in the stands, the television microphones could easily pick up the Devils celebrating on the ice.

And who was the first one to hug Brodeur? Nicholls, who bounced back from the suspension in grand fashion, and operated as if directed by a higher power on this night. Brodeur greeted him, smiled, calmly took off his mask, and went about with his winning tradition. He turned, took a victory drink, put the Gatorade bottle away, wiped off the sweat from his face, and flicked it to the ice, just like he had with all but one shot during the game. As usual, the Devils were professional in their celebration. Indeed, they were the typical Devils at the end: calm, subdued, businesslike, and ready to play the next game.

"You come in every day, and there is an expectation to uphold, and it's an expectation and a reputation that we formed internally, inside the building," said Brodeur, who stopped 25 of 26 Rangers shots on this night. "Sometimes, it's hard to live up to it, because it's not an expectation of the fans or the media, it's an expectation of us, of the management, of the organization. But, without question, it keeps everyone accountable as far as your work habits, and your game preparation."

But in the end, as great as Brodeur, MacLean, and Chorske all were, the night belonged to Nicholls. Perhaps Don LaGreca put it best when describing Nicholls. LaGreca, a talk show host on ESPN-AM 1050 in New York and one of the radio voices of the Rangers, grew up a Devils fan in Hawthorne, New Jersey. On his way up through the business, LaGreca covered the series for Sports Phone, a retro form of the Internet, if you will, in which patrons would dial a number to hear a sports report from an up-and-coming broadcaster. It was indeed a different time for sports journalism in New York back then, but one LaGreca will not forget, for several reasons.

"For Bernie Nicholls to play the way he did, with all that was going on in his life," he said, as he paused, looked down, and shook his head. "Unbelievable."

If you go back to his second goal, the true backbreaker that gave New Jersey a 3–0 lead, Nicholls' celebration couldn't have been more fitting. As he finished his back skate, which ended in the Rangers' slot, he was mobbed by his teammates, at which point Stevens cupped the top of Nicholls' helmet and shook the shake of satisfaction amid the scrum. When Stevens' head shake had subsided, Nicholls, still with an impenetrable smile on, readjusted his helmet and looked up to the Garden rafters to check the time and score.

And at the same time, who knows, maybe young Jack Nicholls was looking down at Dad, and smiling back.

The Guarantee

○ ○ ○ ○

"To know the person that [Mark Messier] is and how he conducts himself on a daily basis, it's not just The Guarantee, it was everything he said from the beginning of the season. He made us feel like every night was a guarantee. If we came to work hard, paid the price, took care of ourselves, then there would be many nights where we'd win. We believed him. We believed in how he believed in us. He was our leader. He was the guy we leaned on the most."
—NICK KYPREOS, NEW YORK RANGERS (1993–96)

THE PUCKS BANGED off the boards a little louder than usual in Rye, New York, on Tuesday, May 24, 1994. The skates, too, carved the ice with a little more animus than a regular Rangers practice at their Playland facility.

Maybe that's because there was no background noise to drown them out.

Indeed, things were eerily quiet as Mike Keenan put the Rangers through their paces that day. Suddenly facing elimination against an upstart rival from across the river, this team was in a hole not many thought they'd ever be in, first of all, and now that they were in it, many of those same critics gave them no shot at getting out.

The Presidents' Trophy, the No. 1 overall seed in the league, the Atlantic Division title, heck, even the six wins over New Jersey in the regular season—none of that mattered anymore. These Rangers were down 3–2 to the Devils, of all teams, and had one game, three periods, to save this magical, momentous season.

"That was a task in itself, obviously, but to win that Game 6 in Jersey only meant that they'd have to win another one," said analyst Al Morganti, who worked the series for ESPN and had a front-row seat to it all as the rinkside reporter. "And the way things were going, it didn't look good."

Morganti wasn't alone in his view. Everybody in that facility on that day—and most everyone in and around the series in general—could feel it. The Rangers—a collection of high-priced superstars who waltzed through some 90 games with hardly a hiccup until New Jersey arrived on their playoff doorstep—were dying on the vine. And the dark, grey cloud that hovered over them for 54 years was back ... and had never been bigger.

"They surely had some great teams in New York in the past," Kevin Lowe said, "but it was like Mark Messier said to me when I first became a Ranger: 'There are so many demons lurking in the Garden, you have no idea.' They're in every corner, and we had to slay each and every one of them before we could get it done. There were no shortcuts. It had to be done that way. It was a lot of pressure, playing in New York, and I understand now how difficult it was for past teams to not make it as far."

But this team was so much better than so many of those other shoulda, coulda, wouldas that ended up in the basement of the Garden, devoured deliciously by those aging demons. This team had it all. Or, at least, it did.

And it was Messier's job to get it back.

So, at the end of practice, in a glum locker room filled with media types anxious to write, broadcast, and deliver the 1994 Rangers' obituary, Messier took a stand.

"There might have been 15 people around him in a semicircle," said Mark Everson, the Rangers beat writer for the *New York Post*. "A few cameras. Everyone was waiting for him to come out and talk. It seemed normal enough. Another day in the series."

Until Messier started talking, of course.

"He came out," Everson said, "and I just asked him, 'Well, Mark, what has to happen here?'"

And ever so simply, in Messier's patented monotone, with a stone face and a sure delivery, he uttered the phrase that penetrated through the notebooks, the tape recorders, and the eyes and ears of the journalists in front of him:

"We'll win."

Short. Sweet. Succinct.

This wasn't the cocky, look-at-me proclamation offered by Joe Namath, author of the most famous guarantee in New York sports history. Messier simply said, "We'll win." Nothing more. Nothing less. And certainly nothing close to the former New York Jets quarterback and his guarantee of a Super Bowl III victory in 1969, one he ultimately made good on with a 16–7 win over the Baltimore Colts in Miami.

This was different. This was merely a captain trying to save his ship.

"My memory was, *What else is he going to say?* It wasn't like he called everyone over, stepped up on a box, and said, 'I have an announcement to make,'" said Larry Brooks, who was covering the Devils for the *Post* at the time but now covers the Rangers. "It wasn't that way at all. The Devils were the better team at that point, and with all the turmoil, guys getting benched, and things like that, Mess had to do something. So, he did."

After just one point and three shots on net in the previous two games—both Rangers losses—Messier authored a promise, a pledge to his teammates, his coaches, and Rangers fans worldwide, that this team, starting with him, would not go gently into that good night.

"We know we are going to go in there," he said as he finally elaborated, "and win Game 6 and bring it back to the Garden."

For the veteran journalists in the room—Everson, Brooks, then–*Post* columnist Jay Greenberg, and others—it wasn't a "Stop the presses!" moment. At least not yet. There were other questions to be asked, and there was a process to run through. There weren't even a ton of glances between the assembled journalists, something that often happens in media scrums where a writer may flash a "Can you believe he just said that?" look at one of his brethren.

"It was a nothing-to-lose situation," said Stan Fischler, a legendary hockey author, historian, and television analyst who covered the series on the Devils' side for SportsChannel. "You were going back to Jersey, down 3–2, and he, who was always exuding confidence, had to say something. That's what made him such a leader in Edmonton and New York, that confidence. And to me, he was a better leader, the real guts of that Oilers team. It was Messier, not [Wayne] Gretzky. So, same thing here. He was the leader. He was the confident one. And he did what he felt he had to do as motivation."

The interview carried on to other matters of importance from that point on. The Devils, what they were doing, Martin Brodeur's prowess in net, the Rangers' injury situation, how was Messier going to get back on the scoreboard, things like that, as the reporters finished up and moved on to the next player.

But make no mistake: Messier knew what he had said and done. While he may not have been a mainstay in the New York media market, he was intelligent enough to know that his two little words were going to make waves in print and on the air. So, as he left the facility and prepared to ride back into Manhattan with Lowe, Brian Leetch, and Mike Richter, he turned to Lowe as they slowly walked through the parking lot. Messier figured that was the best time to let his longtime friend know what he might be up against over the next 24 hours.

"He looked at me, and there was a bit of concern on his face. It was one of those rare Messier moments," Lowe said with a laugh. "He turned to me, and said, 'Well, I think I may have just created a bit of a stir for tomorrow.' And I didn't know what he was talking about. Like I said, there was a look on his face that I didn't often see. So, I responded, 'Well, what did you say?' And he told me, 'Well, I kind of guaranteed that we'd win.' And we looked at each other for a second, one of those silent pauses...and then we both just chuckled. We got in the car, and I just said, 'Well, boys, we better get our hard hats on, and go out and do this. Mess has left us no choice.'"

Most of the Rangers shared in Lowe's nonchalant attitude toward Messier's words. Did the pledge raise the bar for this crew? Yes. Did it put more pressure on the team overall? Sure. But they had to win the game either way. So, to them, it was business as usual.

"It didn't really faze our preparation or anything," Leetch said. "We had no choice but to go out and play well no matter what he said, so that's how we treated it. We had to get on him a little bit. I remember seeing it in the paper the next day; I always used to grab the paper on my way to the skate. And when I saw him, I had to give a sarcastic smile. 'You really got us into it now,' I told him. 'Thanks a lot, Mess.'"

Across the river, though, it was a different story.

In East Rutherford, as the Devils were preparing to clinch their first berth in the Stanley Cup Finals, there were no smiles. Some players, when they first saw the morning papers, brushed it off. Others weren't so happy about it. Either way, there were no jokes to be made.

"I was kind of surprised, to be honest," Bill Guerin said. "All I can remember saying to myself, was, 'Is he serious? What's he thinking?' Well, he's wrong, and we had to show everyone that. But, can I say the guys were throwing the *Post* around the room and slamming doors? No. We just wished him luck."

If nothing else, it was a headache the Devils didn't need. Here they were, having won consecutive games by a combined 7–2 score and about to host an elimination game on home ice. And Messier had to mess with their mojo and bring New Jersey's inferiority complex back into the equation. For the first time in this series, and for first time this season, the Devils should have been *the* story. They led the series. They were the better team. They were on their way to the Stanley Cup Finals.

But all anyone wanted to talk about was the Rangers.

"It was huge that morning," Brooks said. "Huge. At the Devils' skate, they were annoyed. People were asking [Scott] Stevens, I remember, about it, and it was an annoyance. 'We don't do that over here,' he said, or something to that effect. They were really annoyed. And you really got the sense that they were going to go out and play like it."

Every media outlet reported on Messier's words, but the biggest head turner, clearly, was the *Post*, which splashed the story across the back page in true New York tabloid fashion:

Captain Courageous' bold prediction: WE'LL WIN TONIGHT

The headline was wrapped around a Messier photo with perfect symmetry. It was a determined pose, on the ice, in his home uniform, and the shot fit the words perfectly.

"That was a run where we had a pretty standard system each night. There was a playoff game—Rangers and Knicks—almost every night, and so for the early edition, we'd usually go with the advance of the next game for the next day, on the back page, and then for the later editions, we'd go to the live game," said Pat Hannigan, the night sports editor at the *Post*. "Well, on that night, the Knicks were playing Game 1 of the Eastern Conference Finals against the Indiana Pacers, and it was just a Game 1. The Rangers, though, were facing elimination, they were going to Jersey, and it was now or never, do or die for a team that had to win that year. It seemed all along that this was their year, and this was it, they were up against it.

"So, that played into our thinking, and then, of course, Messier said what he said, and it was pretty easy for us that that was the way to go. Now, normally, like I said, that would have been swapped out for later editions because of the live game, but this was big enough, and it was Messier, and it was the Rangers facing elimination. You only have those moments so many times in New York sports, so really, that was the way to go."

The Knicks weren't forgotten, of course. They defeated the Pacers 100–89 in Game 1 and received a headline at the bottom of the back page with a photo of coach Pat Riley off to the left. But on this morning, as commuters stopped by their local newsstands on their way into the office in the big city, they didn't see the Knicks in the prime position. They saw Messier.

"I wasn't there on hand when Mess made The Guarantee, but you know how those media scrums go. It just wasn't one of those bold proclamations," said Neil Smith, New York's always-colorful general manager. "The questions were going back and forth, and Mark Everson asked the question, and Mess replied. There's no question that Mark Everson and the *New York Post* turned that into The Guarantee. And then it took on a life of its own. It didn't start out that way, though. But this was the New York media, after all."

It had already been an interesting series for Everson. He had one unpleasant phone conversation with Keenan regarding an article calling attention to the Rangers' injuries and Keenan's decisions to bench some stars, namely Leetch.

"Oh yeah, that was something," Everson said with a laugh. "He benched Leetch, and said 'He was hurt.' The next day, over at Rye, [Rangers media relations executive Barry] Watkins came along, and said, 'Mike will talk about all the injuries, and he wants it off the record.' And I said, 'Barry, it can't be off the record. All of the other guys said okay to it being off the record, and I'm not going to.' Watkins then said, 'Okay, you can come in, and just don't quote Mike directly.' Well, Mike calls me the next day, and he went … ballistic. I attributed these things in my story—dubious statements as they were—to him. Not direct quotes. But, whatever. So, next morning, he calls me up, and—perhaps he was told this was going to be off the record—and he went ballistic on me. But he got over it."

Ahh, the New York media. Without it, to a certain extent, this series might not have been what it was.

"I think it was a product of the media a little bit, but we ran with it and tried to use it as best we could," Richter said of The Guarantee. "When you break it down, though, Mark is so disciplined about the message that he has for fans, for the team, and for ourselves, and so we all just took it in stride. That was Mark. He does those things, but he does it in a good way. He's a machine, and everything he did was to make us better as a team. He always did the right things at the right time, but he usually backed it up with his actions."

Either way, one of the more memorable New York back pages was born as a result.

"To me," Brooks said, "it's the most famous back page in the history of the *Post*."

That's saying something.

"Whether he gathered everyone around, stepped up, and made a proclamation, that didn't really matter to us," Hannigan said. "It didn't really matter how he said it, it was the fact that he did say it, and all that went with it. It was a simple phrase, but definitely enough for us to go with it."

But, as the city buzzed with talk of the promise—Was he smart? Was he stupid? Would he sink or swim?—Messier just went about his day. He took the good-natured ribbing from his teammates, digested it, and got to work.

"I think he made The Guarantee because we had been through so much adversity that year, and there was a lot of building into the tank of confidence. He wanted us to get the feeling back, confidence-wise, that we could bounce back, get it together, win a big game in New Jersey," said Adam Graves. "He wanted everyone focused, and wanted to take some of the pressure off some of the other players, and put it on himself. And that's why Mark is Mark, and that's why Mess is Mess, and that's why he's arguably one of the greatest leaders hockey has ever known."

For Messier, even years later, he is as simple and straightforward with his explanation of The Guarantee as he was with the delivery way back on that May Tuesday in 1994. It was a matter of pride and passion. Nothing more.

"Putting on the jersey, to see the No. 11, to see the 'C,' there's no question there's something to that. The players that play in New York, there is a lot of pride. I know I had it," he said. "There's a lot of pride in the work that you put in to become a Ranger, and obviously, there's more pride in the work you put in to stay a New York Ranger."

Graves concurred.

"For me, he could show that pride in so many ways, and The Guarantee was just one of them. He never asked us to do anything he wouldn't go in and do himself, too," he said. "To take the pressure off the team, which he did, and put it all on him, really allowed us to just go out and play and do whatever we needed to do."

In a way, it did seem to take some of the pressure off the Rangers. For the first time in a long time, people weren't talking about the team's struggles. They were talking about Messier's confidence. They were talking about The Guarantee.

"To this day, I still can't believe he did that," ESPN's Barry Melrose said. "But that's Mess for you, and that's what that series did to people. The Rangers were in a bad place, and their year was hanging in the balance. Jersey was playing so well."

But even the New York media members probably could not have predicted the long-term ramifications of their efforts. Regardless of how the game would turn out in East Rutherford, Messier's pledge remains one of the most famous moments in NHL history. Even 17 years later, the effects lingered. In fact, during in the 2011 Stanley Cup Finals, Boston forward Mark Recchi uttered a memorable phrase prior to Game 6 at the TD Garden in Massachusetts.

The Bruins trailed the Vancouver Canucks 3–2 on June 13. Boston needed to win at home, and then jump back on a plane to Canada for a Game 7. Fresh off a 1–0 loss in Game 5, a reporter asked Recchi at the morning skate if he was prepared to guarantee a win in Game 6, or better yet, guarantee two wins and a series victory.

Recchi, 43 at the time, began his career in 1988 and took on Messier many times in his long and storied tenure. He simply laughed and lightened the mood in an otherwise tense locker room. "I'm not pulling a Messier, boys," he said.

And in this new technology age, where social media rules the day and everyone has a handheld information tool in his pocket, who could even imagine what another "Messier" might have become. In the end, of course, it didn't matter to Recchi and the Bruins, who won the next two games and lifted the Stanley Cup two days later in Vancouver.

But perhaps that's what made The Guarantee so memorable back in 1994. It was one of those things that comes around once in a lifetime, and win or lose, it was going to be a part of Rangers and NHL lore forever.

"Clearly, it was a different day, and a different era," Messier said. "Who knows what it would have become in today's day and age. Back then, though, it was what it was. It was a big moment for us. What more can you say?"

Game 6

○ ○ ○ ○

"I have to admit, going into Game 6, I wasn't very optimistic at all. And for those first 30 minutes of Game 6, the Devils were just so dominant. And all I could think of was this: let's just do this with running time to get it over with."
—HOWIE ROSE, NEW YORK RANGERS PLAY-BY-PLAY VOICE (1985–1995)

PLAYERS OFTEN MAKE last-minute ticket requests, especially during the NHL postseason. It comes with the territory when you're a professional athlete; people are going to exhaust every possibility of getting into a building if history might be made on a given night. Often, those requests come from acquaintances the players hardly even know.

But that wasn't the case for Martin Brodeur prior to Game 6. No, on May 25, 1994, the request was made by him personally, and it was hardly for strangers. With a chance to secure a bid to the Stanley Cup Finals as a 22-year-old goaltender, this barely-needing-to-shave, aw-shucks rookie, who grew up watching the Canadiens do this with ease in Montreal seemingly on a yearly basis, wanted to make it even more special. He requested that his father, Denis, and his own fiancée, Melanie, be in attendance on this Wednesday night in East Rutherford. He wanted them to come down from Montreal and sit smack dab in the middle of the Swamp as the Devils attempted to derail destiny, eliminate the rival Rangers in six games, and clinch this once-moribund franchise's first-ever conference title.

Denis, a former goaltender himself, knew what it was like to play this great game at a high level. In fact, he helped lead Team Canada to the bronze medal at the 1956 Olympic Games in Cortina d'Ampezzo, Italy. Sixteen years after the Olympics, Martin was born, and 38 years after the medal performance, Martin was suited up in red, white, and black, living every parent's dream in front of 19,040 fans in Game 6.

Of course, with the season already a success—after appearing in just four NHL games prior to 1993–94, Brodeur sculpted a rookie of the year campaign and established a foundation for perhaps the greatest NHL goaltending career of all time—Brodeur had little more to prove, especially given the fact that he wasn't even the starter at the opening of the season. But as long as the Devils were there, they might as well go out and win the damn thing. And to do that in front of Denis and Melanie, well, that would make it extra special.

So, as the teams took the ice at the Meadowlands in front of a crazed crowd for what would be the most important game of the season—and perhaps, history—for both franchises, Brodeur was able to look up 12 rows to his left and see his family watching over him with passionate pride.

The setup, the orchestration, was perfect. And with the way the Devils opened what would easily go down as one of the greatest games in NHL history, it clearly seemed as if the Brodeurs were indeed on track for a celebratory evening some 370 miles away from home.

"There was no question about it, and there was no other way to describe it," Brian Leetch said. "The Devils were all over us."

In a setting that had become all too familiar to everyone, Mark Messier and Bobby Carpenter, the two faceoff demons, lined up for the opening draw, which Messier won. In a first period that can only be described as dominating, that was about the only thing the Rangers would win in the first 20 minutes.

"We came out so fast and so hard, mentally, we had to make sure we controlled our emotions, as well," Bill Guerin said. "Realize that the game is not won in the first period, there's a long way to go, control yourself. But at the same time, don't change the way you're playing."

The Devils weren't about to do that. After all, in a series that saw such ebb and flow and such great stretches of hockey for both sides, this period may have been the best by either team.

"They were all over the ice," said former *New York Post* columnist Jay Greenberg.

Claude Lemieux gathered some momentum early, sneaked into the Rangers' zone on the left wing, and fired a wrist shot from the point that was kicked aside by Mike Richter. The game's first shot belonged to the Devils, and it only seemed fitting, because more were on the way.

"They came right out and dominated the game," said the *Post*'s Larry Brooks. "They should have been up 6–0. They had scoring chance after scoring chance. Honestly, Richter was as good as he's ever been. That, and the Devils hit a bunch of posts, as well."

The Rangers were scrambling from the opening drop, in fact, and the Devils sensed it. Tommy Albelin had a surprisingly open slot, and took a one-timer slap shot off a feed from Lemieux that Richter stopped. The rebound caromed out to Carpenter, whose wrist shot was also blocked by Richter.

With 15:50 left, the Devils entered the zone with Bernie Nicholls and Stephane Richer. Nicholls, also stunned by the amount of working space he had been given, took a slap shot of his own from the right point. Saved with Richter's sprawling glove.

"Mike Richter," Gary Thorne said on the ESPN broadcast, "is holding down the fort right now for the New York Rangers."

Indeed, in a game where the buildup squarely belonged to Messier, it was Richter who was stealing the show. The Devils, with their portion of the crowd gaining in volume with every rush, fired 13 shots on net in the first period, and should have had even more. They also had three 2-on-1s in the first five minutes.

The onslaught was on. But the man who entered the game with a 1.94 goals-against average was living up to his numbers.

"Absolutely, it could have easily been 5–0, 6–0," Howie Rose said, echoing the sentiments of so many who were on hand at the Meadowlands.

"It was one of Richter's greatest moments. He was truly carrying them on the biggest stage."

The Devils refused to let up. Richter had to make a right-leg save on Bruce Driver that pushed the fans to the edges of their seats. A minute later, Valeri Zelepukin waited for Stephane Matteau to give up his body, which he did, allowing Zelepukin to create some room for a slap shot that again caught Richter on the right leg.

"This is not a good sign for the New York Rangers," Bill Clement said. "They are not sharp on their man-to-man coverage."

Seven minutes in, New Jersey had registered five scoring chances to New York's one. And with 13:41 left in the period, the Devils had an 8–1 advantage in shots.

"It's an unbelievable boost sometimes, when you have a player who can carry a team through a tough time," Mike Keenan said of Richter. "It's certainly not the situation you always want to be in. This is a team sport. But if you have talented players, and one of them picks it up when everyone else needs it, it eventually picks everyone up. Mike was pretty sharp that night."

But at 8:03 of the first, the charge finally paid dividends for the home team. Viacheslav Fetisov, paired with Scott Niedermayer in a rare defensive-offensive backline parlay that was oddly forged by Jacques Lemaire in Game 5, pushed the puck out of his own end with a beautiful diving poke to center ice. Zelepukin was able to corral the puck and carried it with steam from center ice and into the right corner of the Rangers' zone. With a swift spin move, Zelepukin caught a charging Niedermayer, pinching into the left faceoff circle. Niedermayer snared the pass and let go of a line-drive wrist shot that deflected off Rangers forward Sergei Nemchinov's stick and past Richter's shoulder. Perhaps it was a sign of things to come for New Jersey, the thinking being that if the Devils were going to beat Richter on this night, they'd need to have a few lucky bounces.

Either way, the Devils didn't care. Nor did their fans. After a thorough eight minutes of play, New Jersey was rewarded with a 1–0 lead that allowed them to utilize the trap and truly suck the life out of the beleaguered Blueshirts, guarantee or not.

It was Niedermayer's second of the postseason, and while it wasn't the prettiest goal of his likely Hall of Fame career, it was arguably the most important. It was hard to tell by looking at Niedermayer's demeanor. In classic Devils fashion, with the crowd in a tizzy, Niedermayer calmly chewed on his mouthpiece, went over to bench to receive congratulations, and simply leaned over the boards in exhaustion and relief.

"When you have a one-goal lead, it brings you close to a two-goal lead," Clement said, "and coming back from a two-goal deficit, for the Rangers, is like climbing Mount Everest. You can make it, but the majority of people that try, fail."

While the Rangers would obviously make an effort and "try" to get back in this game, there was an overwhelming sense of "Here we go again." The Curse was hovering again, and despite Richter's every effort, it seemed that the Rangers were about to make the 54-year drought a 55-year drought.

"It had to fall apart in one way, shape, or form, right?" asked the *Post*'s Mark Everson. "This was the Rangers we're talking about."

In the Meadowlands press box that was so close to the ice, the beat writers had to start thinking about a Rangers obituary, even though the game was still so young.

"Keenan has been under enormous attack in New York by the press, especially a talk-radio sports station, about the moves he's made or hasn't made, and the sitting of some players who are injured or aren't injured," Thorne said, referring to WFAN. "Boy, I'll tell you, it's all because of 1940. In New York, you cannot get away from that year."

The Devils didn't make anything easier, either. Even after killing off a Bobby Holik hooking penalty at 15:12, New Jersey showed no fatigue. In fact, they sustained the pressure and soon doubled the lead. Fresh out of the penalty box, Holik hit a streaking Nicholls, who charged into the offensive zone. At that point, the Devils took the route that worked the first time against Richter, as Niedermayer gracefully pinched into the slot. Nicholls, just off to Richter's right, saucered a crisp pass to Niedermayer, who one-timed it toward Richter. Lemieux not only screened Richter, but was able to get a stick on Niedermayer's shot as well, which altered the direction of it and beat Richter through the five-hole at 17:32 of the first.

Suddenly, it was 2–0 Devils, and the Rangers were one step closer to the death of the dream. Lemieux's seventh goal of the postseason brought the crowd to a fever pitch, as the white pom-poms that were given out upon entry into the arena seemed to rise into the air in unison. There were blank stares along the Rangers bench from Keenan and his players, and there seemed like no end in sight for this Devils flurry.

"All I can remember saying is, 'Don't pull me out of this game. Please. Please.' Because I felt I was at the top of my game, and though we were down two goals, I knew we could come back," Richter said with a passion in his voice unrivaled by anyone in the series. "'Don't pull me out of this game, Mike. Don't do it.' In fact, when I gave up the second goal, I did not look over at the bench at all. I didn't want to give him any chance to pull me."

He was right, of course. Leave it to the best goaltender in American hockey history to know when he was at his best. Was he trailing? Absolutely. But was he struggling? Absolutely not.

"Richter kept the game within reach," Mike Francesa said. "Lot of people forget about that. What a performance he put on in that Game 6."

Keenan agreed. In fact, as Richter hovered around the same net he was pulled from in Game 4 and slowly stared up at the scoreboard that was forecasting the Rangers' doom, Keenan stuck with his top netminder.

"Richter, in my eyes, held the Rangers in there," said Devils play-by-play man Mike Miller. "New Jersey, to me that night, was the better hockey team. The energy level for them was unbelievable."

Indeed, if the Rangers were going to make any changes, it was not going to be between the pipes. Glenn Healy could get comfortable at the end of the bench. The team that changed its personnel drastically at the trading deadline, the team that changed its line combinations drastically throughout the series, and the team that changed its story drastically with each off day, was going to sit tight.

For now.

Not that it made anyone in the organization comfortable at the time. Certainly not general manager Neil Smith, who admirably sat in that famous New Jersey press box with the walls crumbling around him. With two minutes left in the opening period, Smith, in a grey suit, white shirt, and black tie, had his hands over his mouth, looking up at the scoreboard for an answer that wasn't there. As his coach feverishly chewed on ice cubes just feet below him, Smith chose to gnaw on a coffee stirrer.

The press box was at the top of a section of regular seating, instead of the more common halo press boxes that surround NHL rinks from the rafters. To the right or left of anyone in that box were lower-bowl sections filled with Devils fans who were out for Rangers blood. Everyone—and everything—was within earshot.

"I give him credit for that," Everson said. "GMs didn't have to sit there, and many chose not to. He was dying a thousand deaths in that press box that night, for sure, but he stayed right there."

That was no easy task, especially after the second goal.

"There was a guy in an aisle seat the whole time, just working me over," Smith said. "It was bad. It was almost to the point where security was going to have the guy removed. I told them, 'No.' I told them that 'It was okay. Let him stay.' But this guy was killing me. All night, it was 'Back to the drawing board, Neil! Back to the drawing board!' The whole game. It made me sick to my stomach, I have to tell you."

Smith stuck it out through the first period, as did his limping team. In a frame with few positives—and facing the possibility of needing to be the first team in the series at any point to come back from a two-goal deficit—the Rangers, at least, were given a power play, thanks to a Driver high stick on Eddie Olczyk at 19:07. The man advantage would carry over to the second period, and perhaps give the Rangers an ounce of life.

It was something for New York to cling to as the intermission horn sounded and the Devils fans belted out the sing-song chant of their rookie goaltender who stopped nine shots in the period. "Mar-ty, Mar-ty" was the chant of choice, much to the liking of Denis and Melanie in Row 12. Indeed, Marty was 40 minutes from winning a conference championship, and everyone could feel it—including the road team.

"We were playing not to make a mistake at first," Doug Lidster said. "It was more of a mental challenge for us than anything. We had to just go for it."

Lidster was one of two changes to the Rangers lineup for Game 6, replacing the suspended Jeff Beukeboom after his hit on Richer in Game 5 at Madison Square Garden. The other change was Olczyk replacing an injured Brian Noonan, and though the scoreboard didn't show it, both players paid dividends in the first frame. Olczyk drew the Driver penalty, and Lidster, who had one of the harder shots in the league, did enough in Keenan's eyes to replace Alexander Karpovtsev on the first defensive pairing, alongside Leetch.

But none of that mattered to the Devils as the second period started.

"We had them," Lemieux said. "We were playing well, and we needed to stick to our system for 40 minutes."

Easier said than done, though.

The Devils maintained pressure early in the second as both teams seemed to settle into a groove. With 16:20 left, Niedermayer, the best player on either side to this point, again made some room for himself and fired a shot that Richter stopped. But really, that was one of few charges as the Devils began to clamp down with the trap, waiting for their offensive chances rather than keep up their first-period pace. Stopping the Rangers became their top priority, and they were achieving it.

"Even when the Rangers get into the Devils' zone, it's one pass, hardly ever a shot, and Devils out," Clement said. "No sustained pressure, no sustained forecheck by the Rangers at all."

The Devils fed off that. Five minutes in, Richer, from behind the net and with two defenders draped on him, backhanded a pass to John MacLean in front of the net. In a scene that had already played out a dozen times, a Devils forward—in this case, MacLean—could not believe the time he was being given. So, he took it, positioned himself 12 feet in front of Richter, and flicked a shot that stunned Richter under his arm. Richter made the save, though, as the puck fell to the top of his skate, allowing him to cover.

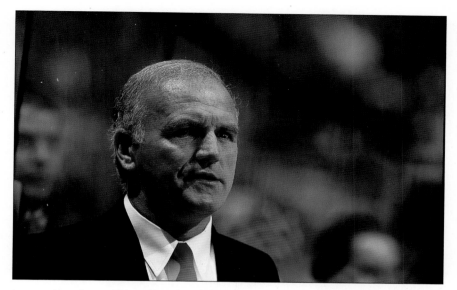

Jacques Lemaire and his suffocating defensive system helped transform the Devils from an NHL also-ran to a perennial Stanley Cup contender.

In 1993, Rangers GM Neil Smith hired Mike Keenan to take over as head coach. The pair had only one goal: to bring the Stanley Cup back to New York for the first time since 1940.

Mark Messier was traded to the Rangers in 1991, becoming the latest in a long line of sports stars that arrived in New York with championship expectations.

Defenseman Brian Leetch anchored New York's back line and matched his career high with 23 goals in 1993–94.

In his first season as the Rangers' top goaltender, Mike Richter posted 42 wins and led the team to the best record in the NHL. (AP Images)

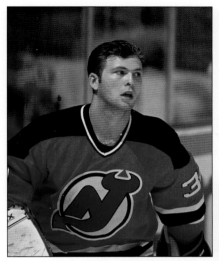

Goaltender Martin Brodeur won the Calder Trophy as the league's top rookie in 1993–94.

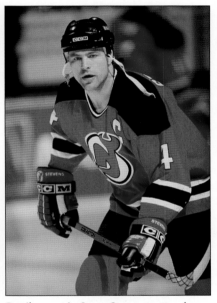

Devils captain Scott Stevens posted 18 goals and 60 assists in 1993–94, leading New Jersey in points.

After being part of the trade that sent Mark Messier to New York, forward Bernie Nicholls landed in New Jersey and adopted the team's defensive mind-set.

In Game 1, a wrist shot by Stephane Richer (44) in double overtime gave the visiting Devils the series lead and shocked the Madison Square Garden crowd into stunned silence.

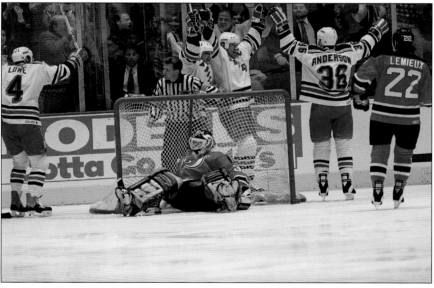

Desperate for a win to even the series, the Rangers swarmed Martin Brodeur in Game 2 and won 4–0. (*AP Images*)

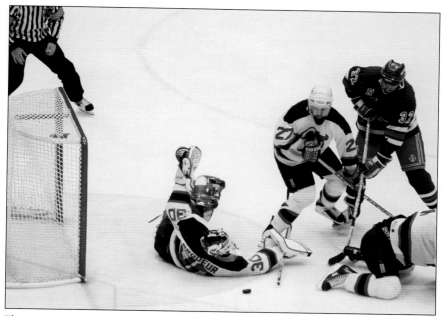

The two teams again needed double overtime to decide Game 3. The winning goal came courtesy of New York's Stephane Matteau, who slid a loose puck past Martin Brodeur at 6:13. (*AP Images*)

After New Jersey won Games 4 and 5 to push the Rangers to the brink, Mark Messier issued his legendary guarantee before Game 6, then put on a heroic, three-goal performance that sent the series to a deciding seventh game. (*AP Images*)

Matteau! Matteau! Matteau! Stephane Matteau's second double-overtime winner of the series sent the Rangers on to the Stanley Cup Finals...

...and sent Chris Terreri, Bruce Driver, and the rest of the Devils home for the summer.

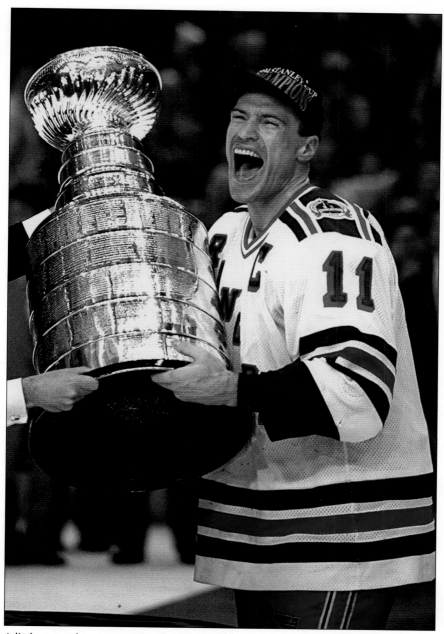

A little more than two weeks after The NHL's Greatest Series Ever, Mark Messier and the Rangers finally broke the franchise's 54-year Stanley Cup drought.

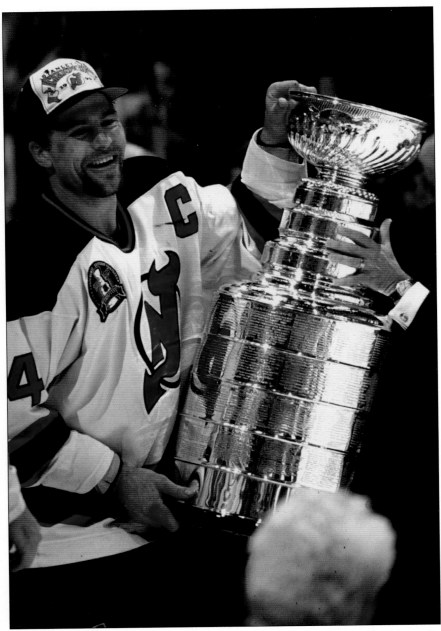

Just 375 days later, Scott Stevens and the Devils redeemed themselves and celebrated the first Stanley Cup victory in franchise history.

That easily could have been curtains for the Rangers. A three-goal deficit on the road in an elimination game against an inspired New Jersey team with 35 minutes to go would not have been overcome, no matter who guaranteed what.

"We knew we needed that third one," Ken Daneyko said. "We were playing well, keeping it up, but if we got to a three-goal lead, it would have been over."

Keenan knew that, too. Still searching for answers, he took advantage of the stoppage in play, and called one of the league's more notable timeouts at 14:28. As Queen's "We Will Rock You" belted out through the loudspeakers, longtime Devils public address announcer Bob Arsena made the call that surprised many in the building: "Timeout, Rangers."

"The Rangers are going to use their one 30-second timeout right here. Mike Keenan just feels, I think, that this thing is starting to drift away," Thorne said. "There comes a point in a game like this, where a team sometime senses it's over. If that happens, it *is* over, and the Rangers may be getting dangerously close to that point, out of frustration."

MacLean and the Devils, frustrated at themselves for not snaring that 3–0 lead, casually skated over to their bench, and Steve Larmer and the Rangers did the same to theirs. The Devils took a drink and enjoyed the respite.

It was a different story at the other bench.

"I just looked straight ahead," Leetch said. "I didn't look back at the coaches at all."

In reality, there was no need to, because Keenan didn't have much to say during the break.

"Mike didn't say anything at the timeout," Matteau said.

So, here were the do-or-die Rangers, some 34 minutes away from being eliminated from a tumultuous series in which some players were benched and others suspended, and the coach called a timeout, only to leave it to the players to figure out what to do next.

Larmer, who was on the ice, not the bench, jawed motivational words to those sitting in front of him. Matteau, who was on the ice as well, looked up at assistant coach Colin Campbell. Among those sitting was Messier, with Glenn Anderson on his right and Craig MacTavish on his left. Messier turned to his right, looked down the bench, and just started to shake his head. He continued to look there, and ultimately said to his teammates, "You good?" When they nodded, he then turned to the left, spit, then twisted back and looked up toward the direction of Keenan. His coach did not return his gaze, so Messier just hopped over the bench and took the ice for the next shift, alongside Anderson and Adam Graves.

Not much happened during the break, and though the Devils continued to control play for long stretches after it, the timeout is remembered as the moment that Messier truly took this team over. He had experienced a decent series to that point—posting one goal and at least one point in every contest before Game 5, plus being a beast on faceoffs—but he certainly wasn't the player Rangers fans had come to know and love. With his famous guarantee now hovering over his head, and a deficit that was still manageable thanks to his goaltender, this was now his team and his time…or else.

But again, like everything else in this schizophrenic season in New York, that time started ominously. As Messier prepared for the draw to the left of Brodeur, Keenan suddenly sprung to life. He put one leg on the bench, leaned down, looked at his players, and said simply, "Let's go." Of course, the Devils won the faceoff, held the zone, and Chorske immediately hit the post in front of Richter, a near-miss that could have ended it right there. Then, Albelin kept it in the zone and fired a slap shot from the right point that hit Chorske in front of Richter, or that, too, might have sneaked in and essentially ended the series.

"They just could not get the third goal," Brooks said. "Just wasn't going to happen. There was just an overwhelming feeling that they were not going to score again. At that point, it was just a matter of time before the Rangers got one."

New York survived the post-timeout flurry and slowly started to mount some offense. At 10:26, Matteau had some open space in the slot and fired a shot toward Brodeur, but it was blocked. Still, the Rangers had some sustained pressure, and ever so slowly, things were starting to even out everywhere but on the scoreboard.

"Sometimes, things come too easy to you. And things were coming so easy to the New Jersey Devils, like they've almost looked to me as if they've let up a little," Clement said. "Yes, the Rangers are still coming, but the Devils seem a little unsure of themselves in their defensive coverage, and the last five minutes, they've been a step behind."

All the while, the Rangers were making quick changes to keep their players fresh. Leetch intercepted a Scott Stevens clearing attempt at center ice, carried into the zone, and left the puck for a streaking Joey Kocur on the right board. With 7:09 remaining, Kocur, left alone, fired a shot from the right circle that Brodeur stopped but couldn't find because Leetch ran into him. The puck caromed to the corner as Kocur centered again, but a sprawled out Brodeur stopped and covered as his helmet flew off.

When putting his helmet back on during the stoppage, he had to pause and laugh. It was clear he was still confident. His teammates? Not so much.

Four minutes later, the Devils broke down in the neutral zone—their home away from home, their comfort zone, their turf—and it cost them. It also changed the course of the series, and history, forever.

Guerin had the puck five feet away from the Devils bench, as a line change was needed. The common New Jersey strategy there would have been to fire it down behind Richter, allowing time for the fresh troops to enter. But with the new line half over the boards already, Guerin instead turned and pushed a harmless backhand about seven feet … right onto the stick of Messier, who graciously turned and headed across center ice.

"Because of the style we played, we probably strayed from our system on three, four, maybe five occasions, and that's it. But it cost us," Driver said. "But that's what happens in the playoffs. You make mistakes that you don't normally make, and the puck ends up in the net. And I can tell you, I remember that stray."

The line change happened, but not in full, and at this point, the Devils were caught behind the play because the clearing attempt hadn't traveled far enough. Guerin was still stuck out there as a result. Confusion reigned, and the Rangers pounced. Messier—who saw a sudden change on his line with Graves at the 10:12 mark, in which Alexei Kovalev replaced Anderson at right wing—aggressively entered the zone and calmly left a soft, seamless backhand pass to Kovalev at the right point. Kovalev, surprised he had as much ice as he had because of the bad line change, created some more space, set up his shot, cocked twice, and fired a slap shot from the top of the right circle that beat Brodeur and cut the Devils' lead in half. Brodeur was in position and had enough time to see the puck, but he was ultimately screened by Daneyko and Graves, who were tangled as they neared the crease.

"Those last two minutes, I'll never forget," Nicholls said. "Everyone's trying to change, and Billy got caught, and then they come down and Kovalev scores. That was it. They were back in it just like that. The momentum was all us until that point. We dominated the game, we knew we were the better team, and we were only up 2–1. If we would have been able to get to the locker room up 2–0 it would have been over."

Instead, at 18:19 of the second, the sleeping giant was awake.

"They scored late, and they scored on a line change," Driver said. "Our forwards changed, and they came off at a point on the ice where they never changed, and in a position where we never changed: when the puck was coming back toward us, instead of deep in their zone. And all that did was create a 3-on-2 opportunity, which gave them a little bit of time to make a play. That's all they needed. Just that little bit of time. Boom, boom, it's in the net, and all of a sudden ... we're done."

Strong words. Keep in mind, there were still 21 minutes to play, and the Devils were still *leading* by a goal.

"But it didn't matter anymore," Brooks said. "They weren't mature enough yet to come back from that."

That much was evident. In fact, when Nicholls was interviewed by SportsChannel's Stan Fischler between the second and third periods in a studio not far from the Devils locker room, the team's psyche was written all over his face.

"They were done," Fischler said. "He looked as if he had seen a ghost."

The feeling was mutual in the stands. Kovalev's tally ignited the Rangers' portion of the crowd more so than perhaps any goal that New York had scored in that building going back to 1982.

"That's 100 percent right. There was a feeling now that, hey, we've got a shot in this game," Joe Benigno said. "But you still never felt 100 percent confident, because this was the Rangers we're talking about. When you travel a lifetime without winning, you just never feel too confident. But they had a shot, and after the way that game started, that was all you could ask for."

But would the inferiority complex overwhelm New Jersey in the third period? Would the Devils be able to recover?

"We never thought of it from where the Devils were in the game," Lidster said. "I do know that we never lost *our* confidence."

So, here were the Devils, trying like mad to get that third goal to win the conference crown on home ice and avoid a Game 7 in New York, and suddenly, it felt as if they were the enemy in their own building.

"It was unbelievable," Lemieux said. "The place just went absolutely crazy for [the Rangers] after that goal. We all knew what went into playing the Rangers at home, and we knew their fans would always be there. But this was different. It was as if everyone turned on us."

Clearly shaken, it was a different collection of Devils that walked down the hallway after the second period than the group that did so after the first. That was evident in the press box, too.

"In their locker room, there was finger pointing and complaining, and obviously, in our room, we had life," Smith said. "They were not a happy group. Imagine how tight you'd be, if you were that team that could have been up 6–0 or 7–0 with the way they started the game."

In the second period, the shots had evened at 13 per side, and the Rangers scored the lone goal. The tide had officially turned.

"It was really Kovalev who broke the ice for us. They were dominating play, they were up a couple of goals, and their crowd was really feeling it. You could sense it," Smith said. "Then, Kovalev scores, and the place erupts…for us? In a matter of seconds, the whole place turned. It was surreal. And the story is the Devils were clearly disheveled after all of that, knowing that they were playing as well as ever. Yet, this goal made it a 2–1 game, and we had all the momentum."

It certainly wasn't the most confident bunch of Devils that headed into the locker room, and the Rangers knew it. Despite being shorthanded to start the third—thanks to an Esa Tikkanen knee-to-knee trip on Richer—everyone in the building knew which team had the more powerful propulsion, no matter what the scoreboard said.

"The reason momentum can change so quickly in that setting is because the teams were so evenly matched," Richter said. "A missed shot here, a post there, a line change, and all of a sudden, everything shifts. It's the little things that can make massive differences."

Truer words were never spoken.

"The Kovalev goal, it gave them hope," Howie Rose said, "but I remember with that one look in Mark Messier's eyes, you could tell that something else was coming later."

As the Vancouver Canucks, who had secured the Western Conference championship the night before, sat and watched like the rest of the hockey world, awaiting their opponent in the 1994 Stanley Cup Finals, NHL history was about to be made in the Garden State.

"We are going to have one hell of a third period," Thorne said.

Messier's Miracle Mile

○ ○ ○ ○

"This is the stuff of which sports history is made. Personally, for [Mark Messier], and for the New York Rangers, if indeed this is to be their year, it's the kind of thing that makes you believe that destiny is really there on your bench."
—GARY THORNE, ESPN PLAY-BY-PLAY ANALYST

WHILE THE DEVILS were in their locker room, contemplating how to keep things all together, maintain their slim lead, and finish what they set out to do, the Rangers were across the hall, experiencing what some players saw as a changing of the guard. It was one that may have been happening slowly over time.

"I think back to Game 4, to be honest, in New Jersey, when the incidents came, and Mike [Keenan] sat some guys, and Mark [Messier] had his meeting the next day with us," said Doug Lidster, who by now was set for a ton of playing time with Brian Leetch in the third period and would be a key factor in those following, critical 20 minutes. "My impression was that it was no longer Mike's team at that point. It really did slip over to be Mark's team at that time. Mike got us to where we were supposed to be. Absolutely. But then the ship moved on to Mark. From Game 4 on, we had lost the momentum. I don't remember anything being said. I don't remember any speech from Mike. I do remember, after the second period, we were down 2–1 then, and I remember Mike walking around, patting everyone on the back.

"To me, that went over like a lead balloon. 'This was not the Mike Keenan that I know,' I kept saying to myself. I don't remember anything specific that Mike said. I suppose, though, there was nothing to be said. If that was part of his method, so be it. If he said something, I never heard it."

An interesting strategy, for sure, considering the most important period of the year was about to begin. But if this truly was Messier's team, everyone was about to find out how it would fare.

"There was a lot of positive talk among the guys. That goal, [Alexei] Kovalev, was the best situation for us," Stephane Matteau said. "'You cannot give up.' 'You cannot get down.' 'You have to keep it up.' Things like that among the players in the room. And with this group, we were confident that we could come back. We knew that we'd all come together and do everything in our power to get it done. And it was strange at times, it was quiet in there for a bit, but really, no one was nervous even though our season could have ended right there."

If the Devils needed a branch to cling to as this third period of Game 6 began amid a persistent buzz from both sets of fans at the Swamp, they only had to remind themselves that when leading in the playoffs after two periods, New Jersey was 8–1. When trailing after two frames in the postseason, New York was 0–3.

"Anytime a team scores a goal at the end of the period, the momentum changes. And that happened, and then you get a breather and a chance to collect yourself, and that momentum gave them a lot of energy," Tom Chorske said. "We knew we'd be in for a battle. It was just two teams with a lot of will going head to head. But yes, you could sense that the momentum was in their favor. And even though we led, we had our work cut out for us."

But it just didn't feel like New Jersey was winning anymore.

"Everybody in the building sensed the momentum, it truly was surreal," Chris Russo said. "Here the Devils were, at home, leading 2–1 headed into the third period, and they should have felt confident. But it wasn't that way at all! It was one of those periods where you were just waiting for Messier to do something special, especially after The Guarantee. It was a terrific atmosphere."

The Devils even opened the period on a carryover power play, but that still didn't matter.

"The Devils were just shell-shocked," said the *Post*'s Larry Brooks. "It was that simple."

Less than a minute into the period, with the Devils still a man up, Messier, already armed with an assist, began his assault for the ages. Instead of a harmless, yet productive, dump into the Devils' zone that would have allowed the Rangers' penalty killers to set up, Messier took a chance on the attack and carried the puck past the blue line. With a few feet of wiggle room, he let a wrist shot go from the right circle that Scott Stevens blocked in front of Martin Brodeur. However, the rebound was kicked right back out to Messier, who carried it around the back of the net and attempted to stuff a wraparound past the goal line not long after the net barely slid off its moorings.

In today's day and age, it was the kind of play that would have drawn a lengthy review. But in 1994, the play was whistled because the net was dislodged, as Stevens and Brodeur slid together back into the right post, knocking the net off its moorings just as Messier was about to slide the puck around the left post.

It was a break for New Jersey, clearly. But it was also a harbinger of things to come. Messier was on the attack, and the Devils were sliding, literally.

"Wow," Gary Thorne said. "The net came loose because of the Devils. And the Rangers had nothing to do with it."

Whether he meant to do it or not, it was a smart move by Stevens. The block from a prone position was a terrific hockey move, and letting the net slip away from its normal position, forcing a stoppage, was far better than getting up and trying to stop Messier, who was five feet away with momentum. That wasn't going to happen.

But no matter—the Rangers just kept pushing. New York ably killed off the power play, and in many instances, the Rangers looked like they were the team with the man advantage. The Devils had just seven seconds of attack time during the minor, and finished with no shots.

How's that for a change of pace?

Plus, Keenan had modified his lines, and a new line of Messier, Kovalev, and Adam Graves debuted five minutes after New York's timeout. Glenn Anderson, remember, took the ice with Graves and Messier right when the timeout concluded. But that shift was a complete disaster, and Chorske almost ended the game. But at 10:12 of the second, with a faceoff just inside the Devils' zone, Kovalev joined the top-line mix, and things changed. All three had their legs on this night, two of them had points in the second period, and together they seemed intent on breaking through New Jersey's trap with speed and skill.

"I think it was pretty simple from Mike's perspective at that point," the *Post*'s Jay Greenberg said. "Put your best players together, get them out there, and see what they can do."

Fresh off that penalty kill, Kovalev and Messier were back at it again, and this time the net would stay put. With a strong push out of their own zone, Leetch hit Kovalev in the neutral zone cleanly, and he carried in. From the left point, Kovalev shoved a flat pass over to a breaking Messier, as the Devils scrambled to get into position, with Bruce Driver and Ken Daneyko on defense. A mere second before the two defensemen caught up to the rush and swarmed him, Messier flipped a backhand shot to Brodeur's stick side that would become one of the more famous highlights in NHL history. Messier's shot fooled Brodeur, sneaked through to the net on the left side, and popped back out. Brodeur, hoping it had never made it to the net, caught the puck with his glove and held on, looking back as if he'd had it all along.

Too late.

Messier had tied the game, and as he swept along the boards with his hands held straight up in another famous pose with a grin as wide as the margin of play over the last five minutes of game action, his teammates mobbed him. At 2:48 of the third period, in a game once dominated by the Devils with the Rangers on the brink of elimination, it was now 2–2, and the sentiment was summed up by veteran New Jersey play-by-play man Mike Emrick's simple television call on SportsChannel: "The man who promised victory has just tied the game."

Messier's 95th career playoff goal, from Leetch and Kovalev, once again inspired the Rangers' portion of the crowd to cheer at a volume previously never heard before in East Rutherford.

"There were more Rangers fans than Devils fans," Claude Lemieux said. "That's the way it was. For us, that was very tough."

Overpowered by the Devils for the better part of the previous eight periods, the Rangers washed all that away in less than an hour's time.

"Once the Rangers tied it," Brooks said, "it was just a matter of time. The game was over."

Steppenwolf's "Born to Be Wild" blared over the loudspeakers, as the arena staff tried feverishly to drown out the Rangers fans, who by now had completely taken over. Perhaps it was a fitting musical selection; after all, consider the first line of the song: "Get your motor runnin.'"

Well, Messier's was runnin' alright. The only question was, when would it stop?

At the 16:23 mark of the third, he had won 17 of his 23 faceoffs. What's more, he had played 16:23, with 21 shifts, two shots, and two points. His best was yet to come.

"[The Devils] changed, for sure, in the third period," Leetch said. "They didn't forecheck as much and allowed us more room. We took advantage of that."

In the first five minutes of the third period, the Rangers had already fired seven shots on Brodeur. The Devils, meanwhile, managed just one quality chance in that time frame—a wrist shot by Driver off a feed from John MacLean—but Mike Richter made a sliding save that he held on to.

The frenetic pace calmed a bit once the game was tied, as—for a change—the contest began to resemble a traditional playoff game, where both teams focused on line changes, not making mistakes, and waiting for the right opportunities to attack.

At 11:32, though, the Rangers caught a break as a 4-on-4 opportunity resulted from matching roughing penalties to Scott Niedermayer and Esa Tikkanen. The benefit was two-fold for New York, and that would prove fruitful. First, 4-on-4s favored the speed and skill of the Rangers, who could do more with the ensuing open ice. Second, while Tikkanen was a valued member of this postseason run, the one-for-one tradeoff with Tikkanen and Niedermayer, the Devils' most skilled offensive defenseman, was no contest. Advantage, New York.

While the Devils did not attack and elected to bide their time on the 4-on-4, a sloppy clear once again proved costly. Bobby Carpenter, one of the Devils' most consistent defensive forwards, got a little lazy on his dump-in from center ice that, like Bill Guerin's from the second period, should have been deposited well behind Richter, allowing for New Jersey to set up with time on its side. Instead, the puck slid only 20 feet off Carpenter's stick and right onto the blade of Kovalev, who turned at his own blue line and raced toward history again.

Kovalev passed to Leetch at center, and the defenseman then carried it into the Devils' zone. Leetch then turned toward the bench but left a backhand pass for Kovalaev's stick at the top of the left faceoff circle. Kovalev, again making the most of the room he'd been given, let a slap shot go that Brodeur stopped but kicked out to the right side.

"Rebounds can kill you sometimes. You have to control those rebounds," said Kelly Hrudey, who, from his post as a CBC analyst in 2011, was part of a McDonald's advertising campaign in Canada that charted the greatest moments in hockey history. In one of the commercials, he was in a McDonald's restaurant arguing with former NHL forward P.J. Stock over the memorable list, all while endorsing The Guarantee as his choice.

Well, this rebound broke free, as if sent down by the hockey gods. And who was at Brodeur's doorstep to bury it from two feet out? Messier. At 12:12 of the third period, Messier's second goal and third point of the night gave the Rangers their first lead at 3–2.

"There are signature games in a player's career, and signature games for a team on its way to a Stanley Cup championship," said Peter McNab, a former Devils center and Emrick's partner, at the time, on SportsChannel. "We are looking at one of those for Messier, and for the New York Rangers."

"Listen, the Rangers were better than the Bruins and Sabres, and it showed right away. But we had them," said Messier's longtime friend Ken Daneyko, noting New Jersey's first two postseason opponents that season. "I've known Mess a long time, and we go back a ways, and I just know him deep down inside. Trust me. And when I saw him down 2–0 in Game 6, I saw him demoralized. He looked done. And then Kovalev gets that late goal in the second period, and the rest is history. We had to close the door on a great team like that and a great player like Mark. We didn't do it. And we paid for it."

As Brodeur looked up to the rafters, the New York celebratory hug drifted behind the net, centered, of course, around Messier. The captain's permasmile had returned once again as his teammates tapped him on the helmet. The first one there was Leetch; Kovalev came in next. Messier and Leetch at one point were almost close enough to have kissed each other, as the Rangers' portion of the crowd erupted again.

It was a different story over in Row 12, just to the left of Brodeur. A dejected Melanie had her feet on the top of the chair in front of her, with her head resting in the white pom-pom she had been waving for more than an hour earlier in the night. She slowly crept out of her cover to see a celebration in front of her, decked out in red, white, and blue. Denis, with a frown on, could only sit and watch as well, as his son picked himself back up and got his bearings about him.

"The third goal was a similar thing, where one of our forwards decided to drift over and help one of our defensemen out, when he really didn't need the help, and it left a guy open," Driver said. "And then? Boom, in the net. I look at those two blatant mistakes, you just feel that lost opportunity. Again, it's easy to say now. But we *did* have them."

The Rangers bench, meanwhile, was simply electric as Messier arrived, and all he kept yelling was the same call that Matteau used earlier in the series, in the same building: "Woooooooooooooooooo!"

"There is no greater theater in sports, and Mark Messier is writing the stuff of which legends are made," Thorne said. "Coming out publicly, saying, 'We will win' Game 6, and now, he has scored two goals in this game."

And his teammates were going along for the ride. In fact, seven minutes into the third period, the Rangers—over the course of the last 20:00 of game action—had outshot the Devils 19–8. At this point, it was all about Messier and what the Rangers were about to accomplish. It appeared as if the Devils' dominant defensive mind-set—where a one-goal lead in the third period meant a surefire win—was actually working in reverse, and it was the Rangers who were playing with that confidence cushion.

"We were finally playing up to our abilities," Matteau said. "We had the best, deepest team, we had four skilled lines, and that's something you don't see in this league all that often. When we were going, it was tough to defend us. And we were going there. But really, it went back to the timeout, and eventually when Mike put Mess, Graves, and Kovalev on the same line. To see them do what they did, it was unbelievable. And I had the best seat in the house."

And the house truly belonged to the Rangers by now. A poster-board sign held by a New York fan behind the penalty boxes told the story succinctly, by way of a Sharpie: "Welcome to the (Second) Home of the Rangers."

But the Devils did show a little fight as the clock ticked down, and in a tight period where more players got away with potential minors than usual, longtime referee Kerry Fraser eventually flagged Anderson for a two-minute slashing penalty on Bernie Nicholls at 17:11. The Devils suddenly had some life. All it took was one goal to send the game to overtime.

Determined not to get cheated, Jacques Lemaire—after a stoppage in play in which the ensuing faceoff was going to be to Richter's right—called a timeout with 1:53 left. In a game where timeouts became a major storyline, Lemaire organized his troops and pulled Brodeur from the net, creating a 6-on-4 opportunity. The break, clearly, was needed: at the time of the decision, the Devils had been outshot 25–9 in the previous 31:30.

"But I just remember thinking to myself," Brooks said, "*This was too early to pull him.*"

The move certainly was debatable. But Lemaire had faith in his power-play unit, and must have believed that as long as the Devils won the faceoff, with six skaters on the ice, they should be able to sustain play in the New York zone.

Well, they lost the faceoff. And to who, of all people? Messier, who beat Nicholls. The rest, as they say, is history.

In a classic sweep through the faceoff dot, Messier backpassed it to Lidster, who was in the right corner. Lidster collected the puck and calmly shoved it around the boards behind Richter. With the extra skater, though, the Devils were able to swarm, and MacLean intercepted the pass and offered up a blind centering pass to Lemieux from behind the net, probably one that he had made 1,000 times before.

Easy enough, right?

But Lemieux was tied up by Leetch, an underrated play by the defenseman that clearly prevented a potential tap-in for Lemieux that would have tied it. Leetch was able to lift Lemieux's stick six inches off the ice, just enough for the centering pass to land right on the tape of Messier, who turned and flipped it from the left faceoff circle. In as straight a line as a puck will ever travel, Messier's shot made a beeline for the Devils' yawning net and completed perhaps the greatest single period of hockey ever orchestrated by a single player in one of the grandest stages that this game offers. At 18:15 of the third, Messier capped off an incredible hat trick that gave the Rangers a 4–2 lead in a game they were severely outplayed in for almost two periods.

"So, what does he do [after The Guarantee]? He goes out and scores three goals in a row, bails them out of a tough spot, and wins a game for them that they *had* to win," Russo said. "Unbelievable. And the idea around New York that we always talked about was to break this kind of jinx, to break The Curse, you had to win a game like that, Game 6. You had to win a game that way. And they did."

Messier knew that better than anyone. In fact, instead of the common celebratory group hug on the ice after a goal, Messier did one better after the empty-netter. He raced over to the bench, where the entire team could share in the moment.

"You always really have to remain consistent in your beliefs and philosophy," he said later.

"That was a real key thing for Mark," Lidster said. "Everyone was important to the cause, to the mission we were on. No matter who it was— the guy who delivered the UPS packages, he had an important role on the team. Everyone was a part of it. Mark created that atmosphere, and we all loved it. He knew just what to do, and when to do it."

Hovering above the mass of blue uniforms and equipment stood an elated Keenan. Dissected every which way by the media, the fans, and even his own players, Keenan's midstream lineup change had paid dividends.

Was it still Mike's team at this point? Did it really matter? The important thing for fans in New York was that their team was still alive.

"That's what this group of Rangers could do so well. We could adapt to a style, to a strategy, a lineup, and make it work for us," Steve Larmer said. "It's an incredible feeling to be around a group of players with that ability. At the end of the day, it was an incredible journey to go through with incredible teammates."

"When you make a bold guarantee like that, and then you back it up by going out and playing like that, certainly Mark became a sports figure in this town that will never be forgotten," Mike Francesa said. "There was so much going on, and Mark kept that team together. It was Mark that did that. Richter kept the game within reach, and what a performance he put on in that Game 6. Unforgettable. But for Mark to rise to the occasion like that, truly, it was one of the great moments in New York sports history. It really puts him in a special place in New York, and it's a different place, because he played and won in Edmonton, and the best part of his career was played somewhere else. But he delivered it, he backed it up, and to make that guarantee at the most critical time? Unbelievable."

From the brink of elimination to riding a momentum wave the size of the city they played in, the Rangers—anchored by a two-word guarantee— were suddenly moments away from tying the Eastern Conference Finals, a series that was already headed for legendary status.

"Do you believe it?" Thorne asked on the telecast with his famous, exclamatory tone appropriating the moment precisely and efficiently as the final goal crossed the line. "Do you believe it?"

The answer for so many was … no.

"Unbelievable," Barry Melrose said.

"The stuff of legends," Mike Emrick said.

"Mark went above and beyond in that series. I clearly remember him turning around, absolutely," Richter said. "And when he flipped the puck toward the empty net, I knew it was going in. Just knew it. It was on a perfect line and I don't even think it hit the ice until the red line. I simply couldn't believe it. 'Did he just do that?'"

Of course, lost in all of the drama was Richter himself. Keep in mind, he held New Jersey scoreless for the final two periods, stopping 17 shots. He was rarely tested in the third, clearly, as a crumbling Devils squad mounted just four shots. But given his margin of error at the time, it was a flawless performance.

"I always thought that Richter did not get enough credit in that series," Russo said. "Messier was great. Leetch was great. But especially after what he did in Game 6, Richter saved the series. He outplayed Brodeur."

In an ultimate slap-in-the-face moment for the home team, the visiting Rangers fans littered the ice with hats in honor of Messier's hat trick. Down they came from all sections in all different colors, extending the misery for a team that just needed to get back in the locker room to focus on the next game in New York. The Devils could only watch and hope that they'd get another chance to play a home game in the next round against the Canucks.

Lou Lamoriello, a study in calm professionalism win, lose, or draw, could only sit in the press box with his hands over his mouth in amazement, his white hair a bit frazzled after a long night, as his counterpart Neil Smith stood, pumped his fist, and smiled the smile of a general manager who just earned a Game 7 on home ice.

"As I watched us come back, things began to change, yes," Smith said. "And when Mess scored the empty-netter and we went up two goals, I turned to see where that guy was, the guy who was killing me all night from the stands. And he was gone! Nowhere to be seen. He had left the building. I'll never forget that guy. But Mess was the stuff of legends that night, and it'll go down in New York sports history, and all of sports history, for sure. It was something to see. Game 6 was truly an unbelievable experience. One I'll never forget."

As the ice was still being readied for play, Messier took the ice again to stay warm, not content to rest on his laurels. In a fitting move for a captain looking to keep his teammates focused on the task at hand, Messier circled and headed back toward the bench, held out his glove for some encouragement, and uttered three simple words:

"One. Four. Five." he said, shaking his head slowly. "One. Four. Five."

His message? That the Rangers still had 1:45 to play before officially registering this victory.

"The Devils were so close. And now, they are so, so far away," Clement said. "What a series."

The Rangers won a faceoff in the final seconds, and again the puck landed on the stick of Lidster in the left corner next to Richter. At that point, the Devils pulled back, Lidster maintained possession, and the final seconds of a 4–2 season-saving victory ticked off.

"Messier with The Guarantee, and Kovalev's goal in Game 6, the whole thing was so dramatic," WFAN's Steve Somers said. "Outside of Namath, the guy comes through with a hat trick. You can't make it up."

The game indeed ended with Lidster in possession. But the night belonged to someone else in blue, and Emrick summed it up better than anyone: "The called shot. The hat trick. The win. Mark Messier."

The effort left the Rangers captain with 10 playoff goals in 15 games.

"To say it is one thing. To go out and back it up is another," Melrose said. "But to score a hat trick along the way? You've got to be kidding me. This was a great series with a lot of special plays and special players. None bigger than Mark Messier."

What could not be lost in New York's euphoria—and it stood to reason that it wouldn't among these players—was that all this victory did was tie the series. Had the pendulum swung? Certainly. Was the series over? Hardly.

"At that point, we still had to win a game," Smith said. "There were no assurances that we were going to come back and run them off the ice in Game 7. I always compared it to Team USA in 1980. The Miracle on Ice was incredible, and beating Russia will go down in history forever, but so many people forget that the Americans still had to win another game, against Finland, to win the gold medal, and they had to come from behind in that game just to do so. We had work to do, certainly."

And that was fine with the media, too. With a day off in between the games, there was plenty of time to get that New York media hype machine firing on all cylinders again.

"This will be the biggest game in these two franchises' history," McNab said on the broadcast, "going back, at least, 50 years. Buckle up."

As that Game 6 horn sounded in East Rutherford, the Devils retreated, gave themselves a few polite taps on the pants, and plodded back into the locker room a beaten bunch, left to wonder what had just happened.

Meanwhile, across the ice a sea of blue gathered around Richter. There were smiles, laughs, hugs, and taps on the helmets. Keenan was off to the left as he walked around the boards and into the hallway with his staff. He didn't look up much, he didn't smile, and he didn't give any hint of satisfaction or contentment. This was, after all, just the third win of the series. Most of all, he seemed happy to leave the celebration to his players. After the turmoil, the tension, and the uncertainty surrounding his relationship with his stars, this moment was the players' to enjoy, if only for a brief time. In a matter of hours, it'd be back to business in New York, preparing for the game of games, the grand finale to what was becoming "The Greatest Series Ever."

As a smiling Messier charged into that celebratory goal-crease hug, with his patented leather helmet chinstrap dangling from his ear, he turned, grabbed Sergei Nemchinov and defenseman Jay Wells, looked them straight in the eyes, and offered two determined words that needed no further explanation:

"One more."

Game 7

○ ○ ○ ○

"For me, to see what [the Devils] had been through—having led in Game 6 only to see it wash away while [Mark] Messier took over—it was shocking. Just how much more would they be able to muster in Game 7? And how was Jacques [Lemaire] and the team going to be able to prop themselves up for another chance at it? As I drove through the tunnel that day, that's what I was thinking about."
—MIKE MILLER, NEW JERSEY DEVILS PLAY-BY-PLAY VOICE (1993–2002)

MIKE MILLER WAS in his rookie season as New Jersey's radio play-by-play man, and already he had witnessed a career's worth of memories. During the two-week-long Eastern Conference Finals, he had seen it all. During Game 6 at the Meadowlands, he admittedly allowed himself—as a broadcaster new to the NHL—to dream a bit about how great it would be to call the Stanley Cup Finals in a matter of days. It would be a dream come true. He could already envision Vancouver in the swamps of East Rutherford for Game 1, with all the pomp and circumstance that comes with the championship round. He had good reason to be looking ahead, obviously. The Devils were cruising, they were at home, and all the pieces were in place.

That is, until Mark Messier and the Rangers woke up.

One improbable period of hockey later, the postseason pendulum had swung back toward New York. Suddenly, with what was sure to be a frenzied, packed house at the Garden on a Friday night ready to usher in a conference title on Memorial Day weekend, it was the Devils who had no shot.

"None," Chris Russo said. "That was certainly the attitude in and around New York. The Devils had no chance. With the way the Rangers had won Game 6, everyone thought there was just no way they'd lose Game 7."

But the Devils hadn't reached this point by doubting themselves. Sure, with media coverage spinning out of control, it was easy for people to ride the hot hand and just bank on what they *thought* was going to happen. But New Jersey had other ideas. Jacques Lemaire wasn't about to let his team lose the opportunity of a lifetime. They were still just three periods away from an Eastern Conference crown, and the simple, classic, cliché-like phrase so often heard in sports rang true here: "At the beginning of the season, if you were to tell me that we'd have a chance at the Finals in a Game 7 setting, we would have taken it every time."

And so they did.

"It wasn't a great couple of days for us, but we knew what we had to do," Jim Dowd said. "We still had that mind-set that never once would a negative thought cross our minds. That's how we got to the point we were at. If something bad happens, move on. That sort of became our tradition."

That tradition was put to the test on May 27, 1994, right from the start. In fact, how the Devils could even hear themselves think during John Amirante's rousing rendition of the national anthem was a marvel in itself.

"Madison Square Garden, worthy of its name as the world's greatest and most famous sports arena, just had its roof taken off with the national anthem," Gary Thorne said on the ESPN telecast. "Will they do it again with a Ranger win? Or will the Devils quiet this building before this night is over?"

As Mark Messier prepared for the opening faceoff with Bobby Carpenter, Frank Sinatra's "New York, New York" blared through the loudspeakers: "It's up to you, New York, New York!"

Indeed it was. But wouldn't you know it, Carpenter won the faceoff, and the Devils got right to work.

"They had to come to play," Miller said. "They were out to set a tone. I remember Bill Guerin was such a force early on, and the Devils were getting their chances."

Stephane Richer, injury and all, was able to break in on the right wing early. He wove around the Rangers defense and let off a wrist shot that was saved by Mike Richter for the first Devils shot. Richer wasn't alone. The Devils were aggressive up front, and were hardly intimidated by Messier. In fact, Messier lost his first three faceoffs of the game, twice to Carpenter and once to Dowd.

But the Rangers weren't being dominated by any stretch. They had their legs early on, and there was little evidence of a letdown after the Game 6 comeback. Mike Keenan was determined to hold nothing back. He shuffled his lines, notably moving Glenn Anderson around during the first period as he adjusted to the Devils' push. With derogatory chants of "Marty, Mar-ty" serenading the Devils rookie goaltender four minutes in, the Rangers sustained some pressure in New Jersey's zone and released some rubber his way. They weren't the best chances in the world, but five minutes in, the Rangers had six shots.

Where New York was imposing its will, though, was on the physical side. Six minutes in, the Rangers were outhitting the Devils 7–5, including a surprising shoulder from Brian Leetch to Claude Lemieux that knocked the latter to the ice as he hit the Rangers' zone. Kevin Lowe also shoved Bernie Nicholls into the New Jersey bench, and almost tried to push him over.

It was clear this was not just another game. In fact, if you didn't know the uniforms and the personnel, you'd think the two teams had reversed roles during the opening frame. Here the Rangers were—with grit and grind—playing Devils Hockey, while the Devils—with skill and skating—were playing Rangers Hockey.

"They were playing hard and physical, but I thought they were playing responsible," Miller said of the Rangers. "They were pulling a page from the Devils, kind of waiting for a turnover or an odd-man rush. And they got a few, but Marty was so strong."

"The benefit of winning Game 6 was getting the Devils to play on their heels just a little bit there early on," Leetch said. "That allowed us some breathing room without having to force the play. There were still opportunities both ways, even though both teams were playing close to the vest. But we liked the flow of the game, and we were getting chances. Marty was playing so well for them, though, and we knew it was just going to be another one of those tight games."

The hits continued for the home team, as the crowd was truly seeing a different type of Ranger on the ice. It was almost as if New York wanted to demoralize New Jersey physically, before doing so on the scoreboard. But with 6:05 to go, and the Rangers outhitting the Devils 18–9, the road team began to fight back. Brian Noonan, a Keenan favorite who was back in the lineup replacing Eddie Olczyk, entered the slot in front of Martin Brodeur and was sandwiched by Nicholls and John MacLean just before getting a shot off. With 3:15 to go, Esa Tikkanen was erased along the boards by Bruce Driver. He fell awkwardly and was cut on the forehead just below his helmet line. Tikkanen left to get stitched up and was largely unfazed, but the Devils had made their statement.

"I don't care who you are," Bill Clement said on the ESPN call. "If you're watching this, you have to like it."

The Devils pushed on. Their fourth line, intent on making the most of its regular turn, sustained some play on their last shift of the period in the Rangers' zone and quieted the crowd a bit in the process.

"We knew, with the way the series had already gone, that it was not going to be easy," Stephane Matteau said. "We knew we had the momentum, but we knew the Devils were going to play hard with the Finals on the line."

From his knees behind the net, Mike Peluso passed the puck to Randy McKay directly behind Richter. Peluso then turned and headed for the front of the net to create traffic, as McKay fed Bobby Holik a soft centering pass. Holik fanned on it, but surprisingly had enough time to gather and let a shot go that hit Richter in his chest. Richter covered to gain a whistle, but it was a quality shift nonetheless and a credit to New Jersey.

Scott Niedermayer fed off that momentum on his next turn. Along the boards to Brodeur's right, he lowered his right shoulder into Joey Kocur, who caromed off the boards, fell backward, and coughed up possession of the puck.

"Some people go their whole careers without getting that chance to win it all," Niedermayer said. "But I got it early in my career, and wanted to do everything I could to make the most of it."

It was just another sign of how different the atmosphere in the building was. In a be-all, end-all game, everyone had to be prepared to do a little bit of everything. Enforcers, like McKay and Peluso, needed to create offense, and the skill players, like Niedermayer, needed to be physical.

"Everybody hits," Clement said. "If you don't hit, you don't play in a Game 7."

And unless you can't skate, you're going to play in a Game 7, too. Take Richer, for example. On a bad knee, he took nine shifts and one shot in the first period.

With 1:02 left, Dowd won a faceoff to the left of Brodeur over Alexei Kovalev, and the Devils cleared the zone with some precision. Dowd connected with MacLean at center, and the latter ripped a slap shot from just outside the zone that Richter calmly stopped as the final seconds ticked away on an emotionally even period.

With the Rangers leading in shots 11–10 and hits aplenty on both sides, the teams and fans were able to collect their breath and prepare for the rest of the night. But the Devils had reason to feel confident. They withstood the Rangers' initial onslaught, settled into the flow of the game, and showed everyone expecting them not to show up that they weren't going away anytime soon.

Keenan again juggled his lines to start the second, as Kovalev returned to the top line and replaced Anderson, as he did successfully in Game 6. But it was a different line that got the Rangers going in the second period. In a region of the ice he'd make forever famous later in the game, Matteau shook free of Scott Stevens' stick and centered a pass from behind the net to Tikkanen, who had returned to action with five stitches in his forehead. From the right faceoff dot, Tikkanen fired a one-timer that Brodeur stopped and held from his knees.

"That was the best scoring chance for the Rangers in this game," Clement said, "and it had to happen quickly because there was about a quarter-of-a-second window for Tikkanen to let it go."

As tense as things started to get, spirits were still up on both sides. As Noonan circled in front of Richter during a stoppage, the goaltender politely whacked at Noonan's pants with his stick at 15:30.

"It was an exciting game, but you had to stay calm and play your game," Steve Larmer said. "But it was definitely exciting. Scary…but exciting."

The officials had made it clear by then that they were going to let the teams play, and let the best one win. In fact, 25 minutes in, despite hits all over the ice, there hadn't been a single penalty called.

"There were such great players on both sides," said linesman Kevin Collins, who worked Game 7, "with great play on both sides."

No line personified that more than the Devils' fourth. Back at it six minutes in, McKay shook Leetch behind the net but fell, though the puck glided over to Holik, who was to the right and behind Richter. Holik sent it over to Peluso at the right faceoff dot, and the latter sent it around the boards where it was stopped by Noonan, who sent it back around Richter as the posturing continued. Noonan's clearing attempt was stopped by McKay behind the net, and with the skill of a top liner, McKay pushed a backhand touch pass between his legs to Peluso on Richter's left. Peluso left it for an unguarded Holik in front of Richter for the Devils' best chance of the night. Holik got some good wood on it, but Richter stopped it and kicked it out with his right leg with 14:00 left.

"Great save by Mike Richter! A magnificent save on the setup with Bobby Holik," Clement said. "Robbed of a goal! That was the best save of the last four games."

"That's one of the things that I remember so vividly about Game 7," said the *Post*'s Larry Brooks. "As the minutes ticked away, and with what was all on the line, there Jacques was, continuing to throw out that fourth line. A regular shift no matter what. And they were unbelievable that night."

As was Richter. With play stopped thanks to an icing at 13:37, a fan in the lower bowl held up a simple sign with a brick wall on it. Richter's number—35—was smack dab in the middle of the wall, and it seemed fitting after that save. A 1–0 Devils lead, with little more than half the game left, could have spelled doom and gloom for the home team. Instead, Richter fired up his teammates and the crowd, and within minutes, the whole tenor of the game changed.

"We knew that with it being such a very close, competitive series, that the margin for success was minuscule," Keenan said. "We knew we were up against a very talented a team, a very strong, physical team that was young enough to stick around for a long, long time. And we knew we needed to make the most of our opportunities."

At 10:36 of the second, they began to do just that. Messier won a faceoff from Dowd to Brodeur's right, and Adam Graves slid it to the right point for Leetch. So began one of the better individual plays ever scripted against the Devils' dominant defense. Leetch collected at the point, right in front of the Coca-Cola sign, and skated alongside the boards and in behind the goal line. Guerin sensed Leetch's strategy, and rushed in behind Brodeur to stop or at least impede him. But Leetch stopped on a dime, sprayed Guerin with some ice, orchestrated a 360-degree turn that completely shook Guerin, and offered up a wraparound that eluded both Guerin and Stevens. The puck ultimately crawled in the net through Brodeur's pads as he hugged the right post.

Perhaps Brodeur wasn't expecting it. After all, there were two defensively sound Devils tracking Leetch's every move. Whatever the case, the crowd erupted as the puck crept past the goal line ever so slowly. Brodeur was left to simply stare ahead as Leetch's sixth goal of the playoffs at 9:31 wiped out the second-period momentum that the wave of Devils forwards had mounted. The goal gave the Rangers a 1–0 lead that—considering the way Richter was playing—might have been all New York would need.

"You just don't see those kinds of moves much against a good defensive team," Matteau said. "Leetchy…what a play."

"Great players rising to the occasion," Thorne said. "Brian Leetch, with his first goal of the series."

Hard to believe, but it was true. Leetch, perhaps the Rangers' best all-around player, who had been benched earlier in the series, finally broke through and gave the crowd reason to relax…though just a little. This was New York, after all.

"[The Garden] was rocking," Russo said, "as you might expect."

In fact, not long after the goal, "Rock and Roll, Part II" came on over the loudspeaker—the ultimate hockey momentum song from 1972, complete with Gary Glitter's "Hey!" chorus—and the crowd rose to its feet. After the ensuing faceoff, the derisive "Mar-ty, Mar-ty" chants returned, and once again, there was celebration in the air.

The Rangers responded in kind. With 9:00 to go, New York was leading in shots 7–2 in the second period and 18–12 in the game. It was a critical juncture for New Jersey, especially considering Richter had kept its offense off the board. The Devils were in danger of losing everything they had worked so hard for.

"Richter's pads were so wide...he always had big pads, and he had this funny walk with them as he came off the ice," ESPN's Al Morganti said. "But his walk was always so confident with them, and they were that night. He was spectacular in that series. Nothing was getting through him."

The Rangers played as if that didn't matter and continued to pressure after the goal. An Anderson wrist shot from the right point was stopped. A Graves shot from the point was deflected. A Kovalev shot from the right circle was blocked. The Rangers were dominating, and the Devils needed a change. Eventually, as often seems to happen when teams begin to scramble defensively, a desperate New Jersey team committed a penalty at 12:13. Matteau carried into the zone on the right point, and with some room calmly waited for Messier to shake Lemieux on his way into the zone. It never happened, because Lemieux interfered with Messier just as Matteau's pass landed in front of them.

It was at that point that one of the recurring themes of the series—a Rangers timeout—returned. In Game 6, Keenan was simply trying to stop the bleeding. But in Game 7, he was the one who smelled blood. Already up a goal with a power play in store, Keenan knew he had a chance to bury the Devils once and for all. So, he called time to give his top man-advantage unit a rest. And just as he had in Game 6, he didn't say anything during the timeout. The team didn't need him to.

"One thing about Mike Keenan," Clement said. "He is on top of every crucial moment of a game."

More times than not, these Devils were, too. With the exception of a Noonan wrist shot with 10 seconds left in the power play that was calmly stopped by Brodeur, the Rangers' opportunity came and went with little danger. It was an important kill for New Jersey, and ever so slowly, the team fed off it. With two minutes to go in the frame, the Devils mounted a rush. With three players hovering at the line, Sergei Nemchinov fanned on a clearing attempt that was intercepted by Guerin, with Valeri Zelepukin and Dowd on his wings. As they raced in, Guerin elected to shoot as Zelepukin crashed the net. But again, Richter made the save with 1:46 left, falling backward into the net after the whistle.

Guerin was left to look down at the ice. He shook his head, spit, and looked back at Richter as if to say, "You got me again." Clearly, as mentally strong as these Devils were, it seemed that Richter was in their heads now. And as the public address announcer gave the one-minute warning, there were cheers and whistles, followed by a heartfelt chant that wasn't heard much throughout this series but probably should have been: "Rich-ter. Rich-ter."

"It really did get lost among everything else just how good Richter played in that series," Russo said.

At the end of the second, the Rangers had a 22–16 edge in shots and a 1–0 lead. They were 20 minutes from a date with destiny in the Stanley Cup Finals. The comeback was almost complete. There was a buzz throughout the Garden during that intermission, as fans got up out of their seats to pace, wander, and do whatever it took to take the edge off.

Steve Levy, an ESPN anchor on *SportsCenter* who cut his teeth in the business on WFAN and was raised a Rangers fan, was one of those wanderers. "I had just started at ESPN, and my career was very much in the early stages," he said. "And it was a strange feeling for me, because I wasn't sure how I was supposed to feel. In a work setting, it would have been different. But I was there with friends, and as a fan, it was impossible not to get caught up in the moment."

As the teams took the ice, history began to creep into the equation. Would those aforementioned demons in the basement that Messier and Lowe alluded to surface at some point in the next 20 minutes? After all, the last time the Rangers won a playoff game by the score of 1–0 was on March 28, 1940, the same year they last won a Cup. No pressure.

Brodeur was ready to meet the challenge, though. He made his best save, and kept the Devils in the game, as Nemchinov and Greg Gilbert created a

2-on-1 at center ice early on in the third. Gilbert passed the puck through Niedermayer's legs and over to Nemchinov right in front of the net, but Brodeur slid along his knees and prevented Nemchinov's tap. Incredibly, it was the Rangers' first odd-man rush since Game 4, a true credit to New Jersey's defense.

But time was running out for the Devils, no matter how strong the goaltending on the other side was. With 16:56 left, as Stevens dumped in behind Richter, the "Let's Go Ran-gers" chants got louder and louder as the fans started to sense a victory. With 16:32 left, the Rangers had a 23–15 edge in shots, and the Devils knew they would have to take some chances and perhaps even break their defensive shell.

"The Rangers are now the ones mucking it up at center," Thorne said.

But that move cost them, and the Devils were given a chance. An elbowing call at 6:32 was levied on Kovalev after he decked Stevens. There was a tangle at the Rangers bench, and Kovalev had been just a little too physical. As the hit was levied, every Ranger on the bench immediately looked to referee Bill McCreary to see if his arm was raised.

It was. The Devils would have an all-important power play.

Unfortunately for New Jersey, it was the Rangers who dominated the next two minutes; at times, it appeared as if the Devils were the team that was short-handed. Larmer easily cleared the zone with 1:15 left in the penalty. Tikkanen did the same with 32 seconds left, and Leetch did the same seconds later. Finally, Matteau casually carried to center and calmly dumped into the Devils' zone as the penalty kill ended.

New Jersey didn't appear frustrated, though. Nine minutes in, Guerin mounted another rush that could've tied it. As Tom Chorske carried out of his own zone, Guerin blew through center between Kovalev and Jay Wells. Wells had no shot from the outset, as Guerin took the pass, entered the zone, and was free on Richter. Guerin turned his back and offered up a backhander with some steam that Richter stopped. Then, Guerin ran into Richter on the rebound and knocked the net off its moorings. As Guerin raced into the zone, the entire Devils bench rose to its skates, sensing a tying goal...to no avail.

"He was a beast that night," Brooks said of Guerin, who didn't give up and had two more shots on his next shift. "He was all over the place."

As they both got to their feet, Richter and Guerin had words for each other. For one of the only times in the series, New York's mild-mannered goalie actually seemed a bit rattled. Of course, it didn't show on the scoreboard. With that save on Guerin, Richter hadn't allowed a goal in the last 91:30 of the series.

The Devils maintained their push, though, and continued to pressure Richter. Nothing changed in the way of lines, and with good reason. Lemaire had no reason to change his system now. The chances were there. The aggression was there. The passion was there. Everything was there…except a goal.

"We're down under eight minutes to go," Clement said, "and Jacques Lemaire will not stray from his game plan."

With 5:55 left, there was a faceoff to Richter's left. Nicholls beat Messier on the draw, but Tommy Albelin fanned on a shot from the point, creating a 2-on-1 the other way for Graves and Kovalev. Graves elected to shoot, and fired from the right point. Brodeur made the save with his right leg, and calmly covered. He was still in this game, and was content to get a whistle whenever he could to keep his teammates fresh. Even as the clock wound down, the Devils still played their game and suffocating defense.

"We really made an impact with the way we played defensively," Brodeur said. "That's us. That's who we are."

Brodeur was right—with three minutes left, it appeared abundantly clear that the Rangers were probably not going to get another goal in regulation. If they were going to win it here and now, it was going to be 1–0. With 1:50 to go, a nervous quiet that had built over a few minutes began to give way to cheers, whistles, and screams. The fans began to rock back and forth in their seats, and often looked at each other as if to say, "Is this finally it?"

All the while, the Devils were changing lines fluidly, giving themselves every possible chance to grab a goal. The Rangers were ready for every push. As time ticked down, Driver sent in the puck behind Richter and to his left. Jeff Beukeboom gathered and tried to clear, but MacLean held, only to give way to Leetch, who took it out of harm's way and into the New Jersey zone.

Devils attempt foiled.

With 1:29 left, Richer gained some steam along the benches but was run into by Tikkanen before he could enter the zone.

Devils attempt foiled.

With 1:18 left, Stevens carried to center as the Devils tried to mount a rush, but Beukeboom intercepted and his clearing attempt reached the seats with 1:11 left.

Devils attempt foiled.

All the while, the boat horns from the upper deck were going off, and the crowd's fever pitch was at an all-time high.

But the Devils were unfazed. As amazing as it seemed, this team that had been built to win in the toughest of circumstances would not stay down on the canvas. Dowd won the ensuing faceoff versus Messier near the New Jersey bench and dumped in as Brodeur headed off for the extra man. Messier gained possession, turned, and iced the puck, as Zelepukin touched up on the play.

As the teams skated toward Richter and the faceoff circle to his right, the Garden's organ rendition of "Rock and Roll, Part II" played, and the crowd vigorously yelled "Hey!" right on cue. Tension, torment, passion, pride—it was all out there for everyone to see. This classic series, one that was already being mentioned among the best ever, was in its final minute.

Or so everyone thought.

With 48 seconds left and an empty net on the other end of the rink, Nicholls again beat Messier on a draw. He drifted to the point, where Stevens held. New Jersey's captain then banged it around the boards back to Nicholls, who backhanded it behind the net. Beukeboom, having his best period of the series, was there. He corralled and cleared. Stevens touched the icing with 24 seconds left, as "Shout" began to play during the stoppage. The 1959 classic Isley Brothers song indeed asked the fans to shout, and they responded. You could sense the anxiety, but it didn't stop them from singing along.

Nicholls and Messier went at it again at the dot to Richter's right. Again, capping perhaps his best playoff series ever, Nicholls won it. He pushed it to the point for Driver, but Driver sensed Nicholls' momentum and got it right back to him. Nicholls, at the top of the right circle, let go of a wrist shot that was stopped by Richter and was held after a quick whistle by McCreary. Richter had tried to play the puck off to his left when the whistle was blown, a play that would have burned a few more precious seconds off the clock. Richter was not happy about the call, but did not say anything at the time to McCreary. After all, Richter needed to remain focused; at this point, he had not allowed a goal in the last 1:02:11 and was mere seconds away from being the first goalie ever to have five shutouts in a postseason.

"I still thought it was a quick whistle," he said later.

With 18.6 seconds left, Messier finally won a draw from Nicholls, as the "De-fense" chants went up at the Garden, as though it was a Knicks game. After Messier took this draw, the puck caromed behind Richter for Beukeboom. But his clearing attempt around the boards was stopped by Driver, who gave to Richer. With a bullet of a centering pass to the crease with 11.2 seconds left, Richer set the stage for the most fitting, frantic regulation finish to The NHL's Greatest Series Ever that anyone could have dreamt up.

"Time stood still," said Joe Benigno.

On his knees, Richter frantically reached to cover the puck as Zelepukin took a whack at it to keep it loose. With 8.4 seconds left, the puck magically appeared back on Zelepukin's stick, and he shoved it past Richter's left skate and past the goal line, as Lemieux jumped straight up in the air behind Richter in a classic photo pose frozen in time. McCreary, from his position behind the net, pointed to the puck in the net; his outstretched arm was like a dagger into the hearts of Rangers fans everywhere.

It was a goal.

Suddenly, it was a 1–1 game with just…

"Seven point seven seconds left. Unreal."

"Yep, 7.7. Never forget it."

"Oh yes, 7.7 seconds left. Will never forget those numbers."

"See what I mean? Cursed. 7.7 seconds."

Those were the words of Neil Smith, Steve Levy, Mike Miller, and Howie Rose, respectively, who all had different reactions to one of the most clutch goals in NHL history. As they so eloquently stated, with 7.7 seconds left, Zelepukin got around Leetch and buried his second chance at glory, stunning the Garden faithful and setting off a turn of events that could only fit this series and none other.

Richter, the model of calm and confidence, simply lost his cool after the goal was scored. Believing he was the victim of a quick whistle just before that faceoff, he surely wanted a whistle when he thought he had frozen Zelepukin's first attempt. Richter pushed himself to his feet in frustration as the Devils celebrated in front of him and raced toward McCreary behind the net. His momentum actually carried him into the referee, giving him a push up against the boards.

"Richter came right out and bodied McCreary against the glass. There was no mistake about it," said hockey historian Stan Fischler. "It either should have been a 2:00 penalty or a misconduct. In the end, it was nothing. He escaped with nothing. It was a terrific break that the Rangers got."

McCreary knew it, too. In a story that Richter later confirmed, McCreary, with 7.7 seconds left and the ensuing faceoff at center ice, told Richter quite simply, "You owe me one."

"It's all irrelevant now," Fischler said. "But it should have been called. It's all an aspect to the business, and you live with it. Things fell right for the Rangers there, no question, and that was it."

The frustration, though, boiled over to the stands, as one might expect. As passionate as the Rangers fans are, sometimes that works against them, and it did here.

"There were so many people broadcasting the game, we had to broadcast from the auxiliary press box," Miller said. "And that was right in the stands, with the fans right there. We were in a plywood box, and the Devils team broadcasters did that game from the seats. We will never forget that, trust me. So, I call Zele's goal with 7.7 seconds left, and the looks, and the deafening silence from the crowd, was unreal. But it was such a big goal, I had to be loud. Well, that didn't go over well, as there was debris thrown at me from the fans. It was a sad scene. But can you remember a bigger moment in Devils history, at that time, than the Zelepukin goal? It was so big. It kept them alive. I had to call it the way I saw it."

After the goal, a surprised, jubilant Zelepukin fell on top of Leetch, but got right back up and was mobbed by his teammates.

"I remember being in front of the net with Claude. We had been locked up together so many times that season, and we knew what each other were going to do. We always had confrontations and battles, and usually he'd try to knock me from my spot with a little cross-check, so I was aware of that, and tried to prepare for that," Leetch said. "So, I angled myself in a spot where— it's just unbelievable—the puck went through both of us. I tried to whack at it, and then I could not believe there was someone on my back side. I was so worried about Lemieux, and there was Zelepukin. Unbelievable. I just looked up in disbelief at myself. I couldn't believe that happened, that I missed that puck with 7.7 seconds left."

Richter concurred.

"For me, what I was thinking, just prior to that, I had made a save and tried to move the puck, and tried to move it quickly, and so I was disappointed because I thought the whistle was too fast," he said. "It created a faceoff in our zone at a critical time, and I wasn't happy about that. When [McCreary] made that quick whistle, I thought he might do it again. On that play, eventually the puck comes to the net, and Zelepukin gets in one clear shot, and I stopped it just under the pad. But there was no whistle! And then came a couple more whacks at it, and eventually it went in. Realistically, more than anything, we were in shock that it went in with that much time left. That moment is unforgettable, and it was incredibly deflating."

Obviously, that scene was played out in several circles.

"When he scored with 7.7 seconds left, I said, 'There's no way they're winning this game,'" Benigno said. "This was Rangers Hockey for you. It couldn't be worse than this, to blow this series in the worst possible way."

Meanwhile, the Devils bench was alive in a way no one had seen since the first period of Game 6.

"We had the momentum," Lemieux said. "We had to carry it into the locker room and back out for overtime."

Before that, of course, there was an anticlimactic faceoff at center ice. As the final seconds ticked away, the fans could do little but look at one another, searching for answers. On the ESPN telecast, a fan could be heard, clear as day, ask, "Do you believe it?" That, of course, was Thorne's line from the game before, when Messier completed his hat trick in New Jersey.

The answer on this night, for many, was no.

"Can you believe this?" Clement asked with a laugh on the air. "Honestly, there have been more momentum swings, more changes of pace in this series than I have ever seen. And I thought, perhaps, we were done with them."

At that point, that same fan in the background said, "Now, it's anyone's game."

Indeed, regulation had ended. The Rangers had a 27–24 lead in shots, but the score was tied at 1–1.

Destiny was derailed, and the Devils were alive ... for the time being.

"And the chants of '19-40,'" Thorne said, "are not dead yet."

(13)

Matteau! Matteau! Matteau!

○ ○ ○ ○

"When you're talking about the Rangers, the feeling was always there that they were cursed. We all know that. But I never, ever, ever said that on the air. Just never could. But in Game 7, here comes [Valeri] Zelepukin, he scores, they play out the final 7.7 seconds, and I finally look at [Rangers analyst] Sal Messina, after I throw it to a break. And I look at him right in the eye and say, 'Now, tell me this fucking team isn't cursed.' It was just the fan in me coming out. And for the first time, Sal let on that he might agree. Cursed."
—HOWIE ROSE, NEW YORK RANGERS PLAY-BY-PLAY VOICE (1985–1995)

STEVE LEVY WAS with friends for Game 7, and like so many New Yorkers in and around the Garden on that festive Friday night, he was prepared for a party. Indeed, Levy had that "dream" job at ESPN, and he was an up-and-coming sports broadcaster. But on this night, in the World's Most Famous Arena, he was a fan above all else, in the seats, living and dying with every shift.

After Valeri Zelepukin's game-tying goal, there was obviously more of the latter than the former.

"People were just walking around aimlessly, looking at each other," Levy said. "There weren't many words, not much could be said, other than 'This is unbelievable.' But mostly, it was just blank stares, and the overriding thought that, *It's just never going to happen for this team. Ever.*"

The hallways—solemn, somber corridors that housed some 18,000 tortured souls dressed in red, white, and blue—slowly started to clear out as the 15-minute intermission that no one saw coming began to wind down. The Zamboni finished cleaning the ice, and as the players walked out of the dressing room—the road team with a little more pep in its step than the home team, of course—there was still an eerie feeling in the building.

"In the locker room, too," Stephane Matteau said. "It was quiet for the most part. Some players were nervous, more nervous than I had seen them before."

Down the hall, it was a different story.

"You tie it up, the momentum was back on our side, we're back in it, and the emotions just changed in an instant. We could all feel it," Tom Chorske said. "Those are electrifying moments, and you start to feel it and act on it. You say to yourself, 'Hey, we can win this game. Let's go do it.'"

The mood eventually turned in the New York room, though, thanks to Kevin Lowe. Still very much a new Ranger, Lowe sensed the urgency to say something…fast.

"In the locker room, yes, some guys were quiet, in shock, some were upset," Mike Richter said. "And, all of a sudden, Kevin Lowe stands up and says, 'If it wasn't so hard, it wouldn't be so much fun to win.' And I have to tell you, why are we talking about that series now? Because it was so hard, and so well played on both sides. And Kevin, in his own vacuum right there, set us straight. We regrouped and went out."

Both teams took a cautious approach to the first few minutes. There was a lot of dump and chase, and a lot of quick, steady line changes. Ever so slowly, the fans began to find their voices, and a few minutes in, the "Let's Go Rangers" chants returned. And they had reason to sing—by the time five sudden-death minutes had been played, the Rangers had become the aggressors, with and without the puck.

Six minutes in, Alexei Kovalev even got away with a high stick on Bruce Driver, as the two tangled behind Martin Brodeur. Eventually, Kovalev's shoulder was wedged between the boards and Driver, and the Rangers sharpshooter fell to the ice as if he'd been shot. He left the shift favoring his shoulder and was immediately tended to.

"At that point, though, it was players playing," said Kevin Collins, the linesman who admittedly was also skating on adrenaline at this point. "With what was on the line, it was going to take a lot to get a call at that point."

The players knew that, of course, so at times they pushed forward and felt free to take a few liberties. At other times, they pulled back and played cautiously. Either way, though, things remained physical. In fact, 12 minutes in, the inspired, suddenly talkative Lowe skated back behind Richter to touch up for an icing, and there was a noticeable cut bleeding profusely from his left eye.

"That group was incredibly tough," Lowe said of the Rangers, "and inspiring and full of character. Everyone battled on that team, on or off the ice."

With 6:55 left, the Devils, easily the more cautious of the two teams, had their best chance as Scott Stevens gave the puck to Stephane Richer at the blue line. With four Rangers still in the Devils' zone, Richer was able to weave a pass through the neutral zone and onto the stick of Randy McKay.

"Every time, it seemed, that you'd look up, that fourth line was doing something," said the *Post*'s Larry Brooks.

And thanks to a perfect pass from Richer, McKay and Bobby Holik broke into the zone on a 2-on-1 against Jeff Beukeboom as the fans slid to the fronts of their seats. Beukeboom chose to defend the puck carrier, McKay, and the Rangers defenseman was able to body him to the left circle. But McKay was able to feather a pass in time to Holik in front. Holik, though, was only able to let off a one-handed backhand tip that popped up in the air. It was caught by Richter, who covered and held for a whistle. A lot of work and a lot of precision had ended in a harmless tip, but that's overtime hockey. From the Devils' perspective, it was a good scoring chance in a period that didn't feature many of them. With 6:45 left, the Rangers led in shots 8–3, and Kovalev had returned, healthy and ready to go.

"Into the overtime, all the Devils seemed to be doing was throwing it to center. And then, the Rangers would take it back up the ice," Stan Fischler said. "It amazed me. The Devils were sitting back! The law of averages was bound to catch up to them, it seemed."

Lowe's rough period continued as he chased a puck that had been swept in behind Richter. An aggressive Bill Guerin lined Lowe up and stunned him with a cross-check. After landing shoulder-first on the ice, face down, the whistle was blown, and Richter rushed to his aid. Lowe returned to his feet eventually, but it was clear that his 186th playoff game was shaping up to be one of his toughest.

The Rangers, perhaps a bit inspired by the hit on Lowe, came to life with five minutes left. Sergei Nemchinov carried out of the zone and hit a streaking Brian Noonan on the right boards as Tommy Albelin scrambled to cover. Noonan had too much speed for Albelin to catch up, and the forward used the surprising space to let off a slap shot from the right circle that would have sailed wide of the net. But this was overtime, and strange bounces have been known to happen. So, even though the puck wasn't going in the net, Brodeur played it safe and calmly snared it with his glove and held for a faceoff.

But the Rangers kept coming. With 4:40 left, Mark Messier won the ensuing faceoff and got the puck to Brian Leetch, but his slap shot sailed wide, as well. The Devils failed to clear, and Kovalev was able to get off a spinning wrist shot from the right circle that Brodeur again calmly stopped at 4:17.

"You better get to the fridge, and get a couple more beers, folks," Bill Clement said on the telecast. "Because this looks like it's going to take a while."

The save didn't faze Noonan, who easily was one of New York's better players in the extra session. As the last minute of play was announced to the anxious crowd, Noonan was able to catch a deflection that started with Albelin's clearing attempt, but was angled off in midair by Craig MacTavish's stick.

In an athletic sweeping motion fit for some of the game's more skilled players, Noonan, right in front of Brodeur, caught the puck, laid it flat on the ice, and let go of a wrist shot that Brodeur had to slide for and stack the pads to stop. It was the home team's best chance of the period, and even though the stakes seemed to be rising with each minute, Brodeur seemed to be gaining in confidence.

"The Devils definitely had great goaltending, and they had several ways to beat you," Richter said. "So, we needed to keep improving with each shift, and be ready for anything. The important thing was to not get frustrated."

Sergei Zubov did just that, though, in the final minute. As he and Bobby Carpenter got tangled behind Richter, Zubov slingshotted New Jersey's veteran center into the boards with a swift swing of his stick. Carpenter was prone on his knees, with his head down, for three minutes. He eventually had the strength to get up and headed for the bench with 39.4 seconds left. No penalty was called. Indeed, the home crowd actually booed Carpenter, as if he might be faking an injury to get a penalty called on Zubov. Either way, the teams played on.

The Devils, thoroughly outplayed, fired the last salvo, as Stevens' blast was stopped by Richter with 4.6 seconds remaining. New York had dominated the frame, outshooting New Jersey 15–7, for a 43–31 overall lead. The Rangers fans could cling to that, if nothing else. But with a composed Brodeur and after the faith inspired by the Zelepukin goal, the Devils were still hanging tough and making life miserable for the Blueshirts' faithful.

"It was the great goaltending at that time, in that period back then, that really, really stabilized us," Ken Daneyko said. "We always had Marty."

But the Rangers were not intimidated or discouraged. Back in the locker room, they were satisfied with their attack time, their shot total, and the way they had controlled the play. They were still one puck past Richter away from elimination, but from a pure hockey standpoint, they had reason to feel confident.

As the third double-overtime period in the series began, Messier won the opening draw against a weakened Carpenter as the "Let's Go Ran-gers" chants returned, despite the anxiety enveloping the ice. But again, there was a distinct feeling-out process early on, and both teams seemed content to fire shots from anywhere, whether they were quality chances or not.

Messier, relatively quiet most of this night, got into the act three minutes in. Leetch was able to hold the zone, and shuttled the puck over to Kovalev at the left circle. Kovalev shot a riser toward Brodeur as traffic gathered in front of the rookie. The puck sneaked through and Brodeur was just able to get his left skate on it, with Messier at the left post. The rebound shot back to Messier, but Brodeur stopped him and the Devils cleared the zone with 16:36 left. The Rangers had two point-blank shots, two seconds apart. But again, Brodeur kept the game alive.

"To be in that building that night," Mike Francesa said, "with the ups and the downs, and the emotions, it was truly amazing."

Even more amazing was how the Rangers refused to get frustrated. They kept pushing forward. They kept attacking. After Richter made a stop on Richer that was made difficult by traffic created by Bernie Nicholls, Noonan, playing his best hockey of the series, carried out to center, gave it to Glenn Anderson, and the two broke in 2-on-1 against Viacheslav Fetisov. Anderson kept it and fired from the circle. It was saved by Brodeur, but the puck drifted behind the net. Eventually, it landed in the left corner, where John MacLean scooped it and lofted it out toward center. Desperate to clear the zone, MacLean's punt didn't work. The fly ball was caught like a center fielder in the neutral zone by Beukeboom. He settled the puck on the ice, and the Rangers got themselves a line change that would end in history.

"The law of averages," Fischler said. "It was just a matter of time."

As Rangers players swapped spots to complete their change, Beukeboom blasted it in from the left point. Brodeur watched it fly off the back boards, the Devils completed a change of their own, and there were now fresh forwards on both sides. Fetisov gathered in behind Brodeur and tried to shuttle it out of the zone, but his clearing attempt was not demonstrative, and it bounced off Esa Tikkanen's skate and off to the left back boards again. Again, the Devils were left scrambling to get back in position; New Jersey was a mess in its own zone, exactly what they were famous for *not* being. Soon, they'd pay for it with their playoff lives.

Looking back, Fetisov probably should have left no doubt and lofted the puck safely out of the zone through the air, à la MacLean, and away from any and all deflections. As it was, the puck found Tikkanen's toe and would stay in the Devils' zone. Matteau, with plenty of jump, had more speed than Scott Niedermayer, and easily won the race for the puck. He gathered, swept in behind Brodeur, used Fetisov as a screen, and let go of a wraparound that seemed like nothing more than a centering pass for Tikkanen.

Turns out, it was anything but:

> Fetisov, for the Devils, plays it cross-ice, into the far corner. Matteau swoops in to intercept. Matteau behind the net, swings it in front. He scores! MATTEAU! MATTEAU! MATTEAU! Stephane Matteau! And the Rangers have one more hill to climb, baby! But it's Mount Vancouver! The Rangers are headed to the Finals!

Those are the immortal words of Howie Rose, and they were a fitting end for The NHL's Greatest Series Ever.

Rangers 2, Devils 1.

Series over.

Cue the crowd.

At 4:24 of the second overtime, Matteau, a selfless, grinding, do-everything-ever-asked-of-him forward who Mike Keenan just *had* to have on the 1994 Rangers, ended this seven-game epic with his third goal of the series. With Tikkanen parked in front waiting for the pass and Dowd right in his back pocket, Matteau's attempt touched Brodeur at the left post and caromed into the net ever so slowly. After a magnificent effort all night long, Brodeur let one in that he should have stopped.

"I got lucky, and you need that," Matteau said. "I learned in hockey a long time ago, if you don't have a play, put it at the goalie's pads or at his feet. So, I did. I tried a spinaround, and I got hooked a little by Niedermayer. And Marty took a half second to move from right to left. I just wanted to put it out front, and I lost control of it a little bit, and it went from there. But I just wanted to get it to Tikkanen, really. I think I was the first to see it go in. It was going so very slowly."

There was a delayed reaction throughout the Garden because the shot was indeed so slow.

"When you're 180 feet away, you don't know what happens until you hear the crowd. You try to keep yourself in the game. And it was fun to watch, trust me, even from that far away. But I didn't know at first," Richter said. "I saw [Matteau] go behind the net, and I'll never forget this. He spins around, lets off the shot, and it goes across the line. But there was this hesitation, at least from my end, that 'Hey, I thought that just went in. But I don't know.' I couldn't hear anything. Nothing. It was surreal. You don't let yourself think it's over, but it's almost like, 'Is it really in?' And then you hear the crowd, and then it's like, okay, now we can go crazy."

Leetch shared in the confusion.

"I was on the line change and was coming down the left side. I remember seeing him go around the net, but I never saw the shot go in, that's for sure. No chance at that. It was too slow," he said. "I looked over at Esa who was at the front of the net, and I saw him jump up. But he was a goofy guy, too, and you just never knew with him what he was doing, so I didn't trust that. But then, finally, to hear the roar of the crowd, you knew it. But just to show you how slow I was to it all, I believe I was the sixth guy to jump into the celebration."

To be honest, the crowd reacted to Matteau's reaction—a memorable, photogenic, jubilant run on skates that ended in the faceoff dot to the left of Brodeur as the Rangers flew over the boards to greet him—and not the actual shot itself.

"For a second there, I couldn't hear a thing," said Dowd, who was in the crease just inches away from the puck. "I saw it go in, and I was numb. It was a line change, and I came up to the breakout. I focused in on Tikkanen and took him to the back post. Matteau turned toward the net, got some space, and it was a simple wraparound, and that's sometimes how games are won in overtime. Doesn't always have to be pretty.

"To be out there on the ice? Well, for me, everything fell silent. I didn't hear the fans cheering, if you can believe it. Like I said, after that series, after all those games, and all those emotions, I was just numb. That's all I can say."

The emotions played out in the Devils' body language as the celebration continued in their zone. Brodeur fell onto his backside and crept inside the net, as if he was afraid to come out. He reached back to grab the puck and push it back out of the net with his glove... and he missed it again.

"We knew we could have beaten them," Claude Lemieux said. "We just didn't."

Fetisov, meanwhile, who wiped out on the play, remained prone, looking at the net. Niedermayer did the same. Eventually, Brodeur made his way out, and by this time, the rest of the Devils had joined him in the crease. The first one to try and lift his spirits was McKay, who tapped him on the pads, as any veteran teammate would do. But it was going to be tough to get over this one, even for this unflappable rookie. After making save after save in the overtime sessions, he allowed a softy that would forever immortalize Matteau and gave the rival Rangers their chance to break The Curse.

"It was a shame that it had to end on a fluky, bad goal," Daneyko said. "But that's hockey."

Chris Russo concurred.

"It was a fluky goal, and you hated to see that for that series, as great as it was. You hated to see it end that way," he said. "But that often happens in hockey series. It's not often the clean, pretty goal that wins games. Especially for a goaltender as great as Martin Brodeur. Even at such a young age, you knew he was going to be great, and you just knew it was a save he probably should have made."

The crowd didn't care. By the time it had sunk in that the puck crossed the line, the fans erupted to a level not heard in the Garden in a long, long time. They hugged one another. They looked up to the rafters. They cried. Some of them even had to sit back down, catch their breath, and check their heart rate. The same scene played out on the ice, as Rangers players and coaches let out two weeks' and 27 periods' worth of emotion.

Eventually, the two teams lined up for the traditional handshake line with the crowd still roaring its approval. As the procession began, Brodeur finally raised up his mask and let the cameras see a face full of emotion. The rookie had made 46 saves on a night where his team just couldn't muster enough offense.

Among the notable handshakes was the one between Lemieux and Richter, two players who made their living in front of the Rangers' net in this series. They shared a moment, as Richter tapped Lemieux on the top of the helmet and the pesky forward congratulated the goaltender.

Brodeur and Matteau paused at their shake as well, two French Canadians who would experience many highs and lows in their long careers. Matteau pulled him tight, and tapped Brodeur on the shoulder. Matteau finished his shakes and let loose the same triumphant yell he did a few days ago when he last won a game in double overtime. He held both hands in the air and simply yelled, "Woooooooooooooooooo!"

By this time, New York's healthy scratches had reached the benches, dressed in suits, and congratulated their teammates in uniform. Nick Kypreos rushed to hug Doug Lidster, and Lidster picked him up off the ground. Matteau did the same with an ecstatic Eddie Olczyk.

As the Prince of Wales Trophy was placed at center ice, Keenan and assistant coach Colin Campbell shared a moment. A hug, one that rocked back and forth for 15 seconds, further illustrated just what had been accomplished. It was not an easy series on the New York coaching staff, clearly, but it ended the way the men had hoped.

Moments later, NHL senior vice president Steve Solomon handed the trophy to Messier. The Rangers captain took it with pride and held it up as the team gathered around him.

"You don't skate around with that one," Gary Thorne said on ESPN. "You hold it up."

Of course, he was right. This wasn't the time to skate around the Garden with a trophy. This trophy only gave them the chance to play for the one that really mattered—the Stanley Cup—and the intelligent, hockey-crazed crowd knew it. In fact, as the trophy was held up, the chant throughout the arena was simple. This trophy was great and all, but "We want the Cup."

Keenan couldn't help but laugh and clap from the bench. General manager Neil Smith, high up in the rafters, finished a swig of Diet Coke, looked down in approval, and turned to walk away, knowing four more wins were needed to complete his mission.

"Well, by a mile, this was the most dramatic series I have ever been involved with," Clement said on the telecast. "And it ended in double overtime on a goal by... Stephane Matteau."

Indeed, it was hard to believe. A player who wasn't in training camp with the Rangers, who two months earlier most New Yorkers didn't even know existed, had scored perhaps the greatest goal in the history of a great franchise. Instantly, Matteau became a celebrity. In fact, not long after the game, he went out with some teammates to an establishment not far from the Garden and received the full rock star treatment. No waiting in line, just walk right in, a king in his castle. The funny part is, earlier in the season, while he was still with the Blackhawks, he went to the same establishment…and couldn't even get in the door.

On May 27, 1994, though, the tables had turned. In fact, one security guard even said to him, "You can do anything you like tonight! You can burn the place down if you want to!"

There is one famous story about Matteau from that evening, however, that does not check out. Matteau, as urban hockey legend tells it, tapped the Prince of Wales Trophy with the blade of his stick before the start of overtime. Of course, touching any trophy in hockey before it is won is a bad omen. It's just something players don't do. When looking back on the biggest night of his career, Matteau was blunt and convincing when debunking a myth that has made the rounds for years. Rest easy, Rangers fans.

"Never happened," he said. "Don't know where that came from, don't know who started it. But it never happened. I never would have even thought to do something like that. There was a game to play."

Lost in the chaos and euphoria of the moment was the man the pass was intended for. Conceivably, it could have been Tikkanen who put the puck in, not Matteau. The pass was headed his way before it ended up in the net.

"I'll be honest, I didn't know Matteau scored it. I couldn't tell," said Al Morganti, who had a rinkside position between the benches for ESPN, but did not have a raised view of the game-winner. "That's why I give Howie the most credit in the world for knowing exactly who it was and when it was. Afterward, when you see Matteau jumping up and down, you can tell, sure. But in the moment, it was such a mangled mess. That's one of the reasons it has to be one of the greatest calls ever. And for him to yell, 'Matteau! Matteau! Matteau!' at that point. He had to be scared to death it was wrong!"

Truth be told, he was.

"The reality is, yes, I thought I had blown it the first time I heard it. Because I had never gotten that out of control before on the air. Never," Rose said. "And when the postgame show aired, here comes Sal [Messina], and he gets in my head. The postgame show airs, and I hear the call, and I say 'Oh, my God. This is so over the top. It's just not me.' And then, while Sal is analyzing the replay, he sees Esa Tikkanen crashing the net, which we really didn't see from our vantage point. The one thing about that broadcast location we had back in those days, all the way downstairs at Madison Square Garden, was that it was perfect for following a play like Matteau's goal. Up and back at the Garden, like it is now? You can't always tell. But back then, the powers of concentration are so acute at that point that my eyes were glued to the puck on Matteau's stick. So, I didn't think it was anyone but Matteau.

"But then you look at the replay, and see where Tikkanen crashes the net, and you say, 'Wow, it could have been Esa! It really could!' So, anyway, Sal says on the air, during the replay, 'Hey, Howie, I don't know, that could be Esa Tikkanen's goal.' And I'm saying 'Oh, shit.' I can just see myself now, having to run into a studio and dub, 'Tikkanen! Tikkanen! Tikkanen!' At that point, I really thought I had blown it. Turns out, I didn't...luckily."

As a result, in many ways, Rose became as famous as Matteau did. Today, they are linked forever. Rose admits he sends a text message to Matteau every May 27. You can guess what it might read: "Matteau! Matteau! Matteau!"

"I've got to be honest with you, it might be the greatest call I've ever heard in sports. Because as an aspiring play-by-play guy, it had all of the elements," ESPN-AM 1050's Don LaGreca said. "The thing that strikes me is, it's not a foregone conclusion that Matteau scores the goal. Some people thought it was Tikkanen, some people weren't sure, and if you listen to other calls—the national call, the TV calls—nobody was more on top of it than Howie. And he put emotion into it, and he got into it, and it might go down as one of the greatest calls in the history of sports...even though it pains me."

Steve Somers worked the overnight shift on WFAN that night, and almost immediately put that call in his files. He played it several times through the night.

"Certainly, in terms of excitement and drama, it's right up there," Somers said of Rose's call. "The emotion you heard from Howie, it was his greatest. He loves the Mets and the Rangers, even though he does the Islanders now, he's so into hockey and baseball. What came from Howie on that night was his heart, his soul, his passion."

Kenny Albert, who now works NFL and Major League Baseball games for FOX, in addition to being the Rangers' radio voice, grew up a Rangers fan, like so many other broadcasters and journalists with New York ties. As such, Matteau and Rose will always have a special place in his heart.

"With Howie, part of his legacy will always be the Matteau call. And what a call," he said. "It's just one of those moments that you can't explain. We'll talk about it forever."

They certainly talked about it through the night on the streets of Manhattan. And that didn't register with Rose until he left the booth.

"As I left the building, as happy as I was that they had won, I was a little nervous as to how the call was going to be accepted. So, I leave the Garden, and there's a guy in his car, sitting on 33rd Street, and he yells out, 'Howie, great call. Great call.' And I just think he's being nice because he saw me, and he's glad they won, and the whole bit. But then I get into my car, and I'm listening to the FAN on the way home, and they're replaying the call every five minutes. Every five minutes! And literally, people are talking about the call as much as they were the game and the series. It was Steve Somers, and I will never forget it.

"The next day, it was Russ Salzberg on the FAN, and he's taking calls, and that's all that everyone was talking about. And as I was driving to Shea the next morning—the Mets had a day game and I had the call—as I was listening to the callers, I finally thought to myself, *Maybe that call wasn't so bad after all.* It's just incredible to me how it has endured for so many years. It's just very, very flattering."

The Devils, and Brodeur especially, would be linked to that call, like it or not, for years. At the time, and perhaps even to this day, they could care less. In the Devils locker room at the Garden that night, it was a scene as somber as you'll ever see in sports.

Tears.

Shock.

Silence.

"They were all so crushed. It was a locker room scene that I will never forget. Ever," Russo said. "I just remember walking up to Ken Daneyko, a true Devil who had been through everything with the franchise. One of the tougher things I've had to do in this business. Very hard. It was pretty somber."

Daneyko concurred.

"It was devastating for us, no question. We gave our blood, sweat, and tears," he said. "To be that close—and I think you truly have to experience that in any sport to really know—and not come away with the prize, it was devastating. The agony of defeat, and all the sports clichés come out at a time like that, but they were true in this instance."

Inspired and motivated by it as they might be in future years, the Devils knew it was going to take a long time to get over it. To lose to their biggest rival, to have a 3–2 series lead and a 2–0 lead in Game 6, and to tie it in Game 7 with 7.7 seconds left, only to see it wash away, the pain was unimaginable.

"I was living day by day at that point, for sure. I was not looking ahead too much. It was tough to think about what it might do to us down the road. It was too fresh," Brodeur said. "When you get so close to winning, you have the feeling, and you go through adversities. Sometimes, you get the better of those, and sometimes, you go in the other direction. Along the way, you learn a lot about yourself and your teammates. We knew we were a team then, win or lose as a team, and it was just a matter of how we bounced back from it."

For Matteau and the Rangers, though, there was another series to be played. It was so important to file this one away—as hard as it might be—and prepare for the Vancouver Canucks, a spunky bunch who had already defeated some big names—Calgary, Dallas, and Toronto—to get to the Finals.

"That's all I thought about, honestly," Matteau said. "People ask that all the time. 'What went through your head as you scored?' Things like that. And honestly, I wasn't thinking about The Curse, and I wasn't thinking about the Devils, or anything other than the fact that we had a chance to go the Finals now. That was it."

That was the right attitude, certainly, and you knew if Matteau's teammates didn't share it, Keenan would change that in a hurry.

"We knew we could feed off what we had done, but we knew we had work ahead," Keenan said. "But that series itself, and in itself, was one of the best series ever in the National Hockey League."

And it ended with one of the greatest games ever. Even neutral participants agreed.

"My feelings are, it's the greatest hockey game that I was ever involved with," said Kevin Collins, now retired from officiating. "I worked 12 Stanley Cup Finals, and nothing came close. It was just the greatest hockey game… ever. So much going on, up and down, and it just had it all. And overall, it was the greatest hockey experience, because of the pressure, because of what was at stake, and because of the media, because it was New York. I will never forget it.

"The magnitude of the game, in Madison Square Garden, to see that level of hockey…just unbelievable. It was just…the greatest."

(14)

The Next Month

○ ○ ○ ○

"To be around it, to feel the buzz. That's the best part of playoff hockey in New York. And everything was focused on hockey, on the ice and off, and people were so wrapped up in it. The good thing, for us, is we were able to focus, and it's that time when you rely on your teammates, you spend so much time with them, and you avoid distractions. And we had to do that because Vancouver was very, very good. And we knew we had our hands full."

—ADAM GRAVES, NEW YORK RANGERS (1991–2001)

THE LEAGUE GAVE the ecstatic, emotional Rangers a bit of a reprieve after The NHL's Greatest Series Ever. Though they probably could have used a full week off after playing what amounted to nine games' worth of hockey against the Devils, at least they were given three full days to regroup, rebound, recuperate, and ready themselves for a flash-and-dash Vancouver team that had already far outlived its No. 7 seed in the Western Conference.

"Pavel Bure was incredible in that playoff year," Barry Melrose said. "Lot of people had the Rangers running right through that team. Bure and the Canucks were going to be ready."

Bure was a 23-year-old Russian right wing who turned the West on its ear in 1994. In the regular season, he had 60 goals, 107 points, and took 374 shots. He was the driving force behind a team that had only three other 20-goal scorers—Trevor Linden, Geoff Courtnall, and Cliff Ronning— and he carried the Canucks on his back in the postseason, as they shook a mediocre 41–40–3 regular season and turned on the jets when it counted.

One by one, teams with better records and more depth fell before them as the Canucks kicked it into high gear. An emotional seven-game series against the rival Calgary Flames in the first round gave way to two thorough series victories in the next two rounds. In the West semifinals, they blasted the Dallas Stars 4–1. In the conference finals, while the Rangers swam through quicksand to eliminate the Devils, the Canucks cruised past the Toronto Maple Leafs, also in five games.

In other words, the Rangers needed to put the Devils series behind them, or else it'd be all for naught.

"As a general manager, I was not a participant, but I felt good about the series," Neil Smith said. "Vancouver was good, and they were playing well, and we knew nothing was going to be easy. But Vancouver was not Detroit, and after everything we had just been through, I'll admit I felt that it was a good team for us to play."

Of course, if the last series proved nothing else, it was that the Rangers, when they wanted to be the best team on the ice, could do it…under any circumstance.

"We knew what was in front of us. But we knew, in the end, it was about us. It was just 23 guys, 24 guys coming together to do something that hadn't happened in 54 years," Nick Kypreos said. "It was a good bunch of guys, real character guys that knew how to come together and battle some adversity and do something that hadn't been done in a long, long time."

But, just like in the New Jersey series, things started ominously at the Garden on May 31. And those demons downstairs, right off the bat, reared their heads.

"No Cup run," Mark Messier said, "none of them, are ever easy."

If the Devils didn't prove that, the Canucks sure did. In front of another frenzied Garden crowd, Vancouver rallied from a 2–1 deficit in Game 1. Martin Gelinas beat Mike Richter in the third period to tie it, and then Greg Adams—a former New Jersey Devil, of all things—scored 19:26 into the first overtime to end it. The Canucks skated off with a 3–2 win, took a 1–0 series lead, and immediately planted those doubts back in the heads of the Rangers and their faithful. Vancouver, in less than four periods of hockey, had already scored three times on Richter; remember, he only gave up one goal to New Jersey in the final seven periods of that series.

"Here we go again," said WFAN's Joe Benigno.

But it wasn't time to jump ship. After all, it was understandable that any team coming off a series anything like the one the Rangers had just endured was going to be a little slow on the draw in Game 1 of the next series. And they did manage 54 shots on net—one for every year of The Curse—including 17 in overtime. It's not as though New York played poorly; perhaps Vancouver goaltender Kirk McLean was just tired of hearing about this Richter character. So, he went out and made 52 saves, stole Game 1, and let all of New York know that this 1940 thing wasn't over just yet.

The Rangers indeed bounced back, just as they had in the Devils series, with a Game 2 victory. The way was led by some unlikely faces, and that was a very good sign moving forward. Mike Keenan knew that if he was going to get goals from players like Doug Lidster, who didn't even start the series against New Jersey, that his team would be okay. Glenn Anderson and Brian Leetch also scored, Richter made 28 saves, and the Rangers evened the series at 1–1 with a 3–1 victory on June 2.

"That's kind of how we were," said Lidster, a former Canuck. "Sometimes you played, sometimes you didn't. We had incredible depth on that team, and you just had to be ready. The guys who came in on a given night did a great job. It was a very unique situation. I've never seen so much talent not get to dress every night. But everybody said okay, let's grab the rope and pull. Do your part. I was happy to be doing mine."

It must have been an incredible lift for the team to see Lidster bang in a goal against his former team. He impressed Keenan with his play in Game 6 of the Devils series, and the coach rewarded him for it. Lidster also made the lineup in Game 7 versus New Jersey, and now had a chance to stick it to a team that shipped him away.

There weren't many natural storylines between these two teams, but Lidster made for a good one. These were, after all, two franchises separated by thousands of miles, from different conferences, and with different skill sets. But Lidster came to play against the Canucks, and clearly wanted to show them something.

Through two games, it was so far, so good.

"There were times when the stars took over on that team—Mess, Graves, Leetch, Kovalev, Zubov—but there were other times when some of the other guys would be the best player on the ice," Lidster said. "I remember Nick Kypreos did that once, and Mike said, 'He did what he needed to do.' Mike played it like a baseball team: play your starters, but also know your pinch hitters, and when it's time to go do your job and get a pinch hit, go in and do your job. That's what I tried to do."

Lidster stayed in the lineup as the series shifted to Vancouver on June 4 for Game 3. There must have been something in that cross-continent flight that got in the Rangers' system. Maybe breaking out of the New York metropolitan area for the first time in a long time was the best thing for them. Maybe with so many Canadian players on the team, getting a chance to play in their home country also fueled the fire. Maybe they had just had enough of the back and forth, and knew it was time to turn it on for good.

"Let's just go out," Richter said, "and win."

Whatever the case may be, the Rangers were all business in British Columbia on June 4 and 7. The Rangers outscored Vancouver 9–3 in Games 3 and 4, took a commanding 3–1 lead in the series, and once again gave their city championship fever.

The goals came in bunches, and from many of the same names. Leetch had two in Game 3, another in Game 4. Alexei Kovalev and Steve Larmer had one in each game, as the momentum continued to build. Larmer was having the time of his life. Rescued from the mediocrity and anonymity of the Hartford Whalers by New York's Smith and Keenan, he was truly making the most of his chance at glory. He had given it a run with Keenan in Chicago back in 1992, but Mario Lemieux, Jaromir Jagr, and the high-flying Penguins were simply too strong.

"It was an incredible moment, and one I'll never forget. Getting a chance to get to the Finals, I think, means different things for different players," Larmer said. "For older players, you have more appreciation for it. When I got there in 1991–92 with Chicago, it was already my 10th year in the league. I remember saying to myself, 'Shit, I may never get back here.' So, to beat the Devils, and for me to get another chance in the Finals, and to be playing well in those Finals, well, it was a dream come true. To be able to have a second chance was an incredible experience. At the end of the day, that's what you play for."

Richter made 52 saves in those two games in Canada, none bigger than an acrobatic, highlight-reel, penalty-shot save on Bure in Game 4. Bure, also known as the Russian Rocket, had crashed to earth; as the series headed back to the Garden, he had scored one goal in four games, and was a prime reason the Canucks were suddenly facing elimination.

But as the teams flew back to the United States, Bure, who would later become a Ranger, was not *the* story. A chance to end The Curse on home ice, in Game 5 on June 9, was all that mattered. The Rangers had won three consecutive games, and five of their last six going back to the Devils series. The offense was rolling, the defense was stifling, and Richter was being Richter.

A title awaited … finally. Or so they all thought.

"Mark Messier talked about it, right from his first year in New York, and I spent a lot of time with him," Leetch said. "We carpooled, and he was my roommate on the road. His focus was always on what do we need to do to be a Stanley Cup champion: back up your teammates. Don't take bad penalties. It was always about preparing for the postseason. Everything we did, everything we talked about, was to become a champion. And, eventually, we had that chance in front of us. It was right there."

At home, no less, with John Amirante on the microphone, past Rangers greats sitting in the front row, a fierce, frenzied crowd behind them, and an overgrown curse that was slowly sinking into the Hudson River, period by period. But as hockey purists like to say, the fourth win, the final win, is the toughest to get. And the Rangers learned that the hard way.

"Oh, yeah. I remember Game 5, in the Garden, and the dragon was going to be slayed on this historic night. You kidding me? Everyone thought it was over. It had to be over," Benigno said. "And I remember saying to myself, when you slay curses, you have to suffer every ounce of pain possible before you get that euphoric moment. And then? Look what happens."

Vancouver, a team that was trying to stay fresh and less fatigued through the postseason grind by using a hyperbaric chamber, somehow came out with more jump than the Rangers on that very memorable June night in 1994. Bure and Courtnall each scored two goals, and McLean made 35 saves as the Canucks shocked an entire city, putting the pride, the party, and the parade on hold.

"Typical Rangers," Benigno said.

A 3,000-mile trip back to Western Canada probably wasn't going to help matters either. Another long trip to look at each other and wonder what went wrong, all while preparing for another tilt less than 48 hours after Game 5? Couldn't be a good thing for a team full of older veterans that was about to play its 106th game of the season.

And all those fears, all those strikes against the Rangers, played out on the ice in Vancouver on June 11. Hyperbaric chamber or not, the Canucks had found new life. Courtnall scored two more, Bure added an assist, and the home team, with its crowd feeding off every new inch of life the Canucks had, cruised past the Rangers 4–1, setting up the ultimate moment in hockey.

Game 7.

Again.

Just like that, Vancouver was on the verge of becoming the second consecutive Canadian team to win the Stanley Cup, after Montreal managed the feat in 1993. The seventh seed out of the West, the team that everyone said the Rangers—or the Devils, for that matter—would skate right on by, was on the doorstep of derailing destiny once and for all.

Who would have thunk it?

"Two Game 7s in two series with all that on the line," Melrose said. "Not easy for the Rangers, or their fans. But it made for great hockey."

But there's something about playing a Game 7 at home. Sure, everything is on the line. Sure, a bounce of the puck can be the difference between going home a goat or becoming a legend. But the home team will always have the crowd on its side. And though there was plenty of pessimism in the stands, given the last two efforts from the Rangers, the New York crowd wrapped its arms around the moment and chose to ignore the recent past, for a change.

"You play all season for the right to play Game 7 at home," Richter said. "And that meant everything to us."

They played like it.

Leetch and Graves, scoring 3:43 apart in the first period, put a dagger into the Canucks early, ignited a surge from the crowd not seen since Matteau's goal in Game 7 against the Devils, and made everyone relax just a little on such a big night. Even though Linden cut the lead in half in the second period with his 11th of the postseason, no one ever really had the feeling that the Rangers were going to lose this one.

There was an aura, an air of invincibility, in Manhattan on this night. Whatever it was—the extra day off between games, the fact that this was their final chance, the early lead, you name it—the Rangers just weren't going to lose on home ice.

"It was just one of those situations," Leetch said, "where you were so confident in your own team on each shift."

That's certainly how it looked this night in the Garden, as this postseason journey fit for a movie script slowly came to an end. Messier's 12th at 13:29 of the second capped the Rangers' scoring, and though Linden's 12th at the 4:50 mark of the third made everyone grip their armrests just one more time, the countdown was on.

The crowd, fueled by the knowledge that a big silver chalice was sitting in the bowels of the Garden, was able to recover from its emotional strain long enough to stand in those final moments. Tears were already flowing, as were hugs borne out of anxiety and passion, as the fans lived out those final seconds of fury.

Below them, their heroes were calmly gutting it out. Clinging to a 3–2 lead, with 1.6 seconds left, there was one final faceoff to the right of Richter, not far from where Valeri Zelepukin tied Game 7 a series before. The Canucks had pulled McLean, and had six skaters on the ice. Craig MacTavish, still one of the best faceoff men in the league, lined up against Bure as destiny awaited.

In a postseason run of amazing broadcasters and even more amazing play-by-play calls, longtime Rangers television voice Sam Rosen ended it for everyone on the MSG Network:

> One point six seconds. Here it is. (Pause) The waiting
> is over! The New York Rangers are the Stanley Cup
> champions! And this one will last ... a lifetime!

The Curse was over.

The demons, the dragons, and all of the doubters who took up residence in that oft-talked-about Garden basement, as Messier put it, went with it. Indeed, as MacTavish swept the puck away to the far right boards, the clock ran down, and sticks and gloves flew all over the ice.

They had done it ... finally.

A huddled mass collected in front of Richter, and at last, the party was on.

"No more curses! This is unbelievable," said John Davidson, Rosen's partner, as fireworks went off in the rafters of the Garden. "These people have waited a long time. Fans, players, coaches. Unbelievable!"

A drained, emotionally spent Vancouver team huddled in its own end, not unlike the Devils had two weeks before, waiting for a handshake that would end its misery once and for all. A skilled group that put together an impressive run of its own, the Canucks just couldn't finish the deal, and were forced to watch a celebration that was 54 years in the making. Back in Canada, it wasn't pretty either. A passionate fan base in its own right, Vancouver supporters took to the streets after the loss and rioted, a scene that would be played out again in 2011, when the Canucks again lost a Game 7 in the Finals, that time to the Boston Bruins.

But that was for another city to deal with. This night—June 14, 1994— was about New York and its Rangers.

"It was a huge victory for the New York Rangers, and probably a tremendous victory for the game of hockey because it was Gary Bettman's first year as commissioner of the league, and it was in the biggest market in the league, and it was a very successful story, winning the Presidents' Trophy and the Stanley Cup," Keenan said. "So, I think it really boosted hockey at that time. The city itself needed a boost, too. At that time, the city itself was a little bit downtrodden, and I think it boosted the emotional level and the psyche of the city itself. All around, it was very important."

When the game ended, Keenan turned to Colin Campbell, his lead assistant, both with smiles and watery eyes, and they simply hugged. A playoff stretch that started out easy and ended anything but had finally reached its conclusion. And for a head coach who had tried with two other teams before—only to come up oh so short—this was the ultimate.

"When you coach in this game for a long time, there are memories that stick with you," Keenan said. "Obviously, there are a lot from this group here. We had a successful run, and I'll carry those memories forever."

But as with any team that wins a championship after such a long drought—the Boston Red Sox come to mind, winning the World Series in 2004 for the first time in 86 years—this title was as much about the fans as it was the franchise. The people who endured the misery for so many years, those who lived and died with the slide of a puck, never wavering in their loyalty on even the darkest of nights, had been rewarded. One such fan, sitting in the lower level, held up a sign from one shoulder to the next that captured it all: "Now I can die in peace."

Steve Somers has perhaps the best perspective of what that night meant to those fans. He worked the overnight shift for WFAN, and even now, nearly 20 years later, he remembers the callers as if he had talked to them yesterday.

"A number of them were in tears, yes," he said. "I don't think I've ever done a program, for sure, in the 25 years at WFAN, that was a more passionate, more emotional program. I've never done a program like that, and I doubt I ever will."

That's saying something. After all, the Yankees have won five World Series since that night, and the Giants have won two Super Bowls since. And though his schedule has changed, Somers is still there every night, taking your calls "on the FAN in New York City!"

"But this was 54 years in the making. And how important it was for them, I cannot tell you," said Somers, who was emotional himself during our interview and spoke with a passion for the game and for the team that his listeners would find very familiar. "To the fans, this title was for their father, for their grandfather, who had been to the doorstep with this team before…only to fail and be disappointed. There was so much emotion. So much passion."

Mike Francesa—like Somers, a longtime member of the FAN and a native New Yorker—remains thankful, to this day, that he was on site that night.

"All the Rangers fans who suffered through all the years of heartbreak, to see them reach the pinnacle, it was something to see," he said. "You just knew those fans were in such a special place, you couldn't help but get wrapped up in it. It was a spring that we will never ever see again. It was just so remarkable on so many levels."

What was so incredible about the power of the Rangers that year was how much interest they garnered. With the blue-collar Knicks making a run of their own in a more popular sport, the Rangers still stole the show and truly changed the game in the metropolitan area forever.

"You knew what was happening. It was tough not to notice. We had plenty going on, and we weren't always in the same town they were in. We were out a lot of the times they were in, and vice versa. But we watched when we could," said Jeff Van Gundy, at the time an assistant coach with the Knicks, and later their head coach. "And to see what that meant to them was great. It was a pretty special time to be in New York."

The Rangers' reach went well beyond the five boroughs, too. Across the country, fans took pride in a title for the first time in a long time. In fact, considering all four of the major sports, this was the city's first crown since the 1990 Giants won the Super Bowl.

"I will never forget that spring. Never," said Joe Gannascoli, a native New Yorker and an actor whose career took new heights when he played Vito Spatafore on the HBO series, *The Sopranos*. "I was in L.A., trying to become an actor. Trying miserably. I was in a shitty apartment, trying to find my way, and I'll never forget checking for scores, waiting for the updates, because I didn't have a TV that could get the games. It was killing me. But when it was all over, what a feeling."

Somers knows that feeling.

"What I do for a living, I consider myself to be very lucky. That kind of night, you're talking to friends. It wasn't a job. It was just a combination of work and personal feelings coming together," he said. "Not when I was kid, starting out, not when I did TV work for 17 years, never a radio program, never was there anything like that. It was a combination of happiness and joy and passion and love and emotion. What I was able to hear was the heartbeat of the Rangers fan, and the heartbeat of the city to go along with it. I also felt the soul of the city."

But that was just the beginning. As the night progressed, the party was just getting started. Minutes before the Stanley Cup was introduced, before it was walked out to center ice for Bettman by two league officials, the screams were deafening.

"Whether you're a fan, four years old, 64 years old, 84 years old, no matter how long you've waited," Rosen said on the MSG telecast, "this is something special."

Bettman then took center stage.

"Well, New York, after 54 years, your long wait is over," he said. "Congratulations to the Rangers and the Vancouver Canucks for a spectacular Finals."

And then he uttered words the city had been waiting to hear for 54 years.

"Captain Mark Messier, come get the Stanley Cup."

As a jubilant Messier left the players' scrum and skated over toward Bettman, Tina Turner's 1989 hit song, "Simply the Best," blared on the Garden loudspeakers. The Rangers had listened to the same song before the game, in their own little world inside the locker room. Four hours later, everyone else heard it.

Messier greeted Bettman with a handshake, then caressed the Cup with a smile as wide as the trophy itself. When he took full possession of it, and Bettman tapped the Cup one last time, Messier, the ultimate captain, called his teammates over before raising it.

He wasn't about to do this by himself.

The Rangers slowly skated over, Kypreos leaned over and kissed the Cup, and then Messier began to skate around with it, holding it high, as his mates followed along.

"How sweet it is," Rosen said.

The streets filled with Rangers fans in Manhattan not long after. There was singing. There was dancing. There was euphoria.

"I remember saying to myself, 'If this doesn't do it for hockey in this town, nothing ever will,'" Chris Russo said.

But the celebration on that night paled in comparison to the parade down the city's Canyon of Heroes on June 17. More than 1 million fans came out to salute the Rangers, further illustrating just how far hockey had come in New York.

One million fans. For a hockey team.

"I'll never forget a poster that I saw that day at the parade. It said it all," Kevin Lowe remembered. "It was held by a little boy, and it said, 'I thank you.' And 'My father thanks you.' And 'His father thanks you.' And I knew right then and there what it meant to so many families who have been following the Rangers through everything for all those years. When you're playing the game, and the series go from one to the other, you're focused on hockey, hockey, hockey. But when you get a chance to step back, after the fact, and see things like that, it just makes it so much more special."

Van Gundy and the Knicks were preparing to play Game 5 of the NBA Finals the night of the parade. Clearly, they were focused on the task at hand, given they were tied with the Houston Rockets 2–2 headed into that game.

"But we still watched the parade, sure," he said. "And I remember that day they were having their parade clearly, because we were having a shootaround before Game 5. And I still remember being in the assistant coaches' office at the Garden. And [then–Knicks head coach Pat] Riley was in his office, and then we heard this incredible, loud noise. And we were all like, 'What was that? We're getting ready for this game, it's a big game, and what's going on out there?' And, wouldn't you know it, it was Mike Keenan driving 40 miles per hour, or it seemed like that at least, right down the hallway of the Garden…on a motorcycle. A motorcycle! And it was just incredible. He was in Madison Square Garden, in the hallways, and there he was, riding a motorcycle, riding around. He had his ways. But hats off to him."

The Knicks were themselves playing with an ultimatum, a win-now-or-else team that also gripped New York in a way not seen in decades. They went 57–25, won the NBA Atlantic Division title, and defeated the New Jersey Nets, Chicago Bulls, and Indiana Pacers to get to the Finals. In the midst of the Rangers' jubilation, the Knicks went out on the same Garden floor that night and extracted a 91–84 victory over the Rockets, gaining a 3–2 edge in a series that would shift to Houston for the rest of the way.

New York, New York.

The Knicks lost the next two games, though, and failed in their attempt to duplicate the Rangers' feat. But, overall, it could not dampen what was clearly the most exciting spring in New York sports history.

"It embodied what New York was all about. I had the same experience in Chicago, when Michael Jordan was winning championships with Phil Jackson, and we had a Blackhawks team that was going to the Finals, and it was the same thing," Keenan said. "Every other night was a huge sporting event. New York experienced the same with the Knicks and the Rangers. That was exciting because the city feeds off each team's energy and success. And in many ways, we pushed each other til the end."

The end came sooner for the Knicks than the Rangers, of course, but titles would soon go away for good for both teams. The memories would always be there, certainly, a banner was raised early the next season, and rings were distributed to the warriors.

But things weren't the same for the Blueshirts. Campbell took over for Keenan in the lockout-shortened 1994–95 season. Content to go out on top, and knowing that a triumphant trifecta of himself, Smith, and Messier probably wouldn't work long-term, Keenan left to become the head coach in St. Louis. He made the playoffs in two of three seasons with the Blues, but never took them to the Stanley Cup Finals.

Meanwhile, Campbell had success, but nothing that rivaled 1994. In 1995, New York discovered how difficult it is to repeat in the NHL. The Rangers limped to a 47-point finish that season and actually entered the playoffs with a losing record (22–23–3). They took fourth place in the Atlantic Division, and though they picked themselves off the mat and upset the Quebec Nordiques 4–2 in the first round, they were subsequently swept by the Philadelphia Flyers in the second round.

The run was officially over.

In the next two years, they would again make the playoffs, including a race to the Eastern Conference Finals in 1997 before again losing to the Flyers. But no one—not Keenan, not Smith, not Campbell, not Messier—could foresee what was coming next.

From 1998 to 2004, the Rangers did not make the playoffs…once. Including another lockout that scratched a full season for everyone, New York didn't take the ice in a postseason game again until 2006.

"I knew, as a scout, the way I built the New York Rangers wasn't the way I would have liked. But New York is such a special place, and things are just different," Smith said. "I had to do what I had to do to break that 54-year curse, and get them a Stanley Cup. So, I did that. Trading new assets for old assets wasn't the long-term solution, and that eventually showed."

Smith left the organization following the 1999–2000 season. The Rangers had just 29 wins that campaign, to go along with two coaches, John Muckler and John Tortorella.

"And that's New York for you. We'd sign players, we lost players, then we'd have to restock again," Smith said. "At times, we'd have a decent run, and things were good, and then all of a sudden, I didn't know what I was doing anymore, they said. But that's New York."

In good times and bad.

The Next Year

○ ○ ○ ○

"We knew [the Devils] weren't going anywhere. You never know what's going to happen with teams. There are very talented teams that never get back to that position in this league. But whatever it was, you knew the Devils weren't going to be one of those teams. You knew they had the pieces in place to get back right there, and give them credit. You have to give credit to Lou [Lamoriello], and Scott [Stevens], and Scotty [Niedermayer], and Marty [Brodeur], and all those guys who kept it going. They did not sit around after that loss to us. They got right back up."
—BRIAN LEETCH, NEW YORK RANGERS (1988–2004)

THERE WERE A couple of different directions the Devils could travel the season after The NHL's Greatest Series Ever. Could they use the gut-wrenching loss as motivation, pick themselves up, and be on the attack from the get-go? Or would they sit around and feel sorry for themselves, knowing all along that it should have been them skating around with the Stanley Cup in New Jersey, rather than the Rangers across the river in New York?

As it turned out, at first, it was neither.

That's because team owners around the league locked out the players on October 1, 1994, over several lingering labor issues, the biggest of which was the institution of a salary cap. The owners wanted one. The players didn't.

Less than six months after Gary Bettman handed Mark Messier the Stanley Cup, ending one of the most dramatic NHL postseasons in history, the commissioner had strain and strife on his hands, and the thought of not being able to build off 1994's momentum was a scary one to the league as a whole.

The Devils, though, had their own problems. Even before the lockout, Lou Lamoriello had several lingering contract issues to work out, most notably that of Scott Stevens, the captain. Stevens was coming off a terrific regular season, posting 60 assists and 78 points, which were incredible numbers when you consider Jacques Lemaire's defensive system. He didn't have a banner postseason, but Stevens did manage two goals and 11 points, and when you're the unrivaled, unquestioned leader of a team that came within a goal of making the Stanley Cup Finals for the first time, you must be doing something right.

The Blues certainly watched The NHL's Greatest Series Ever with admiration, respect, and more importantly, a pad and pen. Not only did St. Louis make a shopping list and check it twice based off that series, they actually went out and acted on that list, plucking Mike Keenan away from the Rangers. Then, they put a target squarely on Stevens' back as Priority No. 2.

Lamoriello, though, never wavered. Although it was a tough contract to sign—the Devils were not then and certainly not now known as free spenders—New Jersey's driven general manager matched St. Louis' offer sheet for Stevens. The Blues, on July 4, 1994, offered the defenseman $17 million over four years. On July 9, so did Lamoriello.

To many, it was a stunning decision. The Devils, after all, had to account for every dollar coming in and going out. They were a team that didn't have a lucrative television deal and did not sell out every game. There were always rumors of a possible move out of the Garden State—in 1995, Nashville would be the rumored, hot-topic destination—so big dollars for big players just wasn't their style. But that goes to show how serious they were about sustaining their success. And it showed how much Stevens embodied the Devils' Way, through thick and thin. So, at crunch time, Lamoriello got it done.

So, all was well in the Swamp, right? The captain was back, the team was still in place for the most part, and another lengthy postseason run awaited, right?

"No. Hardly the case," said Larry Brooks, who covered the Devils through 1995 for the *Post* before shifting over to the Rangers. "They bickered through the whole year. It had a lot to do with money. Who was getting paid? Who wasn't? It was a bad situation."

From the players' perspective, it was pretty simple. As a collective group, they orchestrated the best season in the history of the franchise. They took that horned-and-tailed *NJ* logo for an unforgettable ride, and though it ended just a bit short of its hopeful destination, they believed, as constituted, they could get right back there.

For the right price, of course.

"Everyone was pissed off that Stevens got so much money. It was an unhappy team, it really was," Brooks said. "Claude [Lemieux] was unhappy, Marty [Brodeur] was unhappy. It was not shaping up to be a happy year. And then came the lockout."

But the Devils prided themselves on breeding professionals, and the common perception was, when the time came, they'd be able to put their differences aside and just go out and play. Turns out, that happened earlier than expected...and without the league knowing.

"With Lou, where there's a will, there's a way," Lemieux said with a laugh. "We knew how we all felt after Game 7. But we also knew if we kept it together, and kept our composure and just played together, whenever the season started, we'd be okay. Well, we didn't want to wait that long. So, we were probably the only team in the league that skated through the lockout. Yes. We were probably doing it illegally, but we were doing it nonetheless. We skated through the lockout at South Mountain Arena [the Devils' normal practice facility at the time, in Mennen, New Jersey]. Many of us stayed in New Jersey, and worked together and got ready for the season. But, yeah, looking back on it, that was probably illegal. What are you going to do?"

Wouldn't that have been an interesting news item 16 years ago? As it was, the Devils did start that season they were looking forward to—finally—on January 11, 1995. After 468 leaguewide games were lost, as well as the NHL's All-Star Weekend, the two sides came to an agreement and a shortened, 48-game season was created amid a modified salary cap.

Almost immediately, the Devils became favorites for the Stanley Cup. Not only was the roster virtually intact from the season before, but the season's length, it seemed, favored the Devils, who could grind out 48 games with the trap in place a whole lot more efficiently than 84.

Bernie Nicholls, a good teammate and friend to several of the Devils, signed with the Chicago Blackhawks and figured to be tough to replace. But he was the most notable defection on a team that was still loaded.

"It was pretty clear that he was going to go," Brooks said of Nicholls. "It was a pretty mutual decision. He had really some good games, but his time there had run its course."

It wasn't easy. Lamoriello watched the veteran forward and how he dealt with his family crisis, and always looked at both the player and the person that Bernie Nicholls was with admiration. But a decision was made on both sides, and it was time to move on.

Either way, Lamoriello and Lemaire felt comfortable. Lingering money issues with some of the players aside, they knew what they had and what they were up against. The Rangers were without their Stanley Cup coach. The Canucks needed a little more offense from someone not named Pavel Bure to repeat their run. The Red Wings, with super-skilled forwards Steve Yzerman and Sergei Fedorov, appeared to have all the right pieces but couldn't seem to get it together in the postseason. And the Flyers, another popular choice with a rising superstar in center Eric Lindros, were probably still a year away.

That left the Devils. A team with enough offense, a stifling defense, a returning Rookie of the Year goaltender, and all the motivation under the sun to get it done. It was that simple. At least, that was the idea.

"We had the desire to win," Lemieux said. "We had the best coach, and we had the best goaltender. But for some reason, it wasn't working. A lot of us had horrible regular seasons. I know I did."

The Devils quickly found out it wasn't going to be easy to sneak up on anyone anymore. They were the hunted now, and it seemed clear that opponents had read New Jersey's clippings and headlines. On opening night, January 22, 1995, what appeared like the Devils' most important season in their history began with a thud: a ho-hum 2–2 tie to the abundantly average Whalers in Hartford. Hard as it might be to believe, that contest, which opened a four-game road swing to begin the year, was the Devils' best effort on the trip.

Over the next six days, questions began to surface about this team's drive and desire. With a shortened schedule, even slight slumps could prove costly to a season overall. Teams no longer had 84 games to find themselves. And through four games, the Devils were lost. Clearly:

January 25: Sabres 2, Devils 1
January 26: Bruins 1, Devils 0
January 28: Canadiens 5, Devils 1

New Jersey limped home 0–3–1, having scored four goals total. Forget the Stanley Cup for a second. Making the playoffs, it seemed, might be a stretch for this team.

"It was not a good start," Bruce Driver said. "I don't know that anyone could pinpoint one specific thing. We just weren't playing well."

The Devils won the next two games, both at home, and began to come together just a bit. They weren't easy, but a 2–1 win over the Sabres and a 5–4 decision over the Nordiques, if nothing else, built some confidence.

But a six-game snapshot of this brief season gave many a glimpse of what this Devils team truly was. Despite the talent, despite the motivation, despite the path being wide open for them and their shutdown system, it was clear to see that nothing was going to come easy... and that something was a bit off.

Was the money issue—who was getting it and who wasn't—still lingering for the players? Was it the absence of Nicholls, a reliable, potent center, who could win faceoffs, score goals, and fire up a team when needed? Someone who wasn't afraid to speak his mind, in good times and bad?

"The sad thing is, I don't know how the negotiations went when things got serious, but the thing about Lou is this: no one was *that* important," Nicholls said. "They can replace anybody in New Jersey. I wasn't a huge priority for them, and I was offered a real good deal to go to Chicago, so I did. If I could ever go back, I would have played in New Jersey for free. Trust me. I promise you that. But one thing that always stuck out to me was this: they should have kept me, because they needed my role."

~ It was hard to argue that point, and Lamoriello wasn't blind to that. As the season wore on, as the mediocrity became pervasive, he began to plot out a way to fill that gap. He worked the phones. He listened to his scouts. He needed a center. On February 27, he got his man.

On the same day that the Devils orchestrated perhaps their best game of the season—a 6–1 win over the Canadiens in East Rutherford—Lamoriello shipped Corey Millen, a 30-year-old center who had just two goals in 17 games, to Dallas for Neal Broten, a 35-year-old center who was on the downside of his career, one that began with an Olympic gold medal while on the 1980 Miracle on Ice team.

It was a risk, without question. In many ways, they were similar players—both Americans, both former Olympians, both centers. But Lamoriello thought Broten brought a little more to the table, even though he was older and had no goals and just four assists in his 17 games that season for the Stars.

Perhaps both players just needed a change of scenery. That was Lamoriello's specialty, after all. He could always sense when that was the case.

"At that point," Nicholls said, "they had replaced me, and they really had all the pieces to the puzzle. You just knew that was the kind of move that was going to work for them."

Broten had an assist in his first game as a Devil, and things took off from there.

"I trusted Neal, and I trusted [Dallas general manager and coach] Bob Gainey when I made the trade," Lamoriello said. "I asked him, 'What's he got left?' And it was a trade that was good for both teams. But Neal came in here, and you have to give him tremendous credit. He came in to be a part of a team. Not to be an individual. And that was important. And that's why you see me bring a lot of players back at the trade deadline. You don't have to change their culture. You have to feel it, and guys we know, and guys we have had before, know that. I felt it with Neal."

He wasn't alone. Millen could feel it, as well. He knew what the Devils were lacking, and he knew Broten's skill set could fill that the void. In fact,

Millen remembers the day he first showed up with his new team, the Stars, and found an interesting roommate waiting for him.

"So, I get traded, and I went and met the Stars in Winnipeg," Millen said. "They were on a road trip, and I show up there, and my roommate was Paul Broten...Neal's brother! The team was already there, in the hotel. I fly in, I get to the room, and Paul is one of my best friends from way back. So, we laughed about it, for sure. I walk in, he was happy to see me, but hey, his brother just got traded, so he was a bit down, as well. And the first thing I told him was, 'Holy shit, your brother is going to go win a Stanley Cup.' He looked at me, laughed at me, and said 'What-ev-er.' But I just knew it. I knew Jacques would play Neal with [John] MacLean and [Stephane] Richer, and they would have an impact. I knew Neal fit exactly with what the Devils were trying to accomplish. And he did. When you look back on it, that line was key. I just knew Neal was going to do well there."

Millen was right. In 30 regular season games with New Jersey, Broten had eight goals and 28 points. How different were the Devils from the Stars? Well, he went from being a minus-8 player in Dallas to being a plus-9 player in New Jersey. He meshed well with MacLean and Richer, as Millen predicted, and posted three game-winning goals in his 43 shots on net.

But Broten wasn't alone. Lamoriello also added to the back line, acquiring Shawn Chambers from Tampa Bay. A defenseman with a cannon shot who could help on the power play but needed time to adjust to the Devils' system, Chambers made it to New Jersey in time to play 21 regular season games. He adapted well, and put up Devil-like numbers from a defenseman: two goals, seven points, 23 shots, and a plus-2 rating. He was solid. He was secure. And with Broten, he completed Lamoriello's blueprint.

"We had the orchestra. We had the violins, we had the drummers, we had the piano players, and we had the conductor as the coach," Lamoriello said. "What we needed, at the time, was a center-ice man and we needed a defenseman. Did I think Shawn Chambers was going to turn out the way he played? Come on. Did I hope he would? Absolutely. But did I think Jacques would pair him up with Bruce Driver and be a shut-down guy, and also score some big goals? Come on. And did I think Neal would come in, at his age, and play to that level? Again, come on."

As humble as he may have been, and as subtle as the moves seemed at first glance, they worked. And the league took notice.

"From a GM standpoint, and I've looked at this for years, you can't make trades for a lead dog at the deadline," said Neil Smith, who a year before Lamoriello's moves mortgaged the Rangers' future for a Stanley Cup. "You trade for peripheral players, faceoff guys, a defenseman, but you can't trade for, say, a No. 1 goalie, or a first-line player, and expect them to lead you to the Cup. It's too late at that point. You cannot reinvent yourself when the playoffs start. You simply have to fortify what you've got, and maybe patch up a weakness or two. Lou is a master of that."

Though the Devils were hardly the machine people thought they'd be, Lemaire was able to get enough out of them. They finished 22–18–8 with 52 points, good for second in the Atlantic. A dominant group they were not. But they made the postseason, snagging the No. 5 seed and a date with the Bruins in Round 1. And to these Devils, given everything they had endured over the past 12 months, that was all that mattered.

"I don't know what it was. We stepped on the ice in Boston, the day before we started the playoffs, and it was a hot day there. Will never forget it," Driver said. "Our practice was short because of that. But it was probably the most crisp practice we had all year. The shots, the passes, the flow of practice, everything was just…perfect. There were no mistakes made in practice, and from that session on, it just snowballed and snowballed and snowballed. And it's something that I still can't answer to this day. I just don't know how the switch just went on. We didn't play well down the stretch, and all of a sudden, we have one good, 45-minute practice, and just like that, we were at the top of our game? To this day, I can't explain what, how, or why the switch went on. But it did. And then we get to the playoffs in Boston, we start clicking, and it was like, 'Oh, my God. How did we do that?' I don't have an answer, other than that it just…happened."

The Devils blasted the Bruins in the first two games, stunning the Boston Garden faithful. Combined, they outscored the Bruins 8–0 in six periods of play, as Brodeur notched two road shutouts in a two-day span.

"Once the playoffs came, everything changed," Brooks said. "They were a juggernaut."

They certainly looked like it early, as they dispatched a decent Bruins team in five games, scoring 14 goals along the way. On May 14, 1995, a 3–2 Devils win was the last hockey game played at the old Boston Garden, as New Jersey punched its ticket for the second round for the second time in as many years.

Incidentally, in that final spring of the Boston Garden, much was made of the Celtics' finale, and how Orlando Magic star center Shaquille O'Neal shut the doors on the old building in Beantown. In Game 4 of a first-round series versus the Celtics, O'Neal, one of the game's biggest names, had 25 points and 13 rebounds as the Magic won 95–92 to take the series 3–1. Ken Daneyko, though, was amused by the thought of O'Neal taking credit for the closure. In fact, after New Jersey's Game 5 win, the veteran defenseman was short, sweet, and succinct with his take on the matter.

"Shaq didn't close the Boston Garden," he said. "The Devils did."

The Penguins weren't moving to another building, and they figured to have plenty more scoring punch than the Bruins did, but the Devils treated them just the same in Round 2. After a hiccup in Game 1—a 3–2 loss in Pittsburgh—the Devils woke up and dominated. They would not lose another game in the series, outscoring Jaromir Jagr and the high-flying Penguins 15–5 in the final four contests.

It was onward and upward for New Jersey, and it looked like the sky was the limit.

"It was lights out. Everything we did was working," said Bill Guerin, who had three goals and 11 points in this postseason run. "You see that happen a lot in sports. Every team has to go through some sort of heartbreak and some sort of lesson to get where you want to go. For us, it was getting our hearts broken by the Rangers, and then struggling in the regular season for so long. At some point, we had just had enough. We were too good not to get over it."

The Devils were 8–2 through two rounds and were clicking on all cylinders. And though the jury was out on whether they truly wanted a chance to exact revenge on the Rangers, in the end, it didn't matter. Lindros and a line known as the Legion of Doom dominated the defending Stanley

Cup champions in Round 2. Philadelphia swept New York, setting up a date with the Devils in the conference finals.

In a postseason run as crisp and concise as the one the Devils had scripted, it was hard to believe that any adversity would stand in their way. The Flyers, at the least, put up a fight and challenged New Jersey in a way Boston and Pittsburgh could have only dreamt about. Of course, it didn't start out that way.

The Devils notched two road wins to open the series at the Spectrum—ho-hum, another great start. The games weren't even close, as New Jersey posted 4–1 and 5–2 victories in a 72-hour span. Brodeur made 38 saves en route to the wins, and the Devils cruised home down the New Jersey Turnpike needing just two wins to make the Stanley Cup Finals for the first time.

Lindros and Co. found their stride somewhere along their trip up the Turnpike. And with plenty of Flyers fans in the stands—it wasn't quite like the Rangers fans in East Rutherford, but there was a strong Philadelphia presence nonetheless—the Flyers knocked the Devils off their course. A 3–2 overtime win in Game 3 was followed by a 4–2 win in Game 4, and just like that, the series was tied.

There was worse news for the Devils. On a quick turnaround, they were to face the Flyers in the Spectrum for Game 5 on a Sunday afternoon, less than 24 hours after losing Game 4.

"But we had been through a lot already," Lemieux said. "And when you have great character, anything is possible. We believed in that."

Leave it to Lemieux to save the day. He was already salvaging his poor regular season with a terrific postseason, and he took it to another level in Game 5. With less than a minute remaining in a 2–2 game, Lemieux corralled a loose puck in his own zone, streaked down the far boards, and—surprised he had so much room in a tight game—let off a slap shot from the right point, just beyond the blue line, that beat Flyers goaltender Ron Hextall with 44.2 seconds remaining.

He jumped up in the air with both skates and threw his arms up to the ceiling in another famous, photogenic pose—he was good at those—as the Devils escaped with a 3–2 victory that demoralized the Flyers and their fans, perhaps for good.

"It was a perfect shot by Lemieux," John Davidson said on the FOX telecast.

In a postseason that was looking far too easy, Lemieux stopped the bleeding and put the Devils on the brink of the Finals... again. But would the second time be a charm? A 3–2 lead at home, needing one win against a rival to secure a conference crown? Sure, it wasn't the Rangers that would invade the Meadowlands. But it was still a rival, and one that had tested New Jersey more than anyone else this postseason.

But Lindros was not Messier. And there were no guarantees this time. For the road team, that meant there was no chance.

And so on Tuesday, June 13, 1995, in front of 19,040 fans, the Devils finished the job. A 4–2 win over the Flyers that was not as close as the score indicated erased the monkey that had lived on the Devils' backs for a year. Indeed, through the summer of heartbreak, the fall of a lockout, and the winter of discontent, the Devils had secured their first conference title and were headed to the Stanley Cup Finals.

"[The Flyers have] got a great future ahead of them, but for us, we're running out of time. So, it's great for us, and we can enjoy this for a while," Stevens told Al Morganti on ESPN after the ceremonial handshake. "It was so important for us to get to this next step here. Anything else would have been disappointing."

If you traveled back to that first postseason practice that Driver spoke so highly about and looked at the numbers from that point, they were astonishing. The Devils went 12–4 through three rounds, none of which they had home-ice advantage for. They went a miraculous 8–1 on the road.

Only the Detroit Red Wings, with stars up and down the roster, separated New Jersey from immortality. And clearly, it seemed like the toughest of all tests. The Red Wings had 33 wins and 70 points in the regular season, and were 12–2 in the postseason. They simply owned the Western Conference.

But not even Steve Yzerman, Sergei Fedorov, and a Hall of Fame coach in Scotty Bowman could derail this Devils train. Despite having home-ice advantage, despite having more experience, and despite, perhaps, having more balance, the Red Wings never stood a chance. A 2–1 victory in

Game 1 served notice to all the high flyers in the West that the Devils weren't fazed. And in Game 2, three days later in the Motor City, New Jersey registered two of its more famous goals in franchise history en route to a 2–0 series lead.

"Here's Niedermayer, he can fly, here comes Niedermayer, Richer the trailer, Niedermayer just missed! Niedermayer scores," Gary Thorne exclaimed on ESPN. "Scott Niedermayer! The 21-year-old showing you why, despite the fact that he's played mostly D for the Devils, he is an offensive threat."

In clearly one of the best individual plays you will ever see from someone in a New Jersey uniform, Niedermayer took a loose puck to the right of Brodeur, carried it out of his own zone, created room in the neutral zone, and let off a wrist shot that sailed over the goal and Detroit netminder Mike Vernon. The puck actually caromed off the backboards right back onto Niedermayer's stick, and he easily flicked it past a stunned, sprawled Vernon at 9:47 of the third period.

"You talk about an end-to-end beauty," Bill Clement said.

The goal tied the score at 2–2 and set the stage for a proud kid from Brick, New Jersey, to send the Devils home to his native state with a win.

"A defenseman is down on the ice, a player is hurt," Thorne said. "And Zelepukin's shot…Vernon the save…Jim Dowd scores! A Detroit Red Wing was down on the ice for all of that. Paul Coffey blocked a shot, stayed down, and the Devils have a 3–2 lead!"

Indeed, with Coffey out of commission, New Jersey pounced, and Dowd, the first New Jersey native ever to play for the Devils, and the one who was right in the crease when Stephane Matteau shattered his dreams a year before, scored the biggest goal of his life.

Dowd's second of the postseason at 18:36 was a bit controversial, but he wasn't about to complain. It was a game-winner, after all.

"I was just happy to be on the ice," Dowd said. "Are you kidding me? Happy to be a part of it, happy they had enough faith in me to be out there. Every night, we were adding to an era that really started it all for the Devils, and I'm so proud I was a part of it."

The Niedermayer-Dowd parlay crushed the Red Wings. In a span of 72 hours, they had lost as many games in one series as they had in the previous three combined. As talented as they may have been, it was no surprise that they put up little fight back in East Rutherford, which was gearing for a party with each new shift. A 5–2 Devils win in Game 3 all but ended the series on June 22. With the Red Wings in an 0–3 hole, the focus turned to not if, but when, New Jersey would celebrate its first Stanley Cup.

Turns out, the wait was only two days.

On Saturday, June 24, 1995, in an arena built on a swampland in Bergen County, New Jersey, Lamoriello's plan, Lemaire's strategy, and Dr. John McMullen's dream finally came to fruition. A 5–2 victory that never seemed in question capped a quest for respect, revenge, and recognition in the Garden State. Just more than a year after the Rangers won it six miles away, the dominant Devils had won the Stanley Cup with ease.

"Cleared by Richer, 13 seconds to go. Bouncing puck at the Detroit line. Ramsey will circle in his own end. Seven seconds to go. Six. Five. Four. Three. Two. And one! And the oldest trophy competed for in North America, Lord Stanley's Cup, has made its way through the Lincoln Tunnel! To the Meadowlands! To the Garden State! The New Jersey Devils are the 1995 Stanley Cup champions!"

Those were the powerful, precise, passionate words of Mike Miller, who was in just his second season as an NHL play-by-play man. After calling Matteau's goal—in a slightly less enthusiastic tone than Howie Rose did, of course—he was able to have his moment a year later.

"Anything that was done, was done to be the best. There was nothing ever personal with the Devils. We were, and are still to this day in my opinion, in the frame of mind that we compete against ourselves, more than anything else. We don't compete against anyone else," Lamoriello said. "At the end of the game, every day, every minute, you compete against yourself to be the best."

In 1995, they were the best.

"I remember after we lost the first game Scotty Bowman saying if you're trapped by the trap, you're trapped. Doesn't make a lot of sense, but then again, it does make a lot of sense. I think they could get into your head with the way they were playing," said Bob Errey, a forward for Detroit in 1995, and now a television analyst for Pittsburgh. "And we just wanted to play our game, and they didn't let us. We had a high, up-tempo game, a skilled game, a passing game, and really a game that people enjoy watching, and we just didn't want to play the Devils' way at that point. We weren't going to change our game at that point. But that's the way it was. And they were able to get some bounces and steals, and they stole a couple of early games and really were able to capitalize on that momentum once they returned home."

They did it in front of a crowd that was often maligned and often the scourge of the league. But for one night, and for one season, they ruled hockey.

"The fans are something I will always remember about that night," Niedermayer said. "And really, for all games, for that matter. However many there were from night to night, they were as passionate as they could be. I know that. They knew the game, and they knew how they wanted us to play. I'll always remember that."

As will Bettman, who made his second Stanley Cup delivery in the metropolitan area in just more than 12 months. In this trophy presentation, he was received a little more harshly than he had been a year earlier—the lockout was still fresh in the fans' minds, and there were still those Devils-to-Nashville rumors lingering—but it was memorable nonetheless. The crowd, not unlike the Garden fans a year ago, erupted when the Cup was introduced. And then Bettman took over.

"The Devils' amazing playoff run has taken the word *teamwork* to a new level," the commissioner said, as boos reigned down. "Congratulations to the Devils. Scott Stevens…this is for you."

Stevens didn't skate over alone. He brought his alternate captains—Driver and MacLean—and together they raised the chalice high above their heads and into the Devils' history books.

"The system was awesome and it worked, and we all just believe in it always," Stevens said. "Jacques was such a big part of that. He instilled that belief into us, and once we got going, we were tough to beat."

Though the 31-year-old Stevens liked to talk about his age and the fact that the Devils weren't getting any younger, the fact remained that the system worked with many different parts, and coaches, for that matter.

In fact, New Jersey would go on to win the Stanley Cup in 2000 and 2003 with different leaders behind the bench. Larry Robinson, Lemaire's understudy, won the franchise's second title, over Dallas in six games, and the late Pat Burns won the third, over Anaheim in seven.

But it goes beyond Cups for the Devils. It's a culture of winning, a way of life, and though that didn't always result in championships, it did result in consistency. Headed into the 2012–13 season, New Jersey was the proud owner of five conference championships and nine division titles. All of them came under Lamoriello's watch.

"Once you start to get results, and it starts to sink in, it really starts to feel good," Stevens said. "At many points during that run, we almost felt unbeatable."

Along the way, they became the standard for successful hockey in the post-lockout era. In a period that began in 1995 and ended in 2008, the Devils and Red Wings combined for seven Stanley Cup titles.

"They truly kept it going, and [the Rangers] didn't," Brian Leetch admitted. "You have to give them credit. They kept it together, and we couldn't. That's certainly something that is disappointing on my end, no question."

As satisfying and joyous as 1994 was, one wonders if Rangers fans, looking back on it now, would trade the Devils' three titles for the Rangers' one.

"From a scout's perspective, that was the right way to do it, and I always say that Lou is the best GM of our generation," Neil Smith said. "I wish I could have been given the time to build the Rangers the way Lou was able to build the Devils. But I had to sell my soul to win the Cup. You just knew the Devils were going to be good for a long time, and we weren't. And I think if you ask most Rangers fans if they'd take the long-term plan to win three Cups over all those years, and endure, or just win one Cup, they'd probably say, 'Who gives a shit? Just win one.'"

But that "one" clearly triggered New Jersey. You can make a case that if Matteau's goal didn't go in, and the Devils somehow pulled out a Game 7 win in 1994 and went on to win the Stanley Cup over Vancouver, they may never have gotten back there again. To beat their biggest rival in The

NHL's Greatest Series Ever, and to win a Cup two weeks later? Perhaps their course would have followed New York's. As it was, after losing that series to the Rangers, they were hungry. They were determined. And they were driven.

Before long, a dynasty was born.

"You build history. And I was fortunate, growing up, to be able to watch the Montreal Canadiens and see them grow. They had a history to uphold, and that's a great thing for the fans and for the organization," Brodeur said. "It's a source of pride, and when you want to grow as an organization, recognizing the history of it, is something that you have to do. We do that here."

Along the way, though, no one forgot The NHL's Greatest Series Ever.

"To think that we didn't learn from that series is crazy," Randy McKay said. "To think that it might not have been good for us in the long run … it definitely motivated us. It might have been the best thing to happen to us."

One thing is for sure: it carried them forward for the better part of two decades.

"No question about it. There are many times where you have to lose before you can win," Miller said. "When they beat Detroit, it catapulted the Red Wings into what they became. Somehow, it just works that way. Doesn't feel good at the time, of course, but when you lose like that, many times you eventually win."

Ken Daneyko sure looks at it that way. Clearly, it was awful losing to Messier, his great friend, and the Rangers, his greatest rival. And to say that pain didn't linger through the summer and the lockout and even the regular season would be foolish. But in the end, it was necessary fuel.

"When you look back on it, and you look at other sports, you have to go through that kind of adversity. You have to take responsibility for the tough times, learn from it, and know what you need to do the next time out. You have to go through that, and we did, and we learned from it," Daneyko said. "And that's a tough thing to do when you're in it, and you're going through it. When you retire, and you're older, you can look back on it. But when you're in the moment, it's tough to see the big picture, it's tough to believe that the tough times will eventually lead to the good times. When you look back at the series, you have to take a look at the bigger picture. I look at two things as positives, and they helped, certainly, with the rest of my career. Number one, I was part of the greatest series in the history of hockey. And number two, that was part of the process, part of the transformation into being a champion. I took those lessons with me every game I played from there on. They carried over. And I'll never get away from that series. Never. Not a week goes by before we don't talk about it, or it comes up in passing. It was the greatest series ever."

Lamoriello can't help but laugh when that title comes up every now and again. He admits it was a tough loss—"All of them are," he said—but he's also learned to stomach it.

"As tough as it was, and it was tough, you have to move on," he said with a reflective smile. "Do you realize what it was like to live here then? Every restaurant that you go into, all you heard when you walked in was people saying, 'Matteau! Matteau! Matteau!' But it was okay. There was nothing wrong with that. When you think about that, it was great that people were thinking hockey. People were recognizing it. And people were apologizing to us. People would come up to me and say, 'You had a great year, but I'm a Rangers fan.' And my response to that would always be, 'More importantly, you're a hockey fan.' And that was the atmosphere. It was great to be around."

As Lamoriello savored the memory of those two weeks in May 1994, he was reminded that Daneyko, who won all three Cups with the Devils and played his whole career in New Jersey, admitted—even in defeat—that it was The NHL's Greatest Series Ever.

"Oh, yeah," Lamoriello said with a laugh. "Okay. Well, it was great. No question, it was great. But you can tell Kenny this: do me a favor and you tell him that it wasn't the greatest series ever.

"Only because we didn't win."

Epilogue

○ ○ ○ ○

"It's pretty amazing when you look at the number of years between the two series. A lot of things have changed since 1994. I think it's going to be pretty chaotic at times. For the guys, I think they have to enjoy the moment. It's a great time in their lives, and you never know when you're going to get another chance. Playing against our biggest rival just puts the cherry on top of things. There's a lot of excitement."
—MARTIN BRODEUR, NEW JERSEY DEVILS (1991–)

MARTIN BRODEUR WAS dead on during our interview on May 13, 2012, just as he has been throughout a 19-year career spent chaperoning a six-foot-wide, four-foot-high contraption of red steel. He had to be. His underrated, underappreciated group of New Jersey Devils had unceremoniously landed a berth in the Eastern Conference Finals, and all the talk—surprise, surprise—was about their opponent in that upcoming series.

Yep, you guessed it.

The New York Rangers.

"It's different years, different teams, different results," Brodeur said. "You can look at the matchups we've had in the past, but there aren't many guys who have been here when we played them. It's new, and it should be motivation for them. I think we can expect more of the same excitement."

Indeed, as the 2011–12 Devils—seeded No. 6, without home-ice advantage, and not given much of a chance to accomplish anything beyond making a brief postseason appearance—dispatched the No. 3 Florida Panthers and No. 5 Philadelphia Flyers in 12 games to return to the third round for the first time since 2003, a buzz was building across the metropolitan area. A certain similarity, let's say, to a postseason gone by, some 18 years ago, in which both the Devils and Rangers captured some hearts and broke some others.

It couldn't happen again…could it? The Battle on the Hudson, Part II?

Sure, New York was the No. 1 seed in the East, a seemingly clutch collection of youth, experience, perseverance, and pride, anchored by superstar goaltender Henrik Lundqvist and gritty coach John Tortorella. But the Rangers struggled as the playoffs' top dog. New York actually trailed the No. 8 Ottawa Senators 3–2 in the first round before the Rangers rallied and advanced. In the second round, the No. 7 Washington Capitals had them all but beat in Game 5 of their 2–2 series, but New York rescued itself with two power-play goals—one late in the third and the other early in overtime—to escape with a 3–2 win. They eventually took the series in seven games.

So, though there was no Mark Messier up front and no Brian Leetch on the back line, it still seemed destiny was on the Rangers' side again.

"I know where you're going with this, but it doesn't matter to us," New Jersey forward Dainius Zubrus said as the driven Devils awaited their opponent in the semifinals. "We have to worry about the things we need to do, the things we can control."

And so they did. New Jersey, which clinched the Philadelphia series with a 3–1 win in Game 5 on May 8, sat back, relaxed, waited, and watched as the desperate Rangers fought back and finally eliminated the Capitals with a 2–1 victory on May 12. Just as the calm, cool, collected, confident Rangers had been back in 1994, the Devils sat on their couches, waiting on their opponent. Eighteen years ago, the skate was on the other foot, as the Rangers advanced through two rounds by playing just one game over the minimum.

This time around? Different story. When the Rangers finally caught their breath from the Washington series, they had less than 48 hours to prepare for the rested Devils in Game 1. They didn't have time to read about the hype, much less contribute to it.

But no matter. The media did plenty of that for them.

"You guys are going to make your stories about the Devils and the Rangers," Tortorella said. "Go ahead, I know you will for the next two weeks. I get it. But don't include me in it. I've got a series to coach."

Tortorella, a fiery leader who wasn't afraid to rush to the defense of his team, refused to play the media's games. He didn't care if he was facing the Devils. He didn't care that more people were interested in his team because they were playing the Devils and not someone else. And he certainly didn't care about 1994.

"We're just going to go about our business and get ready for that team," he said. "I can only speak for our team, but that's how we're going to approach that series."

On May 14, 2012, with the ghosts of 1994 swirling around the newly refurbished Madison Square Garden, the new Rangers went to work and made their coach proud.

Defenseman Dan Girardi and forwards Chris Kreider and Artem Anisimov scored goals, and Lundqvist, seemingly on a mission to capture the Cup and add to a sterling career as New York's backstop, made 21 saves en route to a clean 3–0 victory over the Devils. Maybe this wasn't 1994, after all. Back then, New Jersey seized on a surprisingly nervous New York team in the same building, and the Devils escaped with a 4–3 Game 1 overtime victory. But in 2012, the Rangers meant business in the opener, blocking 26 shots and doling out 35 hits.

"We know that's happening," Devils captain Zach Parise said. "That's the way they play."

And they did it well. Brodeur, who turned 40 years old during the previous series and was the only remaining player from the 1994 series on either team, made 25 saves. But he looked pedestrian in the third period, when he allowed two goals before Anisimov buried an empty-netter to seal the victory.

The Garden crowd, still supercharged from the Game 7 win over Washington, was in prime form, especially late in the third. The derogatory

"Mar-ty, Mar-ty" chants grew in vim, vigor, and volume as the Rangers fans' sense of seniority blossomed again. Though many of the fans were too young to remember the roller-coaster ride of 1994, they knew that their team was the Rangers, and the other guys weren't. Same old story.

The team was confident, too. In fact, after New Jersey forward David Clarkson evened the series with the winner in a 3–2 Devils victory in Game 2 on May 16, the Rangers got right back to it in Newark, New Jersey—and in the new home of the Devils, the Prudential Center—by blanking New Jersey 3–0. In a vintage Lundqvist outing, the All-Star goaltender made 36 saves and allowed those boastful New York fans to raise their voices once again. Brodeur had to endure the "Mar-ty, Mar-ty" chants in his own building this time; the Rangers fans eventually gave him a break so that they could support their own netminder with a "Hen-rik, Hen-rik" serenade.

"Their goalie," Devils coach Peter DeBoer said in the postgame press conference, "was the difference."

He was right, of course. And despite the "here we go again" sentiment that was rampant in New Jersey, DeBoer, in his first year with the Devils, remained confident and calm. Those were the kind of traits he exhibited throughout the entire regular season. Given an unlikely opportunity to lead one of the league's most successful organizations over the last 20 years, DeBoer, who failed to make the postseason with Florida the previous three seasons, brought an aggressive, attacking, forecheck-heavy approach to the Devils, who were desperate for a culture change. After all, New Jersey had been dreadful in 2010–11, going through two coaches and failing to make the postseason for the first time since 1996. The team finished with 81 points, good for fourth in the Atlantic Division, and anyone who knew longtime general manager Lou Lamoriello knew that wasn't good enough.

Forget the neutral-zone trap. The Devils needed offense…and then some.

"A change was needed," Lamoriello said. "And I felt that in the conversations we had—because of the questions that were asked—the answers that were given were open, down-to-earth, and honest."

So, he hired DeBoer on July 19, 2011, to the surprise of many. But what does Lamoriello ever do that's expected, right? He trusted DeBoer and his beliefs, and so did the players.

"We were honest with him," forward Patrik Elias said. "When camp opened, he spoke to a few of us, and asked how we wanted to play. And we told him."

Next thing you know, New Jersey posted 102 points and snagged the sixth spot in the Eastern Conference.

"Honored," DeBoer said, reflecting on the job that was offered to him after a four-hour interview with Lamoriello across a hotel table. "I mean, I was out of work last June. And July, I got a call from a Hall of Fame general manager who recognized some of the work I had done in Florida, and gave me a chance to work with a group of guys that have a great blend of veteran presence. They know how to win, and they had a lot of great young players coming through. So, I'm fortunate to be sitting here. It could have been a number of different candidates that he talked to, and I'm thankful that I got the opportunity."

The Devils posted 228 goals in the regular season, and attacked all comers. Three forwards—Ilya Kovalchuk (37), Parise (31), and Clarkson (30)—reached 30 goals along the way, and with Brodeur and backup Johan Hedberg on the other end of the ice, the Devils indeed were the Devils again.

"And they did so by flying under the radar, pretty much all season," Devils radio voice Matt Laughlin said.

But in the end, would they be the same old Devils again? That was the big question once the Rangers showed up on the docket. Stanley Cups aside, New Jersey still needed to defeat its nemesis in a meaningful series to ever rid itself of the nightmare that was 1994. The 2012 series was the sixth time these two teams had faced off in a postseason across New Jersey's 30-year history—and the Rangers had won four of the first five meetings. Even the one the Devils did win—a first-round sweep in 2006—ended up hollow, as they were eliminated in the next round by the faceless Carolina Hurricanes.

Another opportunity was right in front of them, though, and DeBoer knew it. The Devils only trailed 2–1, and they were playing well within their system. They needed more shots, they needed more traffic in front of Lundqvist, and they needed to keep their composure. But he knew they could it.

And in Game 4, they began to prove him right.

On May 21, Parise scored twice and the gates finally opened on Lundqvist. A 4–1 New Jersey win tied the series at 2–2 and infuriated the Rangers, who were outplayed in every aspect. Brodeur made 28 saves and defenseman Bryce Salvador had two points, but the focus after this one was on the rattled Rangers. The East's top team did not like getting pushed around and lost its composure. In fact, forward Mike Rupp, a former Devil, threw a left hand at Brodeur after a whistle that landed around the goaltender's neck and set off total chaos. Arguments broke out on the ice, and a few more were evident in the stands. But the biggest one was between the benches.

DeBoer, incensed that someone would go after his Hall of Fame goaltender after play was stopped, called out to Tortorella and eventually walked down to the end of the New Jersey bench. Tortorella and DeBoer, some six feet away from each other and separated only by the broadcasters' box, pointed and screamed at each other for a whole nation to see.

It was classic, old-time hockey, and a moment befit of this rivalry. In fact, as the melees ensued, Mark Everson, the veteran hockey writer for the *New York Post*, turned to me in the Prudential Center press box and asked, "You'll be putting this in your book, eh?"

Eh.

"This isn't about John and I," DeBoer said in the postgame interview. "This is about the guys on the ice. So, I don't have anything to say about that."

He didn't need to. His team had played with fire and passion. A corner, indeed, was turned in Game 4, whether he wanted to talk about it or not.

The Devils never looked back, and though the media tried to resurrect the ghosts of Messier, Mike Richter, and Stephane Matteau, none of that mattered to New Jersey. The only similarity that remained once the round was knotted at 2–2 was that an extra off day in the series allowed the ensuing games to be played on the exact same days as those games were in 1994. For example, Game 5—a 5–3 road win for the Devils that pushed the inconsistent Rangers to the brink of elimination for the fourth time this postseason—was played on May 23, exactly 18 years after Devils forward Bernie Nicholls scored twice in a 4–1 New Jersey victory at the Garden in that Game 5.

Which meant, of course, that May 24 was the 18-year anniversary of The Guarantee—do you think that was played up a bit in New York? But the new Rangers captain wouldn't bite this time. In fact, forward Ryan Callahan shook his head and laughed at his locker stall when asked if he'd offer up any assurances of a win in Game 6, as Messier once did.

That was a good thing for Callahan, because he would have been wrong. Though the Rangers battled back from a two-goal deficit and controlled play for a portion of the third period in Newark, they could not stop the Devils train that started rolling back in Game 4. New Jersey won the battles in the corners, Brodeur made 33 saves, Kovalchuk scored his seventh of the postseason, and Adam Henrique, a rookie forward who was four years old when Matteau etched his name in hockey history, did the same:

> And Kovalchuk, a shot that's carefully played by Lundqvist. Now, [Alexei] Ponikarovsky with it, threw one in front that's blocked there. Scramble in front, they poke away at it. Still it's loose. Poked at by Kovalchuk…they score! Henrique! It's over!

Those were the frantic, furious words of Mike Emrick, a former Devils television play-by-play man who left the team to take a shorter, national schedule with NBC Sports in 2011. A man the Devils honored with his own ceremonious night prior to a 2–1 loss to Vancouver on February 24 was able to call perhaps his former franchise's most important victory against its most hated rival.

Henrique's winner just 1:03 into overtime gave New Jersey a 3–2 win in Game 6, a series win over its more glamorous opponent, and its fifth conference title. A heartbreak 18 years running—a black cloud that hovered over this proud organization for 6,568 days—blew away on this Friday night, just 10.2 miles away from the Meadowlands Arena, where Messier delivered on his guarantee, scored a hat trick, and kept the Rangers alive in The NHL's Greatest Series Ever.

On this night, though, the Devils exacted their revenge, and it will never seem too late to the loyal fans in that building. Those who stomached the taunts from Rangers fans at the water cooler, at the bus stop, at recess. Those who would walk into rooms sometimes, only to be greeted by chants of "Matteau! Matteau! Matteau!" Those who faced the taunts from the bullies on Broadway who never seemed that impressed with New Jersey's three Cups, because when it counted, the Devils couldn't beat the Rangers.

Until now.

Brodeur, just 22 when his team lost in 1994, diluted perhaps the blackest mark on his stellar career—the Matteau wraparound winner—by winning three straight in this rematch. Of course, he was on the other end of the ice when the Henrique goal went in, so it took the veteran a while to reach his teammates. But what an enjoyable skate it must have been, as he pumped his stick, looked straight into the stands, and held up his arms.

"I don't think you can put into words just how much this win means to this organization," said longtime New Jersey analyst Glenn "Chico" Resch, an original Devil and the franchise's first goaltender.

The Rangers were left dumbfounded. As the Devils' celebration gathered to Lundqvist's left, all he could do was look up at the scoreboard, as his defenseman laid on the ice in disappointment.

"It is shocking," Lundqvist would say later at his locker.

There may well be better days ahead for these Rangers. Loaded with young talent that general manager Glen Sather has acquired and Tortorella has cultivated, the optimism in New York after the series ended was not unlike the feeling Brodeur and the Devils had in 1994. In the NHL, sometimes you have to lose before you can win.

"I think I grew from that [1994] series. Sure, it hurt, no question. It affected me and changed me," Brodeur said. "But if I didn't have that loss, I might not have been the same goalie. Not just me, the whole organization."

The Rangers and Lundqvist may be saying that soon enough. But without question, the stunning loss resonated within this proud Original Six organization.

"It's tough enough to go to bed at night and get up the next morning. You've got to adjust," Sather said at the NHL's general managers meetings a week after the elimination. "It's like having a death in the family."

Well, if it was a death on one side, it was clearly a birth on the other. Make no mistake: the 2012 chapter in this never-ending story belonged to the Devils, who advanced to face the Los Angeles Kings in the Stanley Cup Finals.

"There is only one man in this world who wants to beat the Rangers more than Martin Brodeur," DeBoer said, "and that's Lou Lamoriello."

And as the handshake line reached its end and the Prince of Wales Trophy was awarded to Parise, a fitting song reverberated throughout the five-year-old facility in the center of New Jersey's largest city. "Glory Days," the 1984 hit from Garden State rocker Bruce Springsteen, soundtracked the evening as Devils fans danced up and down the aisles dressed in red and black, celebrating this new arena's proudest night.

One such fan, who inched his way down to ice level wearing a Parise jersey, received some quality camera time when he pulled out a handmade sign he probably scratched together on the train ride to Newark. The sign was blunt, to the point, and perhaps summed up a glorious 12-day span in the life of this tremendous rivalry like none other could. In this case, simplicity ruled the day:

"This is not 1994."

He was absolutely right, in so many different ways.

Postscript: In the Stanley Cup Finals, the well-rested Los Angeles Kings were eager to show the world that a No. 8 seed can indeed win it all. They were a collection of upstart forwards and stingy defensemen in front of a new-world goaltender, Jonathan Quick, who had the flexibility of a gymnast and the glove of a shortstop. Los Angeles defeated New Jersey in six games, and along the way proved just how much the Rangers had accomplished in 1994. After all, the Devils losing to the Kings after eliminating the Rangers continued a trend in the New York–New Jersey rivalry: in the six postseason meetings between the Devils and the Rangers, the fatigued winners were eliminated in the very next round five times. The only exception? 1994.

Acknowledgments

○ ○ ○ ○

"There are several times in the course of a book where you want to throw your hands up and walk away from it, yes. It can be frustrating and agonizing. But that's part of it all, and it's the tough times that make a whole project so rewarding. You have to love it—the story, the idea, the concept. And if you love it, you'll be pushed through those times. When it's all said and done, you'll look back on it and finally be able to take it all in. And trust me, for a writer, there is no greater feeling than holding your book for the first time. Opening up that box that arrived in your driveway, and seeing the book for the first time. At that point, you know you've done it. And your life changes. Trust me."

—MIKE VACCARO, COLUMNIST, *NEW YORK POST*

WHEN YOU DO anything for the first time, you have to lean on those who've already done it. They can be a guiding light. They can be a system of support. A father teaching a son how to skate. A coach showing a team how to play. A general manager informing a staff how to operate.

The same can be said for books. It is true that writing is writing, and if you know how to write, anything can be accomplished. But books are their own entity, far separate from stories and articles and features and essays. To write one without the guidance of those who've come before you would be counterproductive. That is why I leaned on so many authors of my generation, who provided not only insight, but more importantly, the motivation to continue pursuing my dream, through thick and thin.

Mike Vaccaro, a former colleague of mine at the *New York Post*, is a three-time author, and he was certainly one of those driving forces. From the cultivation of this concept, to the plotting out of how I did what I did when I did, Vaccaro was always there, and I cannot thank him enough.

"In this case, you get to write the book that you always wanted to write as your first one," Vaccaro once told me. "That's something."

And he's right.

Vaccaro was not alone. Many authors helped at many different times, including Kevin Kernan and Mark Cannizzaro of the *New York Post*, Harvey Araton of the *New York Times*, Jeff Pearlman, and of course, Stan Fischler.

But there would be no book about The NHL's Greatest Series Ever without willing participants from both sides of it. And with the Rangers and the Devils, that starts at the top. I will never forget my two-hour conversation with former Rangers general manager Neil Smith, on a Thanksgiving Eve, when we broke down 1994 from stem to stern, and shared many laughs along the way.

And I will always cherish a three-hour sitdown in the plush office of one Lou Lamoriello in Newark, New Jersey, before the Devils president and general manager watched his team take the ice on a Saturday night. We both walked away, I believe, impressed with each other's knowledge of Devils Hockey, past, present, and future. It truly was a moving experience.

The passion, the pride, and the unchained truth that these gentlemen spoke with helped make this book what it is. And that sense of emotion was passed down to the players as well.

From the Devils, I will never forget seeing the smiles on the faces of Scott Stevens, Scott Niedermayer, Ken Daneyko, Bruce Driver, Jim Dowd, and Martin Brodeur when certain games and certain situations came up across many passionate interviews.

Many other players from that team knew when to be serious and when to kick back and have some fun with interviews, such as Bill Guerin, Bernie Nicholls, Claude Lemieux, Tom Chorske, Corey Millen, and Randy McKay. The Devils changed their franchise in so many ways in 1993–94, and these players were at the genesis of it. They were building blocks. They were champions. And they were first class, all the way. Lamoriello wouldn't have had it any other way.

From the Rangers, a debt of gratitude must be paid to so many players who probably get sick of talking about the same old year... every year. But to their credit, they never rolled their eyes when asked about that glorious run, and the help from Mike Keenan, Mike Richter, Brian Leetch, Doug Lidster, Adam Graves, Kevin Lowe, Nick Kypreos, Steve Larmer, Darren Turcotte, Craig MacTavish, Mark Messier, and, of course, Stephane Matteau was immeasurable.

What an incredible sense of reality I received from Matteau, who remembers 1994 as if it was yesterday. That team, that year, and this great game of hockey means so much to him, and I felt so honored to have him assist me and grace me with the foreword. So many people know his name—rightfully so—and will never forget it because of what happened in the series: "Matteau! Matteau! Matteau!"

But, indeed, Stephane is so much more than a name. And everyone who knows him understands that. I am proud to say now that I am in that fraternity.

Speaking of memories, you cannot be a respected, admired sports journalist in New York without them, and I certainly found that along this journey. From print to radio to television, the media helped move this concept forward with ease.

There were reporters who covered this series for the *New York Post*— Larry Brooks, Mark Everson and Jay Greenberg—whose passion for this stretch of games helped motivate and inspire. And Pat Hannigan, the night sports editor at the *Post* who authored the famous "We'll Win Tonight" back page, is also a former colleague who spent some time with me reliving that magical moment.

There are also play-by-play broadcasters and analysts who are still now as razor sharp on this series as they were back then. Back then, Howie Rose and Mike Miller were the radio voices of the Rangers and Devils, respectively, and I will never forget a passionate conversation I had with Rose before a New York Mets game, and another with Miller before he went on his sports talk show to talk even more hockey.

Kenny Albert and Don LaGreca are now the radio voices of the Rangers, and this 1994 series is so near and dear to them in their own ways, they were more than happy to share their memories, as well. Albert is a Rangers fan, LaGreca is a Devils fan, and that give and take worked perfectly for this book.

Who can forget the crew at WFAN? At the time, the nation's first all-sports outfit was the Rangers' flagship station, and now, it's the Devils' flagship, so this series is forever embedded in its history. Many, many thanks go out to program director Mark Chernoff, as well as Mike Francesa, Joe Benigno, former host Chris Russo, and, of course, Steve Somers, whose emotional memories of those days and nights in New York City made even this author choke up at times during an unforgettable interview.

During a trip to the Stanley Cup Finals and in and around several primetime sporting events, I was able to get the pulse of the national and international media with regard to this series. They provided much information and inspiration, and their memories, too, are also crystal clear. For that, I offer many thanks to Barry Melrose, Darren Pang, Kelly Hrudey, Steve Levy, Mark Recchi, Bill Clement, Gary Thorne, Al Morganti, Bob Errey, Jeff Van Gundy, and Joe Gannascoli.

In its final stages, when looking back on everything, Dan Gelston of the Associated Press was an inspiration and a terrific source to bounce concepts off of.

Showing how far-reaching this series went, a memorable interview with actor Patrick Warburton, who played crazed Devils fan David Puddy on *Seinfeld*, broke new ground on what that team and that time meant to people. It was one of the more entertaining meetings I will ever have.

Team information is not what it used to be, and there are many sources to research hockey history now across many platforms. But you can't beat the real thing, and to have the help and guidance of Sammy Steinlight, Brendan McIntyre, and John Rosasco with the Rangers' media relations team, and Mike Levine with the Devils' crew—especially during the season when they had so many other items on their list—was especially appreciated.

A party that often is forgotten in moments like this is the officials, and what a task the referees and linesmen had during that series in 1994. Kevin Collins, a linesman for Game 7, still has to give pause before talking about that series because of what it meant to him and his career. In a locker room interview after he retired, he became emotional before succinctly labeling it The NHL's Greatest Series Ever.

Also, thanks to the NHL for game film, for Devils and Rangers media guides, and for the league's official statistic and record book. And without question, this book would not have happened without hockey-reference. com.

No team, no championship, no series is anything without its fans, and there are so many passionate, proud ones on both sides. It was a pleasure to share stories with them, and to hear and see the emotions that rose to the surface when I talked to them. Many thanks to Denis Gorman, Rob Garomo, Lloyd Hollabaugh, and Rob and Noelle O'Shea, among so many others, for sharing.

You always will remember the people you shared such a series with, as well. For me, in 1994, this series was played after I had just graduated from Duquesne University, and I will always cherish playoff game nights with Jim Stewart, Andrew Romer, Frank Rodichok, James Orsino, Gene Pebworth, Gianni Floro, Mike Wattick, Garrett Jordan, Randy Stoernell, David Garth, Pete Aldrich, Troy Grunseth, John McMahon, Tom Blades, and Dave Freeman.

The crew at Triumph Books gave me my start. Without question, if it wasn't for the vision and forward thinking of Tom Bast and Adam Motin, we would not be here today. They believed in this concept, they saw potential in its entirety when others didn't, and that will never be forgotten.

My family means everything to me, and to have so many members of it be hockey fans made this easy. Many thanks to my mother, Kathleen Sullivan, and my sister, Anne Marie Sullivan; to Terry and Johnny Sullivan, brothers of my late father, for providing memories; to my stepmother, Carol Smyth; and to my brother and godson, Drew Sullivan, too young to remember 1994, but old enough now to carry the Devils' flag with pride. And that makes me more proud than words can illustrate.

My wife, Amy, never let me slip when those "tough times" that Vaccaro mentioned came across our path—and there were plenty of those times. I will never forget her strength, determination, enthusiasm, and pride through this entire process. This is not a book without her.

And my children, T.J. and Sara, were also so proud to say their father was going to be an author. They helped me break down game film, they bragged to all of their friends, and they wanted to read the book before I even finished it.

This book is for them…and our future together.